Early Adopter Ha.

X. B.!!

Robert Eisenberg

Daniel Maharry

P.G.Muraleedharan

Jon Pinnock

2002 г.

г. Пало-Алто

В. И. Гальчин

Wrox Press Ltd. ®

Early Adopter HailStorm

© 2001 Wrox Press

Published by Wrox Press Ltd,
Arden House, 1102 Warwick Road, Acocks Green,
Birmingham, B27 6BH, UK
Printed in the United States
ISBN 1-861006-08-X

Trademark Acknowledgements

Wrox has endeavored to provide trademark information about all the companies and products mentioned in this book by the appropriate use of capitals. However, Wrox cannot guarantee the accuracy of this information.

Credits

Authors
Robert Eisenberg
Daniel Maharry
P G Muraleedharan
Jon Pinnock

Additional Material
Miloslav Nic

Series Manager
Christianne Bailey

Technical Architect
Daniel Maharry

Technical Editor
Benjamin Hickman

Technical Reviewers
Johann Dumser
Adam Dutton
Dan Kent
Julian Skinner

Production Manager
Liz Toy

Production Co-ordinator
Natalie O'Donnell

Proof reader
Chris Smith

Cover
Chris Morris

About the Authors

Robert Eisenberg

Robert Eisenberg is currently an independent consultant specializing in Web Services. In 1999 he was the CEO and cofounder of an e-Commerce consulting firm that was acquired by Framfab Inc., the largest Internet Professional Services firm in Europe. Prior to that, as a consultant he was in charge of many production systems for Ocular Science Inc., one of the largest manufacturers of contact lenses in the world. Prior to that he ran a computer consulting firm working with many companies including Pacific Bell, the Federal Reserve Bank, and Cushman & Wakefield. He has written for DevX and spoken on .NET at Microsoft and at local user groups. He can be reached at robert@reassociates.net.

I would like to thank my wife for her understanding and support. Our first son was born during the writing of this book, so it was a challenge. I would also like to thank Sean O'Brien for his essential help and support writing this book.

Robert Contributed Chapters 1 and 5.

Daniel Maharry

Dan Maharry was born in a small seaside town recently notable only for the BBC blowing up a bus on its harbor and for being the birthplace of artist and enfant terrible Tracy Emin. While this may have hindered others, Dan has used this foundation to come to Birmingham, England a city famous for only one feature – the exit.

Here he ponders life and the next words he'll shove in this bio and the several chapters he's rewriting from a small flat with a large stereo and several hundred CDs, which multiply like rabbits despite their inanimate nature. It's possible they may be breeding with the DVDs on the shelf above too. His neighbors live in the constant hope that he'll actually get better on his guitar at some point in time.

He humbly thanks his friends and especially Lou for putting up with his eccentricities and his family for being exactly that. Thanks also to the other authors on this book for keeping up their end of the deal.

*"Switch off the monitors, unplug the comps,
Cease the typing and close down the apps,
Send out one e-mail - 'They are dead, they are dead'"*

Dedicated to the memory of those lost September 11 2001 in New York, Washington, and Pittsburgh.

May they Rest in Peace.

Dan contributed Chapters 2, 3, and 4.

P G Muraleedharan

Muraleedharan lives in Trivandrum in India, where he works for XStream Software India (P) Ltd, a subsidiary of XStream Software Inc. Ottawa. He graduated in Electronics and Communication Engineering and worked for two decades in the electronics manufacturing industry. Subsequently he did his Masters in Computer Science and Engineering and has 14 years of programming experience. He has written many technical papers for professional journals. Muraleedharan is a regular contributor to international conferences and is a member of several professional organizations. His areas of interest include Image Processing, Artificial Intelligence, Internet and web-based applications, and Multimedia applications. He can be reached by e-mail at: pgmurali@vsnl.com

To my Parents and Teachers for their love and blessings. My thanks go to the Wrox team for helping with this book. In particular, I want to thank the reviewers for making innumerable corrections to the structure and style, and my colleagues at XStream Software India for their help and encouragement. Finally and most importantly, I would like to thank my wife, Valsalakumari, and our children Abhijith, Abhinand and Aiswarya for the support and love they have given me.

P.G. Muraleedharan contributed Chapter 7.

Jon Pinnock

Jonathan Pinnock started programming in Pal III assembler on his school's PDP 8/e (which had a massive 4K of memory) back in the days before Moore's Law reached the statute books. These days he spends most of his time developing and extending the increasingly successful PlatformOne product set that his company, JPA, markets to the financial services community. JPA's home page is at: www.jpassoc.co.uk.

My heartfelt thanks go to Gail, who first suggested getting into writing, and now suffers the consequences on a fairly regular basis, and to Mark and Rachel, who just suffer the consequences.

Jon Pinnock contributed Chapter 6.

early adopter

Table of Contents

Table of Contents

Table of Contents

early adopter

Foreword

It's strange how things can be misconceived. A day before I wrote this, Linus Torvalds was in the news for his dismissal of 'worries over the centralized control implicit in HailStorm' at LinuxWorld Expo in San Francisco. Good for Torvalds and bad for those who jumped to the wrong conclusion all at once. Ever since the project codename for Microsoft's new web services-based application platform appeared in the community's subconscious, a lot of the copy written about it has been misguided.

It *is* a collection of web services that can store information securely for you if you choose to use the service. It *is* a great way for web sites to keep their user information up to date. It *is* entirely at the user's discretion who has and hasn't got access to their details. It *is* completely standards-based so you can work with the services on any platform or device with any server-side technology. It *isn't* Microsoft's latest attempt to inveigle its own big brother/Skynet/1984/THX-1138 scenario on the world at large and yes it will be as secure as possible. It is a part of the all-encompassing .NET strategy but it isn't reliant on .NET at all.

What it noticeably isn't, is anywhere near completion. The first developer alpha of HailStorm is to be released at Microsoft's Professional Developer Conference in October 2001. That's what this book is written to, setting some records straight along the way and getting you thinking about what you can do with the technology. It's pretty cool stuff when you actually look at it.

Here's to Microsoft's first try at a totally web services-based platform for applications. We can only learn from here on in. It's either the right way to do it, or it's the wrong way, but whichever it is, it's valuable.

Dan Maharry
Wrox Press, September 2001.

early adopter

Introduction

HailStorm or .NET My Services as it has been rechristened is the latest web-based technology from Microsoft. A suite of fifteen web services, although the number does tend to fluctuate, the aim of HailStorm is to provide an online central information store for user's preferences, documents and details that other sites can then latch on to and use. Its potential to become ubiquitous, combined with its essential simplicity and extensibility, could finally bring web services into the mainstream of web development.

In this book, we'll look at the first public release of HailStorm in A Box, or .NET My Services Developer Edition to give it the official name, the HailStorm emulator that you can install and run on your server to start your initial development against. We'll look at the differences between it and HailStorm when v1.0 is finally released and how to develop against it.

> Please note that although HailStorm has been given an official name – .NET My Services – by Microsoft, we will be using its more familiar (and, let's face it, catchier) original project name throughout this book. Similarly, we will be referring to HailStorm in a Box (HSiaB) rather than .NET My Services Developer Edition, and the XMI Manual rather than the .NET My Services documentation.

Who is this Book for?

This is a Wrox 'Early Adopter' series book, so we're going to assume that you are already a capable web application developer who needs to know everything they can about working with HailStorm. This book goes into as much depth as it can on this new technology as it stands today, but please bear in mind that this book was written against alpha technology that is very subject to change. To this end you'll find a stop press appendix at the back of the book noting the changes made to HailStorm after the rest of the book went to press.

The technologies and internet standards that HailStorm is based upon (Passport, Kerberos, SOAP, XPath) are covered in enough depth to get you started, although it is assumed that you already have some knowledge of them prior to reading this. If you want to learn more about a specific topic, we've included links throughout the book and in Appendix A to more complete sources.

What does this Book Cover?

Early Adopter HailStorm looks at this exciting technology from two different angles:

The end-user overview of HailStorm as it is expected to operate when v1.0 is released in 2002 and the developer's point of view, looking at what we can work with now and the technology we need to be familiar with in order to do that work.

Chapter 1 illustrates Microsoft's vision for Hailstorm is and where it fits in to the overall scheme of things focusing on what Hailstorm will ultimately be rather than what it actually is now.

Chapter 2 examines the differences between the blue sky vision of Hailstorm and the first release of the HailStorm in a Box emulator released at PDC, October 2001.

Chapter 3 looks at how to communicate with the HailStorm services focusing first on establishing a secure connection before looking at actual communication using SOAP.

Chapter 4 looks at the structure of a HailStorm content document and investigates how to navigate through it using XPath.

Chapter 5 continues chapter four's exploration of the HailStorm content documents, including a detailed look at HailStorm Data-manipulation Language (HSDL).

Chapter 6 presents the first of two case studies. In this one, we implement a basic online auction site using HailStorm services to store user information. We'll also see how we might use the myAlerts service to let users know that they have been outbid.

Chapter 7 presents the second case study in which we create our own set of Hailstorm compatible web services.

What do I Need to Use this Book?

To follow this book you will need a copy of HailStorm in a Box, which you should be able to download from the Microsoft .NET Downloads page (http://www.microsoft.com/net/ downloads.asp). This in turn has a number of pre-requisites for installation:

❏ One of Windows 2000 Server, Windows 2000 Professional, or Windows XP Professional

❏ SQL Server 2000

❏ Windows Script Host 5.5 or higher

❏ SOAP Toolkit 2.0 Service Pack 2

If you want to follow the case study in Chapter 7, you will also need a copy of Visual Studio.NET and the .NET Framework installed.

Conventions

To help you get the most from the text and keep track of what's happening, we use a number of conventions throughout the book.

Code examples are generally highlighted like this:

```
<s:Body>
    <insertRequest select="/myDocuments">
        <Document href="cid: <DocumentToStore.doc@wrox.com"/>
        ...
    </insertRequest>
</s:Body>
```

If the example is repeated again, for example, when updating it with some new code lines, the sections you have seen before will no longer be highlighted:

```
<s:Body>
    <insertRequest select="/myDocuments">
        <Document href="cid: <DocumentToStore.doc@wrox.com"/>
        some more new code
    </insertRequest>
</s:Body>
```

We also use several styles in the text:

❏ Important terms, when first introduced, are highlighted as follows: **important words**

❏ Filenames and code within the text appear as: `test.curl`.

❏ Text in user interfaces, and URLs, are shown in this style: File | Save As...

❏ Keys that you may be required to press are indicated in italic, like so: *Ctrl, Alt, Ctrl-z, F12*

In addition:

▶▶ * * *

These boxes hold important, not-to-be forgotten information, which is directly relevant to the surrounding text.

■

! * * *

These boxes hold information about quirks or bugs found in the early releases of a technology.

Important bits of information you shouldn't ignore come in boxes like this!

While this background style is used for informational asides to the current discussion.

Customer Support

We always value hearing from our readers, and we want to know what you think about this book: what you liked, what you didn't like, and what you think we can do better next time. You can send us your comments, either by returning the reply card in the back of the book, or by e-mailing us at feedback@wrox.com. Please be sure to mention the book title in your message.

How to Download the Sample Code for the Book

When you log on to the Wrox site http://www.wrox.com/, simply locate the title through our Search facility or by using one of the title lists. Click on Download in the Code column or on Download Code on the book's detail page.

The files that are available for download from our site have been archived using WinZip. When you have saved the attachments to a folder on your harddrive, you need to extract the files using a de-compression program such as WinZip or PKUnzip. When you extract the files, the code is usually extracted into chapter folders. When you start the extraction process, ensure your software (WinZip, PKUnzip, and so on) is set on to Use Folder Names.

Errata

We've made every effort to make sure that there are no errors in the text or in the code. However, no one is perfect and mistakes do occur. If you find an error in one of our books, like a spelling mistake or a faulty piece of code, we would be very grateful for feedback. By sending in errata, you may save another reader hours of frustration, and of course, you will be helping us provide even higher quality information. Simply e-mail the information to support@wrox.com; your information will be checked and if correct, posted to the errata page for that title, or used in subsequent editions of the book.

To find errata on the web site, log on to http://www.wrox.com/, and simply locate the title through our Advanced Search or title list. Click on the Book Errata link, which is below the cover graphic on the book's detail page:

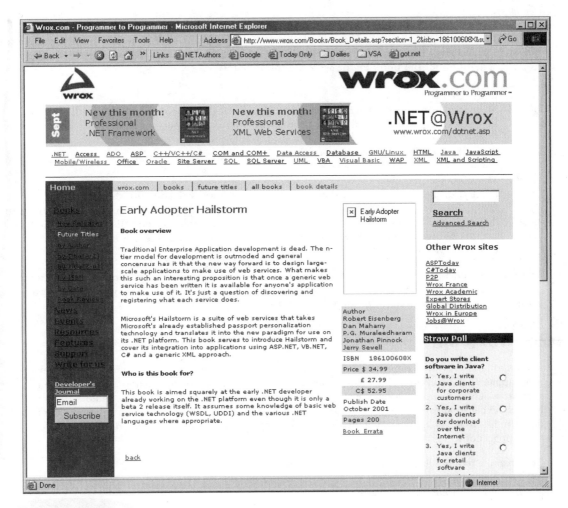

E-Mail Support

If you wish to query a problem in the book with an expert who knows the book in detail then e-mail support@wrox.com, with the title of the book and the last four numbers of the ISBN in the subject field of the e-mail. A typical e-mail should include the following things:

❑ The **name, last four digits of the ISBN,** and **page number** of the problem in the Subject field.

❑ Your **name, contact information,** and the **problem** in the body of the message.

We **won't** send you junk mail. We need the details to save your time and ours. When you send an e-mail message, it will go through the following chain of support:

1. Customer Support

Your message is delivered to one of our customer support staff, who are the first people to read it. They have files on most frequently asked questions and will answer anything general about the book or the web site immediately.

2. Editorial

More in-depth queries are forwarded to the technical editor responsible for that book. They have experience with the programming language or particular product, and are able to answer detailed technical questions on the subject. Once an issue has been resolved, the editor can post the errata to the web site.

3. The Authors

Finally, in the unlikely event that the editor cannot answer your problem, they will forward the request to the author. We do try to protect the author from any distractions to their writing; however, we are quite happy to forward specific requests to them. All Wrox authors help with the support on their books. They will mail the customer and the editor with their response, and again all readers should benefit.

The Wrox Support process can only offer support on issues that are directly pertinent to the content of our published title. Support for questions that fall outside the scope of normal book support is provided via the community lists of our http://p2p.wrox.com/ forum.

p2p.wrox.com

For author and peer discussion join the P2P mailing lists. Our unique system provides **programmer to programmer**™ contact on mailing lists, forums, and newsgroups, all **in addition** to our one-to-one e-mail support system. Be confident that your query is being examined by the many Wrox authors and other industry experts who are present on our mailing lists. At http://p2p.wrox.com/, you will find a number of different lists that will help you, not only while you read this book, but also as you develop your own applications.

To subscribe to a mailing list just follow this these steps:

1. Go to http://p2p.wrox.com/

2. Choose the appropriate category from the left menu bar

3. Click on the mailing list you wish to join

4. Follow the instructions to subscribe and fill in your e-mail address and password

5. Reply to the confirmation e-mail you receive

6. Use the subscription manager to join more lists and set your mail preferences

early adopter

Laying it on the Table – HailStorm as it Will Be

The purpose of this chapter is to provide an overview of HailStorm and to describe the most important points of its architecture. We start with an explanation of what HailStorm is, then move on to a description of the HailStorm business model. A detailed section discussing the security and privacy issues that have raised so much concern follows this. The final section of this chapter focuses on the HailStorm architecture, in particular its XML characteristics.

This chapter focuses on what HailStorm will be services when it goes live in 2002 rather than what is available now. Hopefully this look into the future will provide enough encouragement for you to read the rest of the book and then start developing your own HailStorm-enabled applications.

What is a Web Service?

A few years back we progressed from procedural software to component-based software, thereby improving the software development process. Software components could now be created, tested, and then used in multiple applications. These components expose functionality that can be used by other components or applications. While these components were an improvement over the procedural model, they still were still restricted by location and proprietary object models. Web services are the next step in this evolution. They are capable of ubiquitous interoperability and communication. Web services communicate over the Internet via HTTP and exchange messages via XML.

Web services are programmable objects that are accessible to users and applications across the Internet. HailStorm is a new set of web services from Microsoft that has the potential to change the way we work with computers and access our data. Several industry trends are turning this vision into a reality; they are combining to create a new interactive and programmable Internet:

❑ **XML** – Which provides a platform-neutral mechanism for various services and applications to communicate and exchange data.

❑ **Falling communication costs** – Which permit applications, devices, and services to connect in a cost-effective way.

❑ **Falling hardware costs** – Which permit users to access services by means of powerful but portable products with adequate screens and powerful communications abilities. The power of these devices now approaches the power of notebook computers.

❑ **Emerging standards** – The industry agreeing upon XML-based languages including SOAP for application communication, UDDI for service location, and WSDL for service description.

HailStorm is an ambitious set of services from Microsoft that will serve as a foundation upon which other services can be built and that attempts to deliver the first major set of services that leverage and benefit from these new trends.

What is HailStorm?

Many people have been following HailStorm over the last six-months, trying to figure out what it is and assessing what it offers – articles about HailStorm claim that:

❑ Microsoft is moving to a subscription-based software model

❑ Its Microsoft's attempt to compete with AOL

❑ Its Microsoft's first set of industrial strength web services which validate .NET

In my opinion, HailStorm is all of the above, and more. It is an enabling-platform built on web standards, Microsoft Passport, and other HailStorm-platform services, including myApplicationSettings, myAlerts, and myDevices that permit a new breed of web-based services and applications to be developed. The best way to provide a holistic view of HailStorm is to describe its individual components. The next few sections will describe HailStorm:

❑ From a user-centric view

❑ From PUID-centric view

❑ As a set of building block services

❑ As a platform

❑ As the largest application ever created

User-centric View

The most obvious view of HailStorm is the user-centric view. This is geared to an individual utilizing HailStorm to access services and store data across the Internet in their HailStorm digital safe deposit box. These services will include e-mail, calendars, contact management, file storage, music, photos, and payment. These services will be available to all types of endpoints, including mobile phones, handhelds like Palm Pilots and Pocket PC devices, PCs, and other applications.

Паспорт

Individuals who currently need to manage multiple devices each containing separate islands of data will benefit greatly, because their HailStorm digital safe deposit box can be accessed from any of them. HailStorm makes it easy for individuals to share their data in a secure way with only the services they want. It also enables individuals to access web sites, web services, and applications with only one sign-in. Further, individuals will also benefit from notifications that utilize this centralized point to route them important reminders wherever they are and whatever device they are using.

HailStorm may offer individuals who use it targeted promotions and information via its Instant Messaging aspect. HailStorm's Instant Messaging will be much more robust than the teenage chat that Instant Messaging is most commonly used for now. This Instant Messaging will deliver messages from a system that knows your preferences, how to reach you, and which device is most convenient to you at any given time.

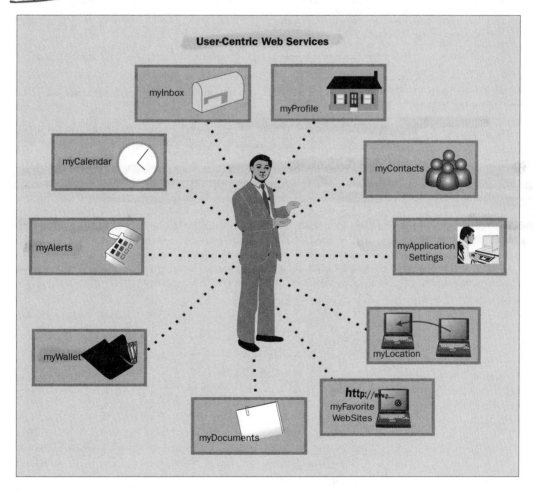

PUID-centric View

HailStorm is identity-centric, but that identity is not limited to only an individual. It provides identities for all sorts of groups and organizations as well. HailStorm utilizes a **PUID** (Pairwise Unique ID) to create a global Internet identity system. This HailStorm identity system does not require proof of identity to obtain a PUID, just an e-mail address. PUIDs are not assigned only to individuals but also to groups and organizations. People may have multiple PUIDs, for example, you could have one PUID associated with your personal identity and another with your professional identity. With the person's consent, both of these PUIDs will be referenced in their myProfile service. Other global identity examples of PUID usage in HailStorm are:

- ❑ Payment providers found in the myWallet services are referred to by a PUID

- ❑ Work information elements found in the myProfile service which, refer to an individual's boss and secretary via PUIDs

- ❑ Passport and all HailStorm services use the PUID as the key field for data storage and connectivity between each other

- ❑ Third party HailStorm-compatible services will access and create cross-reference tables based on the PUID

- ❑ PUIDs are a pointer-based reference system. An employee of MS can be referenced by a personal PUID, by their Microsoft PUID, or their softball team PUID

Understanding the role of PUIDs in HailStorm provides a great deal of the insight necessary for figuring out HailStorm itself. PUIDS will be the foundation with which HailStorm delivers the variety of services. These services will be decentralized, extendable, and deliverable to individuals, groups, and organizations.

The PUIDS are also the key to one of the more ambitious aspects of HailStorm, creating a truly intelligent notification and preference system. In order for HailStorm to provide a mechanism to send you an e-mail or ring your cell phone, it needs to be knowledgeable about your personal and professional life. The more PUIDs HailStorm obtains, the more information it will be able to provide to service providers. This will provide more value to the service providers who utilize the HailStorm network.

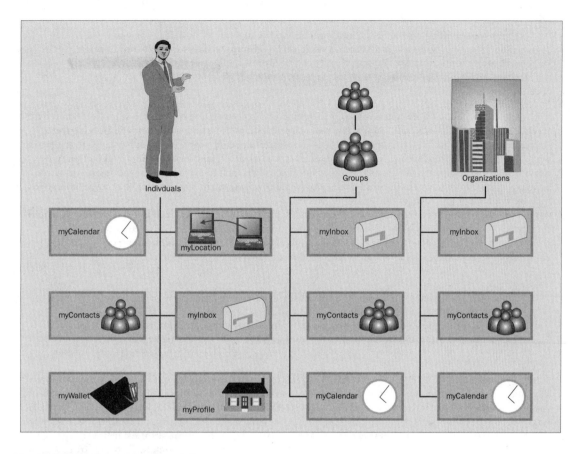

Building-block Services

The paragraph reproduced below in several gray boxes below is taken from the Microsoft HailStorm site white paper at http://www.microsoft.com/net/hailstorm.asp. This paragraph provides a good example of how HailStorm building-block services will be used in applications to provide standard preference, notifications, payment, and calendaring functionality.

While many people label HailStorm a set of services for an individual, the example below reveals that some of the other aspects of HailStorm go much further. We have split the paragraph in to sections and provide some analysis directly below:

> **With HailStorm services, booking a flight using an online travel reservation service becomes much simpler because with the user's consent, the travel service automatically accesses the user's travel preferences and method of payment.**

The travel service integrates the preferences and wallet services into its application. This integration provides the travel service with off-the-shelf preference and payment support, which its simply then has to customize. It also provides the travel service with access to all the users in HailStorm that have consented to this. Obviously, this function is an additional revenue stream for Microsoft, permitting Microsoft to license the use of this service into other applications.

> If you're traveling on business, and your company has travel policies that you need to adhere to, your individual affiliation with your company's HailStorm group identity will make it possible for the travel service to automatically show you only the choices that meet both your preferences and your company's requirements.

It is unclear how much of the functionality is provided by HailStorm and how much is implemented by the travel company via custom code. At a minimum, it appears that the travel company will provide the logic to process the combination of the individual's preferences and the company's travel policy rules to determine what flights are most appropriate for the individual. It is unclear if HailStorm or the travel company is providing the tools to store the company's travel policies. This lack of clarity about who is providing the service will be common in HailStorm because it is a platform. As such, if something is not available today, it may be available tomorrow. In this example, Microsoft, a travel company, or an independent software company could create a service that enables company travel policies to be input into HailStorm. It would then be up to that company to decide if it would like to make this service available to other HailStorm companies and, if so, to determine the price. There is a policy for adding HailStorm services that the company would have to adhere to that is discussed in the developer section below.

> Once you've chosen your flight, the travel service can use HailStorm, with your explicit permission, to figure out which calendaring service you use and then automatically schedule the itinerary directly onto your calendar; further, it will automatically update that itinerary and notify you if your flight will be late.

The travel company can use the individual's PUID, to update the individual's HailStorm calendar. HailStorm will be responsible for synchronizing the individual's calendars. The travel service will use the HailStorm notification service as the vehicle to alert the individual if the flight changes. This is a huge service because tracking an individual and processing the rules, roles, and routing necessary to deliver a message to the individual is a giant undertaking. With the foundation established by HailStorm, all this functionality is now accessible as standard building-block technology from Microsoft.

> Through HailStorm, you can share that live flight itinerary with whomever you're going to visit, so that they will also know when and where to expect you.

This is another example where it is hard to know what needs custom code and what is HailStorm functionality. However, it is safe to say that the group travelers will be identified by their PUIDs and probably stored in some type of list by this PUID, making it easy to select them.

It is worth pointing out that these building-block services are not only potentially useful to custom applications. They may become standard functionality in enterprise resource planning, customer relationship management, and (of course) Microsoft software. Another potentially lucrative market for these services are equipment manufacturers, including cell phone companies, PBX companies, elevator manufacturers, and providers of any of the other devices that need to contact people. The cell phone and PBX companies could simply pass the phone number on to HailStorm and let HailStorm deal with the internal logic of determining the best way to reach or leave a message for the individual being called. Elevator companies and other manufacturers could use it to notify the proper repairperson when there is a malfunction.

There is yet another point about these building-block services and most other HailStorm services in general. They are freely accessible from anywhere by anyone (with the correct permissions) and allow data access to all sorts of data through a single interface. The HailStorm Inbox can contain all e-mail, fax, and phone messages. HailStorm services are a central repository with an easy-to-use XML-based interface that can interact with other applications and devices. Many of the HailStorm services have parallels in Microsoft Exchange or Lotus Notes, but because the HailStorm engine is open to the world, it is much more powerful and flexible.

HailStorm is a Platform

HailStorm is a set of Microsoft web services and a **web services platform**; the real power of HailStorm lies in its platform component. The platform allows Microsoft and third parties the ability to add many more services, all of which will be able to access the functionality and the data stored in all the other services, if this access is authorized. In essence, now that Microsoft has built the basic platform, new services will be able to expand it and add value. HailStorm provides a service fabric that makes creating services for HailStorm easier than creating generic web services. The service fabric contains support for security, metering, and many other infrastructure items. The platform aspect of HailStorm is very similar to Windows, where Microsoft creates the platform and third parties develop applications that add value to the platform.

HailStorm could be the Largest Application Ever Created

To sum it all up, HailStorm could be viewed as the largest application ever created. If successful, it will provide a significant portion of user services, business services, transaction processing, identity, and building-block services across all platforms. Microsoft is trying to define a standard set of web services that everyone, even other web service providers will rely on. A main revenue stream will be that these standard services will be products themselves. It is not too hard to envision a situation where the HailStorm services are so useful and widely acceptable that you almost have to use them. With all that said, in the long run HailStorm is going to be what Microsoft and third parties add to it. Not even Microsoft can do it itself. Microsoft needs a huge pool of companies creating products for HailStorm in order to deliver the most feature-rich web service environment around.

Business Model

Obviously one of the main motivations for anyone using HailStorm (and Microsoft in creating it) is to make money. Therefore, in this section, we'll look at how a business might use HailStorm web services to generate revenue, but first we'll look at how Microsoft will charge for it.

HailStorm Services won't be Free

"The business model for HailStorm is breaking new ground. We will reboot the Internet, and get Users familiar with the model of paying for services. What is it worth for users to have all the devices in their lives synchronized, to be able to get urgent notifications on any device, any time, anywhere, to be in full control of their personal information; to harness the power of the Internet to work on their behalf?" Microsoft statement on charging users for HailStorm services.

Microsoft has three different groups it will charge for HailStorm services: end users, service operators, and developers.

Microsoft will charge end users a subscription fee for using HailStorm services. Microsoft is convinced users will pay for their digital safe deposit box, any device notifications, and the many other features in the HailStorm services. Microsoft will announce pricing details in October 2001. It is assumed that Passport will remain a free service for end users, as it does not seem in Microsoft's interest to charge for it.

Microsoft will charge service operators and developers for development tools and live test support. These charges will be nominal, as Microsoft wants to encourage development for HailStorm. Microsoft will charge service operators annual certification fees and additional fees for large volume use or other additional requirements. The details of these prices will be available in October 2001.

The fact that Microsoft is charging for HailStorm services is significant for three reasons:

❑   This is another step towards Microsoft's apparent aim of changing to a subscription-based business model.

❑   Microsoft is attempting to convince Internet users to pay for these new services. This is a great opportunity for if as it currently only earns revenue from about 2% of its Internet customers.

❑   Microsoft is adamant that because it is charging the end user for using HailStorm services, it will not have to rely on generating income from user data. It feels that the fee-based model will provide the user with security and privacy.

HailStorm as a Business Opportunity

HailStorm provides many business opportunities to other organizations as well. Any business that wants to connect its devices to people and the Internet can benefit from HailStorm. Any business that has a need to notify people will benefit from HailStorm. This may mean that business save money by notifying employees and business partners of important events. For many hardware manufacturers, including cell phone providers and PDA makers, the ability to deliver HailStorm services will provide additional revenue, a competitive advantage, and may become a necessity over time.

Businesses can add services to their products or web sites and gain additional revenue streams by charging for these services as HailStorm-compatible services. Microsoft is generally interested in products that sell to many millions, so services with that reach may receive competition from Microsoft. Microsoft also states that it will create services in areas where it has vertical knowledge; however, not even Microsoft can come close to creating services for all the potential markets.

New levels of selling and marketing will be made possible by HailStorm with the location, notification, wallet, and other HailStorm services. Conference tickets can be offered to people who like a particular band; restaurants with no wait within five blocks can be located, sales on products in the mall you are located in that meet your preferences, and many other targeted sales opportunities are possible with HailStorm. In reality, it is impossible to know what will be the most successful and useful services but the potential applications are very wide ranging.

Web services and HailStorm may provide web sites with needed revenue. One of the problems with the dot com era was the reliance on the browser. Sites that expose themselves to HailStorm services are also available to applications and other services as well as browser-based users.

Businesses Opportunities for Developers

HailStorm creates business opportunities for software companies, developers, and any other companies that want to utilize HailStorm services to create applications. HailStorm's success depends upon the level at which developers embrace HailStorm. One of the primary reasons that Windows was successful was the enormous support from developers and software companies. HailStorm also needs lots of developers and applications to add features and functionality if it is to succeed on a major scale.

HailStorm creates a tremendous market opportunity for companies and individuals capable of writing useful web services. Write an application, load it on a server, obtain HailStorm certification, and start benefiting from it. The potential customer base is very large. Developers who create services for the HailStorm platform do not have to build the authentication, location, messaging, notification, and preference logic. It is already part of the HailStorm service fabric. They also benefit from being able to expose their services to the 165 million Passport accounts.

The section earlier that described HailStorm integration with the travel service offers a glimpse of the massive development opportunity created by HailStorm. Think of all the travel companies, phone companies, software companies, and web sites, to name a few, that will need to integrate HailStorm services with their applications or create HailStorm-compatible services to work with their products.

So much for what might be, here are some examples of real-world applications that are being created by companies using HailStorm:

- ❑ EBAY is planning to use the HailStorm notification service to notify bidders using its auction service, permitting EBAY to concentrate on its core business

- ❑ American Express Blue Card is using it to notify customers of back orders and to cross-sell them other products

- ❑ Expedia is planning to use HailStorm for filtering travel plans that match the travelers' preferences, update their calendars with travel itineraries, and send notifications when the traveler and the people the traveler is visiting experience travel itinerary changes

- ❑ Groove Networks, founded by Ray Ozzie, creator of Lotus Notes, is using HailStorm to provide security, contacts lists, and other infrastructure support to its new peer-to-peer product

Microsoft released the first set of services itself. Going forward, it will work with other companies via the Microsoft Open Process. This will ensure the naming, schema, and the general functioning of new services. Microsoft will create services where it feels it has industry expertise and rely on third parties in areas where it does not. At the time of writing this book, the specific procedures that developers are required to follow to create services that tie into the HailStorm platform or create their own HailStorm-compatible services have not been made publicly available by Microsoft. Developers should make sure that they obtain this information when it is available if they wish to engage in HailStorm development.

Identity Services

HailStorm uses Microsoft Passport for authentication purposes. Passport permits a user to log in once and have access to HailStorm and all Passport-enabled sites.

The identity market is critical because the next generation of computing will involve tying services around an identity, and the company that controls the identity market will have a significant competitive advantage. As software begins to be delivered to individuals across all types of endpoints, Software licensing will no longer be based on a license to a specific computer, but rather to an identity or user. Any firm that controls this identity market is well placed to benefit from this new revenue stream.

As networks become more advanced, there is a big push to offer services to connected users. Microsoft is battling AOL to deliver services anytime, anywhere. Whoever controls the identity market will have a big edge in this battle.

Dispelling the myths about HailStorm

Since HailStorm's was first announced, there has been a lot of speculation about what Microsoft's aims are. Due to the distrust of MS that exist in some parts of the Internet community, some of this speculation has been very negative. In this section, we try to assuage some of the fears that have arisen in relation to HailStorm.

Privacy and Security

Microsoft states that because it is charging the users a fee for using HailStorm services it will not need to mine or benefit from their data in other ways. Microsoft is also building a system that will allow users to control who has access to their data and to set time restrictions on it. This service is not available yet, so it is hard to know how useful it will be, but it does seem to have considerable potential.

The part of HailStorm that seems to have attracted the most attention is Passport authentication. Passport is the single sign-in service that permits a user to log in onto HailStorm and all Passport enabled sites with one login. Windows XP users can extend the single sign in to log themselves into Windows XP also. Windows XP users will be required to sign up for a Passport account if they want to use some of the Internet features built into Windows XP, including Instant Messaging. HailStorm is built on top of XML, SOAP, UDDI, and WSDL: all open Web standards; the sole proprietary feature of HailStorm is Passport. Microsoft is not permitting using a standard UDDI lookup to locate competitive identity services. It is requiring the use of Passport.

Passport and HailStorm Security Technology

Passport collects personal information from users and stores the data by PUID. This enables Passport to validate the PUIDs from all HailStorm users, services, and applications. It is important to understand that Passport provides authentication, not authorization. Passport will return the PUID of the user, but it is up to the application, web site, or service to control what, if any, access the user is allowed.

Passport v3.0 will use a modified version of Kerberos (developed at MIT) for security. This requires the service to determine the client's identity without asking the client, and the client to determine the service's identity without asking the service. Kerberos uses a third party to authenticate a client to a server. The official release of HailStorm will use Passport 3.0; here is a list of some of the security features that will be built in to Passport and HailStorm:

❑ Data sent from Passport to Passport sites is delivered in a triple-DES encrypted format

❑ Sites using Passport have to have their own encryption key that is used to send user data between Passport and the Passport site

❑ Passwords are only delivered directly to the Passport service. They are never seen by participating web sites/services

❑ HailStorm data is never sent in the clear; it is contained in the SOAP message body in an RC4-encrypted format.

- ❏ Passport cookies are encrypted

- ❏ Passport-enabled sites are required to use SSL or disable caching on pages that display users personal information

- ❏ All the HailStorm and Passport data will be stored in an encrypted form; the Microsoft data operators cannot read the data

- ❏ Digital certificates and other authentication technologies will be available for Passport 3.0

- ❏ Services that utilize HailStorm data request it by passing a PUID to HailStorm. Microsoft has no access to the data that the service holds for the user and the service can only access what the user allows them to

Passport and HailStorm Policies

This section will cover some of the commitments Microsoft requires from HailStorm service operators, some information on privacy and security groups they are working with, and some of its reasoning about why it is in its interest to ensure Passport and HailStorm are and remain private and secure:

- ❏ Microsoft is working with industry security standards such as Truste and BBB Online

- ❏ Sites using Passport and HailStorm have to sign security and privacy agreements, where they commit to not mining or selling the data without the user's permission and to following security procedures to keep the data safe

- ❏ By default, only the user has access to the their data

- ❏ Microsoft is building a tool that will permit users to grant other people, devices, and applications access to their data

- ❏ Microsoft will not sell, mine, or target user data stored in Passport or HailStorm

One point frequently brought up by Microsoft is that it is in its vital interest to ensure that users' data is secure and private in HailStorm. It insists that if it cannot achieve this goal, users will not sign up for HailStorm, and HailStorm will fail.

Will Microsoft Change the Rules in the Middle of the Game?

Some people are concerned that Microsoft will increase prices and change its policies on data mining after HailStorm reaches critical mass. Microsoft claims it will not do this because changing the privacy rules will chase users away from the safe deposit boxes. Also consumer protection laws prevent Microsoft from using data in ways that are inconsistent with the terms under which it was collected.

If Microsoft increased the prices to HailStorm services providers it would risk the platform becoming less attractive. Therefore it is almost certain it will keep prices reasonable to end users because Microsoft wants HailStorm to be used by millions rather than by a few people paying higher fees. Service providers will be protected as Microsoft can only cancel contracts with a provider if they violate the terms of the HailStorm agreement.

Availability

Availability is an area that has received a lot of attention because Microsoft has been hit with multiple denial of service attacks this year. On top of that, distributed web services, as a whole, pose interesting challenges to uptime commitments. If multiple services from multiple vendors process a transaction, how then does any one vendor guarantee the entire transaction? In some cases, some of the suppliers may be generic and located via a UDDI lookup on a per transaction basis.

Here are Microsoft's commitment and record on uptime and availability:

❑ Passport has a history of high availability (98.1%). Most of the down time has been due to other entities as Microsoft Passport, itself, has only been down for 43 minutes over the last two years. This is a 99.995% availability rate. These availability rates are much higher than most internal authentication systems. Passport performs over 2 billion authentications every month.

❑ There are now built-in protections against denial of services attacks.

❑ There is an indemnification clause in the Passport contract that releases Microsoft from incidental damages.

❑ Microsoft will provide service level agreements and will announce details in October 2001.

❑ HailStorm services will run in geographically distributed physically redundant datacenters and the data will be synchronized across them.

HailStorm's Relationship to .NET

You may have seen some publications that use HailStorm and Microsoft .NET interchangeably, but that is not correct. This is partly Microsoft's fault as its marketing of HailStorm has been a little confusing on this issue. While HailStorm is a part of the Microsoft .NET Initiative it does not depend on any part of the .NET framework. Microsoft .NET is both a vision and a suite of products that includes the .NET languages, enterprise servers, and development tools. In fact, Microsoft.NET contains the all the tools needed to build generic web services that are completely unrelated to HailStorm as well as HailStorm-compatible web services.

HailStorm Architecture

Access to HailStorm services is via a SOAP messages containing HailStorm specific header and body content. The content of the soap message is written in HailStorm Data Manipulation Language (HSDL), which allows you to access and modify the information stored by the HailStorm services. HSDL is an XML-based language that consists of the elements used in all method calls. Although XPath is not part of HSDL, it plays a key role as it is used for node specification in every method used.

Microsoft will hold user data for the core HailStorm services. Companies that access HailStorm services should keep a user database with the PUID as the key field. This will permit them to access HailStorm services by passing the PUID to the HailStorm service. The HailStorm service will then return the data for that PUID that the company is authorized to receive.

It is important to remember that HailStorm is not directly accessible by users. It is a set of XML web services that store data and exchange it across the Internet. Other applications and devices called endpoints provide the user interface.

Endpoint is a term that has evolved from software being accessed anywhere, anytime, on any device. The reason for this is that the software services will not only be accessed by devices, but also by other applications and endpoints. You can think of these as intermediate points, because it is just as likely that software will talk with many services, applications, and, maybe, even with multiple devices when processing requests.

HailStorm Service Fabric

As a programmer, it might be hard to understand exactly what HailStorm brings to the table. Why should you create web services with HailStorm? Why not just create generic web services? We have already covered some of the marketing aspects of this in the *Business Model* section of this chapter. However, the other compelling reason to use HailStorm is that it will enable you to develop and deploy web services with out having to provide the complete infrastructure yourself from scratch. The HailStorm service fabric is a common infrastructure that all the HailStorm services run under. Here is a brief list of the different components of the service fabric will provide:

- ❑ Authentication
- ❑ Security and Privacy
- ❑ SOAP processor
- ❑ Dispatcher
- ❑ Metering
- ❑ Monitoring
- ❑ Defense
- ❑ Audit and Logging
- ❑ Operations

By using HailStorm you can stop worrying about these 'dull' but essential aspects of your web service and concentrate on the actual services you will be offering.

Is HailStorm an Open Platform?

HailStorm services are accessed via SOAP messages, enabling any device that can send and receive a SOAP message to access HailStorm services. This is surprising news from Microsoft, which has traditionally created software that runs only on Windows. One reason for this change is that personal computing is increasingly expanding into areas other than the desktop PC market that Microsoft dominates. Microsoft operating systems do not dominate the non-PC world as they dominate the PC world. Microsoft is making a lot of progress with Win CE, but still has only a small portion of the high-growth hand-held and mobile phone market.

While Microsoft is committed to using open standards, it is also adamant that it will make its Windows-based platforms the preferred endpoints for HailStorm. Microsoft knows that they are competing in a completely open market and that the only way to sell its operating systems is to make them the most compelling endpoint for these software services.

There is talk from Microsoft about supporting the running of HailStorm services on other platforms, but as of now, there are no more details. The current situation is that the HailStorm services can be accessed from any platform but the alpha SDK is only available for Windows platforms.

Here are some specific items where Microsoft is currently supporting Hailstorm or will add HailStorm support to its products:

❑   Integration into all of its endpoints including XBox, Stinger, and future versions of Windows

❑   ASP.NET and Visual Studio.NET make it easy to build web services, which complement HailStorm, and can utilize HailStorm as a platform

❑   Microsoft web sites such as http://www.msn.com and http://www.bcentral.com/ will be able to offer additional services to their customers based on HailStorm services

❑   Microsoft applications such as Office will be enhanced to take advantage of the capabilities of HailStorm such as authentication, application settings, personal data, and notifications

HailStorm is XML

HailStorm Services rely on XML for messaging, as most or all web services do; however, HailStorm Services are also stored and manipulated as XML documents and defined using XML schemas. Exposing the data as well as the operations in an XML format provides HailStorm services with very strong interoperational abilities. HailStorm is a first generation, distributed XML application designed to aggregate the data and functionality of remote services.

> "Now, schema is the technical term you're going to be hearing again and again in this XML world. It's through schemas that information can be exchanged, things like schemas for your appointments, schemas for your health records. The work we're announcing today is a rather large schema that relates to things of interest to an individual. And you'll recognize very quickly what those things are, things like your files, your schedule, your preferences, all are expressed in a standard form. And so, by having that standard form, different applications can fill in the information and benefit from reading out that information. And so it's about getting rid of these different islands." Bill Gates in the HailStorm press announcement March 19th 2001.

One way to look at HailStorm is as an identity-based system revolving around XML schemas. Any data can be securely accessed and manipulated via standard XML operations based on the PUID. HailStorm will achieve critical mass if there are enough schemas and PUIDs defined.

The figure below shows several HailStorm Services, each exposing an XML interface.

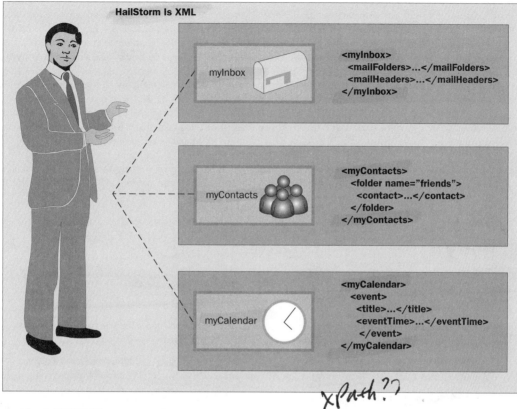

HailStorm Is XML

```
myInbox

<myInbox>
  <mailFolders>...</mailFolders>
  <mailHeaders>...</mailHeaders>
</myInbox>
```

```
myContacts

<myContacts>
  <folder name="friends">
    <contact>...</contact>
  </folder>
</myContacts>
```

```
myCalendar

<myCalendar>
  <event>
    <title>...</title>
    <eventTime>...</eventTime>
  </event>
</myCalendar>
```

XPath??

Querying XML Documents

HailStorm documents are accessed using XML queries. At the time of writing, a subset of XPath (xpQuery) is supported and, according to Microsoft, xmQuery is working but not documented. xpQuery is based on XPath, and as it is the only query mechanism currently documented, we'll use XPath as the de facto querying method in this book.

HailStorm data will be stored in a database but because of the XML layer in between the developer will never need to directly access the database. Programmers familiar with XPath and XML document processing will, in general, feel right at home. Those who are not will have to learn to query against, insert into, and update XML documents rather than a relational database. Learning the XPath syntax is straightforward; however, a couple of issues remain that are a little more challenging:

❑   HailStorm documents are stored in a hierarchical and not a relational format. This requires learning to work with hierarchical documents.

❑   XPath is more of a node selection tool than a querying tool and can only query elements within the data being selected. This means that in order to select the e-mail address for Patricia, you have to pull the entire contact down and use the DOM or XSLT to extract the name. xmQuery and other XML querying tools are being certified by W3C, and HailStorm is designed to work with other query tools as and when they become available.

How to Code with HailStorm

Visual Studio.NET will add support for HailStorm. Some or all of this functionality may be available with the beta release, but was not available at the time of writing this book. How far Visual Studio.NET will go to make it easier for HailStorm developers is unknown. At the very least, it will probably provide a way to reference the HailStorm services, add code snippets to begin and end each statement, and add IntelliSense support (a feature common in Microsoft development products that guides the developer through coding) for all of the properties and operations exposed by the services. There will probably also be support added to assist in building the XPath queries, but it is not clear how this support will be added. Visual Studio.NET is Microsoft's developer tool and HailStorm its platform for web services, so you can be sure that Microsoft is going to put a lot of effort into making HailStorm development with Visual Studio.NET as easy and efficient as possible for developers.

Keep in mind this is very early-staged software and that, at the time of writing this book there was no support for HailStorm in Visual Studio .NET. There is supposed to be some support added by the time this book is published.

Summary

Microsoft has a great opportunity with HailStorm if it can overcome the following obstacles:

- ❏ Convince developers to embrace HailStorm and use it as their development platform

- ❏ Convince users that their HailStorm digital safe deposit box is a safe and reliable place to store their data and convince users that they should pay for it

- ❏ Successfully run the large complicated datacenters required to operate HailStorm it has experience with four of the largest Web Sites but this is still not Microsoft's primary business

- ❏ Work out the privacy and security concerns with governments, businesses, and users

- ❏ Win consumer customers from AOL and other competitors

If Microsoft is successful with the items listed above, we will have access to XML documents containing the most updated user data and this data will be accessible on any device.

As a developer the area that is most exciting is the new type of notification and calendar-based systems we will be able to create. The travel agency example and some others were mentioned above. Inserting this functionality into business applications in the enterprise including customer service, order entry, and sales force management is currently difficult. The data and rules for each one are contained within each individual system. HailStorm will enable businesses to create one set of preferences and notification rules and benefit from the data stored in all applications.

Developers who want to embrace HailStorm should become familiar with XML schemas, XML querying, web service technologies, and the HailStorm SDK. So in the next chapter we'll start by looking at what you can do with the HailStorm SDK now and how to get it up and running.

early adopter

2

Reality Bites – HailStorm in a Box

The vision of HailStorm as Microsoft would like it to be is far reaching and it's not too difficult to conceive several blue-sky projects that could make full use of its services when they become available in 2002. Wrox may have even released Beginning and Professional .NET My Services Programming by then to make those projects somewhat easier to realize. However, for now, those books aren't available and neither is a great deal of HailStorm. What is available is HailStorm in a Box (HSiaB), a cut-down, alpha quality emulator that will run on a LAN. This should be released at Microsoft's Professional Developers Conference in October 2001 and be available for download from http://www.microsoft.com/net/.

In this chapter, we'll look at what you can and can't do with it right now. In particular, we'll take an overview of:

❏ HailStorm's current security mechanism

❏ How the messaging between HailStorm endpoints and HSiaB works

❏ The actual services currently available

❏ The various other SDKs and Microsoft releases we can use to 'fill the gaps' that currently exist in this alpha software release

We'll also discuss the current environment for developing a HailStorm endpoint on any platform and the three-step certification process it will need to undergo before public release against the production HailStorm servers.

Finally, we'll get HailStorm in a Box installed ready for some work in Chapter 3.

A Quick Recap – HailStorm as it Will Be

So to the guided tour – a vision of HailStorm as Microsoft sees it is this:

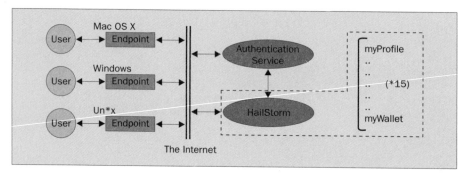

Via HailStorm endpoints, users will be able to access their Digital Safe Deposit Box (DSDB) over the Internet. The endpoints will all be Passport-enabled and use Passport to authenticate a user to the HailStorm services. Once authenticated, the user can then add, modify, or delete information in their DSDB, and designate who else can access this information. The endpoint communicates changes to the stored information by sending a SOAP message to one of the HailStorm web services responsible for that particular piece of information. The service then sends back a response – again a SOAP message – stating the success or failure of the change. The information sent back and forth across the wire meanwhile is always encrypted and thus secure. Likewise, the information remains encrypted on the HailStorm servers at all times as well.

HailStorm as it Stands

The system described above may have arrived by next year, but it's not what we have to work with today. Let's start on the HailStorm side and see what we have and what we'll have to look forward to while HailStorm in a Box matures.

Authentication

The authentication mechanism by which a user is identified and given permission to access the information in his digital safe deposit box is the biggest hole for now and will most likely continue to be so until 2002. When it's operational, HailStorm will use Passport v3.0 (which is Kerberos-enabled) to authenticate users over the web. However, HailStorm in a Box is LAN-based rather than web-based and Passport v2.0 has only just arrived on the scene (September 2001). Unfortunately, this version adds only some extra PIN-based security to Passport v1.4 and we'll have to wait until v3.0 for a Kerberos environment.

▸▸ Kerberos in Brief

Kerberos is a distributed authentication service that allows a client to prove its identity to a server without sending confidential data across the network. Under Kerberos, a client can be either a user or a service, and it sends a request for a "ticket" to the Key Distribution Center (KDC). The KDC generates a "ticket-granting ticket" (TGT) for the client, encrypts it using the client's password stored locally as the private key, and sends the encrypted TGT back to the client. The client will only successfully decrypt the TGT if it uses the correct password. The decrypted TGT is then kept with the client as a proof of its identity.

In Kerberos, the client's encryption key derives from and should be considered as a password. Kerberos uses the Data Encryption Standard (DES) as its method of encryption. This method ensures that encrypted data can only be decrypted by the same key that encrypted it. Otherwise, the result will be unintelligible and the checksum in the Kerberos message will not match the data.

For the time being then, HSiaB uses a pseudo-security mechanism that generates a temporary Passport User ID (PUID) for you to use when your account is enabled on the server. This PUID takes the place of both the actual Passport user ID and the Kerberos TGT ticket that would be given to the endpoint when the user is successfully authenticated, and which subsequently would be embedded in the SOAP messages to the web services to validate the user's identity. The actual interchange between Passport/Kerberos and the user endpoint is covered in Chapter 3, as is how to discover this temporary ID.

While we wait for Passport v3.0 to become available, however, it would certainly not go amiss to download a copy of the Passport v2.0 SDK and learn how to incorporate it into one of your web sites. At this point, one can only assume that the procedure for incorporating v3.0 will be the similar although given that passport is expected to become the next technology behind the Windows OS login, it may become even simpler. Theoretically, a user would be automatically identified by any passport-enabled web sites once logged into that version of Windows. Talking to HailStorm would then be just a matter of talking to the local authentication system, rather than to the Passport server over the web.

For developers using non-Windows platforms, there's obviously the problem in that Passport is a Windows-only technology, however this will be remedied soon, as we'll see later.

Messaging

The sending of requests and responses to and from the web services maintaining users' DSDBs is of course the key to working with HailStorm and the mechanism to do that is already fully implemented. The messaging mechanism uses SOAP messages written in raw XML; this is topic is covered in detail in Chapters 3, 4, and 5. The list of implemented services that you can send messages to is (unsurprisingly) not complete yet, but we can still get a good idea of how to put things together. The only mechanism missing here is the cryptographic engine that encodes the payload of the message for transport over the web and decodes it again on the server.

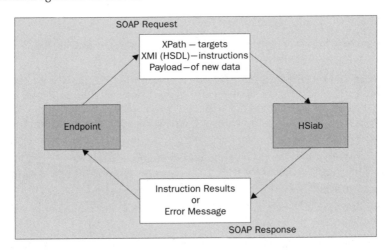

Each SOAP message contains an instruction to a web service written in HailStorm Data-manipulation Language (HSDL). Specifically it targets one of the three XML documents (content, system, or roleList – see next section for more on these) that each service contains and a set of XML nodes within that, containing the information to be retrieved or altered. This set is identified using an XPath expression and may contain zero or more nodes. The payload (body) of the message is the alteration to the document that we'd like to make, written out to obey the schema of that particular document.

Because this messaging mechanism is completely XML and standards-based with no Microsoft proprietary extensions in sight (yet), it remains accessible on any platform. HSiaB provides alternatives for sending the messages as well – via the command line, a script making use of a SOAP API, or an application using the HailStorm reference libraries. Admittedly, the command line remains a Windows-only option and there's only one (C-based) run time library now, but there are at least a dozen SOAP APIs out there already.

The standards-based nature also leaves HailStorm open to make use of new web standards as and when they are ratified. For example, SOAP 1.2, XQuery 1.0, and XPath 2.0 have all just begun the standards process, and will offer more versatility to our requests. XML Blueberry could bring full Unicode-compliance to HailStorm, meaning that information could be stored in the user's native script, whatever area of the world they are from.

The only 'standards' likely to change between now and HailStorm's release are the schemas defining the structure of the actual XML documents sitting under the web services. It will be up to us as developers to keep a track on changes as new releases appear. To give an example, the myAddress service was merged into myProfile not so long ago (August 2001) and the schema for myProfile is now even larger than it was previously.

Actual Services

With various mergers and renamings having taken place, the initial feature set currently comprises fifteen HailStorm services and even they may be rolled out across more than one official version. For now though, HailStorm in a Box contains eight services for you to develop against:

❑ myServices holds the locations of the other web services, looking after the information in your DSDB.

❑ **myCalendar** will mimic the diary service available in Outlook.

❑ **myCategories** allows you to create categories and subcategories with which you can classify the other information stored in HailStorm.

❑ myContacts holds addressing information on your business and personal contacts, organized by category. This is much the same facility as the Contacts folder in Outlook, except that this version stores 'live' information. If the people you hold information about also have DSDBs and give you permission, myContacts can update the contact information from their myProfile service when it changes.

❑ myFavoriteWebSites works in the same way as your browser's Favorites folder, allowing you to store and categorize URLs for later use and even subscribe for notification when information about that URL changes.

❑ **myLists** allows you to create and qualify lists of things to do, much like the Tasks functionality in Outlook.

❑ myProfile acts as a storage place for your own personal information, much as would be seen in myContacts for other people.

❑ myWallet is designed to store the details of one or more methods of paying vendors over the web. Typically, this could mean credit card information or bank account details.

The remaining seven services are still in development, but should appear in subsequent versions of HailStorm in a Box. Remember that one service's functionality might be rolled into another's by the time they do appear but we can at least be aware of what to expect:

❑ **myLocation** and **myPresence** will hold details of a user's current location and connection status respectively.

❑ **myInbox** will round out the traditional collaboration information available online, mimicking or at least approximating the functionality of Outlook's e-mail facilities.

❑ **myDocuments** looks to be the secure area where you can store your own files online.

❑ while **myApplicationSettings** will hold the settings preferences for various applications, much like the Documents and Settings folder does for each user in Windows 2000. The number and size of the documents a user can hold here will probably determine for the most part whether they pay the basic subscription fee or some higher rate.

❑ **myDevices** should keep a list of the settings and capabilities of the devices you use, much like the System Hardware Profile facility in Windows.

❑ Finally, **myAlerts** will hold a list of entities that can send the user messages based on the subscriptions that they have previously set up. We'll look a bit more at the precursors of this service in a minute.

As mentioned earlier, each service is responsible for three documents per user. These carry read-only server information ('System'), the list of entities that can access the information the service holds sway over ('RoleList'), and the content itself ('Content'). Each is written in XML according to various schemas. The schemas for the System and RoleList documents remain the same across all the HailStorm services, but each Content document uses a different one specific to the information that it will be holding. These schemas also define the points in the documents that we can navigate to and alter, through a type of 'color-coding'. We'll look at this in much more detail in Chapter 4.

Each service also has six standard methods: `Insert`, `Delete`, `Replace`, `Update`, `Query`, and `ChangeNotify`. These are atomic methods – if they go wrong, they roll back the changes they have made so far to the original state of the content. There are also domain- or service-specific methods. For example, myInbox will include the `sendMessage` and `getMessageAttachment` methods. We'll look more at these HSDL methods in Chapter 5.

Each service incorporates an element of server-side version history into the information stored in its three documents – a change number to note what came last, so to speak. Microsoft is currently investigating the feasibility of extending this to include client-generated version histories, which would enable multi-master replication. It's only in design though, so there's not telling whether this will come to fruition.

When finally released, the services might have different names but they will be the same underneath. The Hailstorm team wants people to build on top of Hailstorm but not to expand the suite of web services. Their message is 'Make use of ours, but go and build your own if you so choose'. Indeed, that's what we try to do in Chapters 6 and 7.

MyAlerts and MS Alerts

The myAlerts service is a little bit different from the others in that extra work is going on in the background to get its subscription facilities working across all platforms and operating systems. The oft-used example is that of an online auction you are participating in. By using myAlerts, the auction site would send you a message when you are outbid rather than you having to checking back every five minutes.

When it's released, myAlerts will be able to send SOAP-based messages synchronously or asynchronously to any device over any transport protocol – which is pretty powerful. Senders (for example the auction site) will also be able to specify routing data, send to services other than the myAlerts service, and interact with myAlerts through the standard HailStorm methods, as well as do a few other fancy things.

For those of you who'd like to start working on a subset of this functionality, 'myAlerts 0.5' is available for download in the guise of the forthcoming MS Alerts 1.0 SDK from Microsoft. It does have its limitations though:

- ❑ MS Alerts can only be sent to an e-mail account, MSN Mobile device, or MS Messenger client, and they can only send over HTTP

- ❑ MS Alerts can only push notifications to a client; they will not wait for them to be picked up

- ❑ The structure of an MS Alerts notification is largely similar (but not identical) to those in myAlerts

- ❑ The backend of MS Alerts is closed source

The way that a Subscription is defined may vary between MS Alerts and myAlerts as well, although that seems up in the air still.

If you were contemplating installing Passport at this time to get a feeling for that technology, it's worth noting that MS Alerts also uses Passport as its authentication mechanism, so the interaction between the two should give you a closer picture of how HailStorm might work with Passport v3.0.

Development Platforms

There's not a lot to the HailStorm big picture at the moment, which makes it all the easier to realize how useful it could actually be to users and developers alike. However, what about from our point of view as developers attempting to create and integrate endpoints on various platforms? From the user's perspective, it shouldn't matter what device they're using; access to their safe deposit box should always be possible. That means that the onus is on us to make that access transparent and on Microsoft to provide us with the tools for the job. The core technologies – raw XML and SOAP – are cross-platform, which is a good start, as are Kerberos and the algorithm to encrypt the payload of each message. What we need is the ability to authenticate the user then send messages to, and receive them from, the server.

Windows

Naturally enough, developers basing their endpoints on Windows platforms are the best catered for. Passport and MS Alerts can be downloaded to develop against the precursors of the technology that HailStorm will use, and HailStorm in a Box runs natively on Windows 2000 Server.

Likewise, there are several messaging options you can use with HailStorm in a Box even at this early stage:

❑ Using raw XML via a command-line executable bundled with HSiaB

❑ Scripting against Microsoft's SOAP Toolkit 2.0 or some other SOAP API, sending and receiving messages using the functionality of the API

❑ Incorporating HailStorm functionality into an application using code written against the HailStorm Runtime APIs

These run-time libraries will also incorporate the Kerberos-standard DES3 algorithm used for encrypting the payload of the message for safe transfer across the Internet. The algorithm for this encryption is in the public domain so you can implement your own version, but for now HSiaB itself doesn't have the en/decrypt facilities built-in. Microsoft plans to build versions of the run-time library for several programming languages and make them available as shared source code, so that others may implement it in languages of their own choosing. Only one version, the C library, is currently available with HSiaB.

Although HailStorm in a Box is likely to remain a download from http://www.microsoft.com/net/ rather than to be subsumed into another product, it seems inevitable that a plug-in for a 'HailStorm Project' will appear for Visual Studio .NET as well (maybe even Visual Studio 6) to assist the development of Windows-based endpoints even further.

Non-Windows Systems

The first thing to realize, if you want to develop a HailStorm endpoint on a non-Windows platform, is that you are still going to need access to a Windows box on your LAN in order to run HailStorm in a Box and test against it. HSiaB isn't going to be ported across to another platform. Likewise, MS Alerts will remain Windows-only although, since this is an interim technology, this needn't necessarily matter too much.

On the other hand, the current Passport SDK (v1.4), which presents itself as the other sticking point for non-Windows developers, *is* being ported to other platforms by Ready-to-Run Software (http://www.rtr.com/) at the behest of Microsoft. Only time will tell how far behind Microsoft's releases these ports will appear, but it's a start. Underneath the covers, all that's needed of the SDK by an endpoint is to verify a user with the MS Passport server and retrieve the user's Passport User ID for inclusion in the SOAP message.

▸▸Passport v1.4 on Other Platforms

Ready-to-Run Software is porting Passport v1.4 to Solaris and Red Hat Linux for Q3 2001 and has plans in the works for ports to AIX, HPUX, FreeBSD, and SunOS.

Passport v3.0 isn't likely to include any of the Microsoft extensions to the industry-standard Kerberos authentication mechanism, so an alternative implementation making use of that fact could perhaps be engineered for a swifter release. Indeed, MS is using Kerberos so alternative implementations can be created. On September 20 2001 it challenged the internet world to create a 'federation of trust' using Kerberos as the link, envisioning a day when an AOL or Yahoo login would be as valid for accessing MSN or HailStorm as a Passport login, and vice versa.

The outlook continues to be bright when we look at the actual sending and receiving of SOAP messages to the server. There are several excellent implementations of SOAP in the open source world (SOAP::Lite and Apache SOAP to name two) that can do the job here. Like the SOAP Toolkit, they don't have the functionality for encrypting the payload yet. However, once Microsoft opens up the way it has integrated the DES3 algorithm into the construction of the message, it shouldn't be too long before they do. Likewise, the HailStorm Runtime Library is now available in C and will shortly be available for C++ developers so everyone can integrate them on any platform. The APIs will apparently be made public as shared source code as well, so interested parties can port them to JSP, PHP, Perl, and so on as they deem necessary.

Application/Endpoint Certification

All in all things look good for endpoint developers who want to start developing against HSiaB, regardless of the platform they are working on, but what of the live HailStorm servers to deploy a release against?

In an ongoing, open source-like trend, HailStorm v1.0 is slated for calendar year 2002 and looks likely to appear 'when it's ready' and not before. It may have all 15 slated services in it, or it may not, with the emphasis on making sure that those released really do work to the best standard possible – which is all to the good of the developer really.

On the other side of the equation, live HailStorm test servers for developers to deploy their endpoint solutions on are a way off yet. Indeed, Microsoft has already identified a few ways that ill-behaved applications could cause problems with a live server, to the point of emulating a full denial of service attack by mistake, so they will introduce a three-point certification process for HailStorm-enabled applications:

❑   Stage one is to develop the application against HailStorm in a Box. This shares a good deal of common code with the live servers and the interactions are very similar to the real thing.

❑   Stage two is to set the application up against a live (cluster of) test server(s) and configure the application to work over the net with whichever transport protocols you think necessary. (This is the point where serious performance testing can be done)

❑   Stage three is deployment of the application against live production servers and performance monitoring.

Each application will need certification from Microsoft to proceed to the next step, although what the certification will require is so far unknown.

Timeline

Don't be discouraged that there's a way to go before a full SDK or indeed HailStorm v1.0 appear. A lot of the code you create now against HailStorm in a Box will still be valid as beta and final versions of this emulator appear. Don't forget that it will be part of a long-term developer solution for initially testing your applications against the my* services of your choice, so there's plenty of reason for Microsoft to keep it alive and up to date with all the developments in the web services world as well as those of HailStorm itself.

To the best of our knowledge, here's a table of what technologies (which might have a bearing on your development) to expect when, in the forthcoming year and a half:

Previously	H2 2001	H1 2002	H2 2002
	HailStorm in a Box alpha (Oct)	HSiaB beta releases	HailStorm v1.0
Passport v1.0 (Apr 99)	Passport v2.0 (Oct) MS Alerts v1.0 (Oct)	MS Alerts v1.1	Passport v3.0
	SOAP 1.2 Working Draft (Jul) XQuery 1.0 Working Draft		SOAP 1.2 Ratified? XQuery 1.0 Ratified?
SOAP 1.1 (May 00) SOAP-SEC (Feb 01) XPath 1.0 (Nov 99)	(Aug) XPath 2.0 Working Draft (Aug)		XPath 2.0 Ratified?

We've added in a little speculation concerning the two W3C specifications that concern HailStorm most – SOAP and XPath. The next versions of these two standards were recently released as Working Drafts for discussion among the Internet community. It remains to be seen exactly how long it takes them to become Recommendations, but when they do, it would seem only prudent for Microsoft to look and see if it can make use of any new functionality in the standards within HailStorm.

Installing HailStorm in a Box

Now that we know exactly what we're getting ourselves into, let's get HailStorm in a Box (HSiaB) installed ready for some code in Chapter 3. The SDK itself isn't that big, but the prerequisites are quite substantial if you've not got them already installed. In a suggested order of installation, you'll need the following before you can install HSiaB:

❑ **Windows 2000** – Service Pack 2 recommended. Alternately, you can use Windows XP Professional.

❑ **IIS 5.0** or higher – This will probably be installed with Windows 2000 or XP, but you ought to make sure. This gives HailStorm in a Box its presence on the LAN, allowing you to query its services via the Web.

❑ **SQL Server 2000** – Service Pack 1 recommended. Note that blank account passwords are unacceptable for any accounts to be used for HailStorm. Likewise, setup is not currently compatible with case-sensitive SQL servers. This acts as the HailStorm data store sitting behind the web services that you and the user will see.

❑ **Windows Scripting Host 5.5** – Available from http://www.microsoft.com/msdownload/vbscript/scripting.asp to download or as part of Internet Explorer 5.5; the latest WSH 5.6 also works fine. The Windows Scripting Host is needed to install HSiaB and as the one of the ways to access HailStorm once installed.

❑ Microsoft SOAP Toolkit 2.0 – Needed only to run the samples that come with HailStorm in a Box. Some of the examples in this book also make use of this. Download it from http://msdn.microsoft.com/soap if not already installed.

Many and varied errors can occur if you don't have all the prerequisites installed before attempting to install HSiaB. You'll also need the IIS and SQL Server services running before you start to install. If you don't have copies of either Windows 2000 or SQL Server 2000, you can use the 120-day evaluation copies that are available from http://www.microsoft.com/windows2000/edk/default.asp and http://www.microsoft.com/sql/evaluation/trial/2000/default.asp respectively. Note, however, that you cannot apply service packs to these evaluation copies.

The latest build of HSiaB has a GUI-based installer, which, while easier than installing it from the command line, offers you less control in the way it is installed. Unfortunately, the installation process has become sufficiently complex that using the command line to set up HSiaB is no longer an easy option.

Using the GUI Installer

Installing HailStorm in a Box is very simple thanks to the GUI installer that now ships with the SDK. Assuming you have installed the prerequisites listed above, just run the file setup.msi that you'll find in the root directory of your HailStorm CD or download and work through the following steps:

❑ Accept the license agreement then Click Next.

❑ Select which pieces of the SDK you want to install. Currently there are only two choices, HailStorm in a Box and the Documentation and Sample Code. Check both if they aren't already checked then click Next.

❑ The third window lets you specify a SQL Server account username and password with the administrative privileges to create new databases for HailStorm and insert tables into them. Note that this account cannot have a blank password. If you haven't set one up, you can use the default option and use Windows authentication to enable access to your SQL Server. The account you are currently logged on as will be used. Again, this NT account must also have a SQL Server administrator's rights. When you've made your choice, click Next.

❑ Finally, you need to specify the installation directory for HailStorm itself, the documentation, and sample code. Click Next.

Behind the scenes while you're looking at the time remaining dialog, the installer first creates an XML file containing all the configuration information needed to install HSiaB. Using this file, it then sets up each service, performing the same two tasks – copying files to the network share and creating the appropriate virtual directory and database tables – for each service. Finally, the backup and temporary files used in the installation are removed (this can take some time) and with that done, HSiaB is installed on your computer and you are ready to go.

There are now just a couple of tasks you need to do manually to get yourself and any others interested ready to work with HailStorm.

Setting SRVLOCATOR

Several of the command-line tools that come with the installation make use of an environment variable called SRVLOCATOR to establish the HTTP address of the server running HSiaB. By default, this variable doesn't exist and needs to be created on each client machine that will be using those tools. This can be done in one of three ways:

For a temporary solution, to be repeated after each reboot of your machine, simply type:

```
>set SRVLOCATOR=http://HS_server_name
```

at the command prompt (not forgetting to replace *HS_server_name* with your own server's name) and then close the window. For Windows 9x and Windows Me clients, a more permanent solution is to save it in `c:/autoexec.bat`, inserting the above line of code into the file, then saving it and rebooting the computer. For Windows NT, Windows 2000, and Windows XP machines, this can be done even quicker (and without a reboot) from the Environment Variables dialog box you'll find under the Advanced tab of the System control panel.

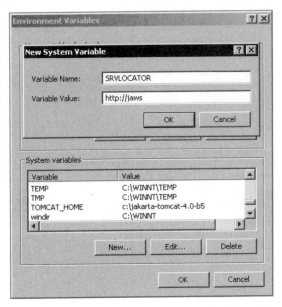

Hit the New... button in the System variables half of the screen then enter SRVLOCATOR for the variable name and `http://your_HS_server_name` for the variable value. Press OK twice and you're done.

Note that once this variable has been created, client machines can then copy the command-line tools across to their machines from the Bin subdirectory where HSiaB was installed and run them there.

Provisioning

Provisioning is another name for setting up a user account on a HailStorm server – creating a digital safe-deposit box for a user if you will. HSiaB automatically provisions the server for the Windows user account logged on when the installation took place, but you'll need to follow this procedure for provisioning the server for any other account. This we do using hsprov.exe, which you'll find in the bin directory of your installation. For each service, barring myServices which is provisioned automatically as soon as you provision any of the other services, you should call hsprov.exe like so:

```
>hsprov.exe -s service_name -o NT_Domain_username -l http://HS_server
```

with appropriate values for each of the flags. Therefore, for example, if you want a digital safe-deposit box with access to all eight services, make the following calls on the command line:

```
C:\HailStorm\Bin>hsprov.exe -s myContacts -o danm -l http://jaws
C:\HailStorm\Bin>hsprov.exe -s myFavoriteWebSites -o danm -l http://jaws
C:\HailStorm\Bin>hsprov.exe -s myProfile -o danm -l http://jaws
C:\HailStorm\Bin>hsprov.exe -s myWallet -o danm -l http://jaws
```

```
C:\HailStorm\Bin>hsprov.exe -s myCalendar -o danm -l http://jaws
C:\HailStorm\Bin>hsprov.exe -s myCategories -o danm -l http://jaws
C:\HailStorm\Bin>hsprov.exe -s myLists -o danm -l http://jaws
```

Do make sure you've spelled the service names correctly.

If you have many people wanting an account on this server, it's easier to use a short script to speed things up.

```
@echo off
hsprov -s myContacts -o %1 -l %2
hsprov -s myFavoriteWebSites -o %1 -l %2
hsprov -s myProfile -o %1 -l %2
hsprov -s myWallet -o %1 -l %2
hsprov -s myCalendar -o %1 -l %2
hsprov -s myCategories -o %1 -l %2
hsprov -s myLists -o %1 -l %2
```

Using the code above and saving it as provuser.bat in the same directory as hsprov.exe, we can provision the services for a user with a single call on the command line:

```
C:\HailStorm\Bin>provuser.bat NT_Domain_username http://HS_server_name
```

Alternatively, you could send hsprov.exe to each user. Provided they've set SRVLOCATOR on their machines, they can provision the server locally.

Reinstalling

If you'd like to reinstall the SDK, or uninstall any components thereof, simply double-click the setup.msi file you used to install it, select Reinstall, and work trough the following steps:

❑ Select the components you want to (re)install or uninstall by checking or unchecking those boxes against them (those components already installed will be checked initially) then click Next.

❑ If you've chosen to alter a component of HSiaB, you'll be asked for an administrator's account to access SQL server. Select an NT or SQL Server account as appropriate and click Next.

❑ Click Next again to begin the reinstallation.

When the reinstall is over, don't forget to provision your services again.

Note that if you'd like to upgrade your HSiaB installation from a previous version, you should uninstall that version first. Included below are details for a manual uninstall which will work for any previous build of HSiaB that does not use a graphical installation mechanism.

Removing HailStorm in a Box

If you want to uninstall HSiaB from your system, double-click the setup.msi file you used to install it, select Remove All, and click Next:

❑ You'll need to give the NT or SQL Server administrator's account again to remove the databases from SQL Server

❑ Click Next twice to begin the uninstall process

> ## ! Check IIS
>
> At the time of writing, the uninstaller did not properly remove the HailStorm-related virtual directories from IIS. You'll need to complete the first step of the manual uninstall procedure below to make sure they are removed.
>
> ■

A Manual Uninstall

At the time of writing, there were still versions of HSiaB available for which the install and uninstall processes were not automated. While we assume that everyone reading this book now has access to the current copy of HailStorm in which these processes are automated, if you've still got an old version and need to upgrade, you'll need to manually uninstall it first. Thankfully, it is a quick process. There are just three steps:

❑ From IIS, (Start menu | Programs | Administrative Tools | Internet Services Manager) locate the virtual directories corresponding to the HSiaB services – usually in the default web site. For each service installed you'll find a directory with the same name; delete all of them.

❑ From SQL Server Enterprise Manager (Start menu | Programs | Microsoft SQL Server | Enterprise Manager), locate the list of databases running on your HSiaB box. For each service, there will be two databases running; delete all of them.

❑ From Windows Explorer, delete the HailStorm files you installed to the server.

With those three tasks done, HailStorm in a Box will have been removed from your computer.

Summary

In this chapter we've looked at the current state of the HailStorm SDK aka HailStorm in a Box, as opposed to the blue sky version due in H2 2002 that was covered in Chapter 1. We've looked at what is available and what's not in the current version. We've also checked out the state of play for developers, Windows-based or not, and how to start getting to grips with the HailStorm platform from their end.

In the next chapter, we'll drill down into the core part of HailStorm in a Box – the SOAP messaging system – and see how to communicate with our newly installed LAN-based server.

early adopter

3

Talking To HailStorm

Microsoft surprised a lot of people with the release of its initial white paper on HailStorm. It contained the frank proposal that HailStorm services would be completely accessible from any platform, and not just Windows. As the white paper put it:

> "The HailStorm platform uses an open access model, which means it can be used with any device, application or services, regardless of the underlying platform, operating system, object model, programming language or network provider. All HailStorm services are XML Web SOAP; no Microsoft runtime or tool is required to call them."

Over the next three chapters, we'll look at the standards Microsoft has chosen to use and what we need to know to get HailStorm working for us.

In this chapter, we'll look at:

- ❑ The Kerberos Authentication Service, which Passport uses to validate users
- ❑ How to construct the SOAP packets that contain instructions for HailStorm web services
- ❑ The transport protocols we can use to send our SOAP packets to the HailStorm server
- ❑ The different ways currently available to generate and send SOAP packets to HailStorm in a Box

Bear in mind, that where possible we'll be looking at only the relevant pieces of each standard for use with HailStorm. There will be links and references outside of the book for those wishing to find out more as appropriate. We'll also flag up where things might not go so well in this quest for technology agnosticism.

Making Conversation

When HailStorm is finally released in the first half of 2002 it will sit behind the identity/security mechanism offered by Passport v3.0, which is due be released some time earlier. At the time of writing, Passport v2.0 had just been released and there were no more specifics on v3.0 beyond the knowledge that it will stop using its current proprietary authentication mechanism in favor of the industry-standard Kerberos system. This would suggest that Passport might become the authentication mechanism in the next version of the Windows OS family; Kerberos is already the Windows 2000 security mechanism. If this happens, a user logged on to their computer would automatically be logged into all Passport-enabled web sites as well.

As we saw in Chapter 1, HailStorm offers a set of services in the form of a digital safe deposit box for which a user pays a small subscription fee. This sits behind Passport as an additional, decidedly useful feature, which clients may make use of if they want. Users log on to a HailStorm endpoint (a web site, XBox game, Stinger smart phone, PocketPC, etc.) in the usual way through Passport. If they already have a digital safe deposit box, the endpoint should give the user the option to alter the information stored within the DSDB. They don't have a DSDB then they should be given the option to create one.

A Secure Future

So how will an endpoint perform a security handshake with and send a request to the Passport/HailStorm servers once HailStorm v1.0 has arrived? Let's look at the interaction with the Kerberos part of the Passport system first.

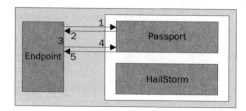

1. Once a user has clicked on the Passport login icon, the endpoint sends a request to Passport (which acts as the Key Distribution Center or KDC) for a ticket-granting ticket (TGT) for the user.

2. Passport returns a session key encrypted with the user's secret key and the TGT encrypted with its (Passport's) own secret key. The TGT also contains the session key.

3. The endpoint asks the user for their password and generates their secret key. If the password was correct, the endpoint can now decrypt the session key.

4. The endpoint now asks Passport for a ticket to access the HailStorm servers. Along with the request, it sends the still-encrypted TGT and some information that authenticates the user (UserID, PlatformID, and ApplicationID) encrypted with the session key.

5. Passport decrypts the TGT, retrieves the session key from it, and decrypts the authentication information. All being well, it generates a new session key for the endpoint's talk with HailStorm and incorporates the key and the various IDs into a new ticket. The ticket is then encrypted with a secret key it can share with HailStorm on demand and is sent back to the endpoint along with the new session key again encrypted with the user's secret key.

The endpoint now has the information it needs to talk to HailStorm – the Kerberos ticket and the session key, which it decrypts with the user's secret key. It can now build a message to HailStorm, authenticate it, and expect a response.

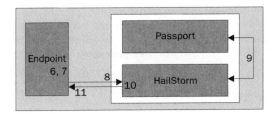

6. The header of the SOAP message holds the address of the server hosting the appropriate web service and the still-encrypted TGT and User PUID for identification.

7. The body of the SOAP message to HailStorm contains an instruction to retrieve or amend information. This and the rest of the body are encrypted with the session key.

8. Once completed, the endpoint sends the message to the named HailStorm server.

9. On receipt of the message, HailStorm sends Passport the PUID and asks for the appropriate secret key to decrypt the ticket, which Passport delivers.

10. HailStorm decrypts the ticket and attempts to decrypt the body of the message with the session key.

11. All being well, the instruction is carried out and either the appropriate results or an error message are returned in the body of the SOAP response message encrypted by the session key.

In overview, it's apparent that only encrypted information is ever sent across the wire to ensure that the request, response, and user information remain as secure as possible.

At this point, it may not be too surprising if you find yourself questioning the wisdom of Microsoft's choice of Passport as HailStorm's authentication mechanism. It is after all a Windows-only technology in the main. The key thing to remember is that Kerberos is an industry standard and not originally from Redmond. By adopting this, HailStorm can be accessed by any endpoint that can produce the right ticket and session key – not just Passport. Should other community-based sites like Yahoo or AOL decide to adopt Kerberos as their login mechanism, their users will have access to their own digital safe-deposit boxes as well. Likewise, Passport users will be able to access the facilities available to AOL and Yahoo.

It's not just the major players on the net either that can take advantage of this step. If you can implement a Kerberos-based login system, regardless of platform or operating system, you will be able to log in to HailStorm with it. Have a look at http://www.microsoft.com/windows2000/techinfo/howitworks/security/kerberos.asp for more information.

An Insecure Present

As we have already said, the Kerberos-based interchange is naturally still a while off. Therefore, the initial release of HailStorm in a Box skirts entirely over the issue of security, replacing the Kerberos ticket with a simple ID number generated when first provisioning a HailStorm service for the user. If you've already installed the SDK, you can discover your identity and your temporary ID using the hspost executable in the Bin directory of the installation:

```
C:\HailStorm\Bin>hspost -p

Your username is danm - PUID = 7525
```

Similarly, the bodies of the SOAP packets sent between endpoint and service are not currently encrypted either. We'll see when we construct an example query inside a SOAP packet where this current shortcut fits in and the final solution that will replace it.

▸▸ SOAP in a Nutshell

The Simple Object Access Protocol is described in its specification as "a lightweight protocol for the exchange of [structured and typed] information [between peers] in a decentralized, distributed environment". As this is the sort of environment we will be using when programming against HailStorm SOAP is ideal. Intended as a simple alternative to other over-the-wire protocols (like DCOM, CORBA/IIOP, and RMI) that could work within the generic Internet infrastructure with no other assistance, its sole function is to define the format of the message sent between clients and servers. Other internet protocols – in this case, HTTP, TCP, and SMTP – define the (synchronous and asynchronous) transport mechanisms used to send the messages.

Each SOAP message is an XML document with three main elements: the SOAP envelope, the SOAP header, and the SOAP body.

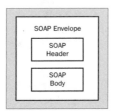

- ❑ The `<Envelope>` element is the mandatory top-level element of a SOAP message, wrapping up both the message itself and any information about the message that might be necessary for its successful delivery and processing.

- ❑ The optional `<Header>` element lets you specify extra information about the message that is not the message itself. For example, authentication, transaction management, and delivery routes.

- ❑ The mandatory `<Body>` element contains the actual payload of the SOAP message, be it a request from an endpoint or a response from a server. The latter might contain a `<Fault>` element indicating that an error or glitch occurred in the processing of the request.

- ❑ SOAP also defines a namespace for the envelope at http://schemas.xmlsoap.org/soap/envelope/. This takes the attribute `encodingStyle` that allows you to set the serialization rules used in the SOAP message.

```
<s:Envelope
    xmlns:s="http://schemas.xmlsoap.org/soap/envelope/"
    s:encodingStyle="http://schemas.xmlsoap.org/soap/encoding/">

    <s:Header>
        ... some additional info about the message here ...
    </s:Header>

    <s:Body>
        ... actual message payload in XML here ...
    </s:Body>
</s:Envelope>
```

This schema is actually stricter than XML in an effort to keep things simple (which is the aim of SOAP after all), preventing the use of DTDs and processing instructions in a message for example.

For further information on SOAP, check out the W3C specification at http://www.w3.org/TR/SOAP/.

SOAP

The choice of SOAP as the communication protocol between HailStorm endpoints and servers is not a surprise. Microsoft's open access strategy and HailStorm's web service-centric nature matches SOAP's language and platform neutrality. However, SOAP never figures in HailStorm as an RPC medium (its original function), carrying objects and serialized structured data across the web. Instead, it uses SOAP's ability to route XML messages over the web to a server – via zero or more intermediaries, synchronously or asynchronously – and receive them back the same way. Indeed, a lot more information goes into the header of a SOAP envelope than in its message payload.

Deconstructing a HailStorm Request Message

Let's take an example and briefly look at each part of a request message before we go into the real detail. Say a friend has just got married and you need to update her last name in the contacts list stored in your digital safe deposit box by the myContacts service. The message you'd need to send HailStorm would look like this:

```
<s:Envelope xmlns:s="http://schemas.xmlsoap.org/soap/envelope/"
            xmlns:srp="http://schemas.xmlsoap.org/rp/"
            xmlns:m="http://schemas.microsoft.com/hs/2001/10/myContacts/"
            xmlns:hs="http://schemas.microsoft.com/hs/2001/10/core"
            xmlns:ss="http://schemas.xmlsoap.org/soap/security/2000-12">
```

First, we have the definition of the namespaces at work inside this SOAP envelope/message. These are all pretty standard except number three which changes depending on the service you're addressing.

```
<s:Header>
  <srp:path>
    <srp:action>
        http://schemas.microsoft.com/hs/2001/10/core#request</srp:action>
    <srp:to>http://this.cluster.myContacts.msn.com/danm@wrox.com/</srp:to>
    <srp:fwd>
      <srp:via/>
    </srp:fwd>
    <srp:rev>
      <srp:via/>
    </srp:rev>
    <srp:id>uuid:764CBFB8-A9FF-46D0-BAEC-3D11F9AA44A8</srp:id>
  </srp:path>
</srp:path>
```

At the top of the header is the routing information describing what type of message this is, its ultimate destination, and any intermediate points it will need to take on its trip there or on its trip back. Finally, there is the unique identifier for the message that the response will quote back for reference.

```
<ss:licenses>
  <hs:identity>
    <hs:kerberos>0123456789ABCDEF</hs:kerberos>
  </hs:identity>
</ss:licenses>
```

Second in the list is the Kerberos ticket used for talking with HailStorm. Later in the conversation, you may also include here the role the server has assigned to you as this expedites the carrying out of your instructions.

```
      <hs:request service="myContacts" document="content" method="replace"
          genResponse="always">
        <hs:key puid="4D36E96A-E325-11CE-BFC1-08002BE10318"
              instance="danm@wrox.com" cluster="this.cluster"/>
      </hs:request>
    </s:Header>
```

Last in the message header is information about the request itself; its destination, purpose, notes for the response, and so on.

! echoBack and adminRequest

We could have included two further elements in the header – `<echoBack>` and `<adminRequest>` – but the former is specific to sending SOAP message asynchronously which we can't do at the moment and the latter, which replaces the standard request, wasn't working as we went to press. The XMI manual contains full details of what they should do.

As noted before, the body of the message contains the actual instructions to HailStorm – in this case, a request to replace your friend's maiden name with her married name.

```
    <s:Body>

      <hs:replaceRequest select="/hs:/myContacts/contact[@id='33']/lastName">
        <m:lastName>Simon</m:lastName>
      </hs:replaceRequest>

    </s:Body>
  </s:Envelope>
```

In overview, the construction of the SOAP message remains simple, just as Don Box and company intended when they designed SOAP. The usually optional `<Header>` element has become mandatory, but that's about it as far as rudimentary SOAP is concerned. To grasp the HailStorm specific pieces, we'll need to start from the top again and look at each message segment in detail.

<Envelope> – Setting the Namespaces

One of the main reasons that SOAP will become at least the basis for XML web service communications (if it isn't already anyway) is its extensibility. In this particular case, we need to make use of four other namespaces in our message besides the standard one to cover the elements we need to get everything working.

```
  <s:Envelope xmlns:s="http://schemas.xmlsoap.org/soap/envelope/"
              xmlns:srp="http://schemas.xmlsoap.org/rp/"
              xmlns:m="http://schemas.microsoft.com/hs/2001/10/myContacts/"
              xmlns:hs="http://schemas.microsoft.com/hs/2001/10/core"
              xmlns:ss="http://schemas.xmlsoap.org/soap/security/2000-12">
```

In order of declaration, the schemas that define these namespaces represent:

> **srp** – The SOAP Routing Protocol or SOAP-RP for short. This Microsoft protocol lets us define very precisely the route our message will take to and from the HailStorm server. You can find the SOAP-RP specification at http://www.gotdotnet.com/team/xml_wsspecs/soap-rp/default.html

m – The 'Content' document for the myContacts web service containing all the contacts information. Each my* service contains its own unique set of data elements as defined in a schema created specifically for that service. If you were querying the myAlerts service, you would specify the myAlerts schema here instead of that for myContacts. These schemas are covered in full in the XMI manual that accompanies the HailStorm SDK and to a lesser extent in Chapters 4 and 5 of this book.

hs – The core, non-service-specific elements that HailStorm needs to interject into the message.

ss – The security extensions to SOAP 1.1 ('SOAP-SEC') that allows a SOAP header entry to carry digital signatures – in this case the Kerberos ticket for talking with HailStorm. You can find the specification for SOAP-SEC at http://www.w3c.org/TR/SOAP-dsig/

The <envelope> element also omits the declaration of the SOAP serialization namespace that is usually present in SOAP messages. HailStorm messages will only ever be raw XML and won't need to hold any objects, so the reference is redundant.

! These Namespaces Change!

Note that the URIs for these namespaces change quite often between releases of HailStorm and it's worth keeping an eye on them when a new one arrives. A change here will signify a change in the way the contents of the SOAP messages are structured.

■

<Header>/<path> – Defining a Target

The <path> header, as defined by the SOAP Routing Protocol, lets the creator of the message define its ultimate destination and the routes that message and replies will take to get there and back. It is a mandatory part of every HailStorm message, be it request or response.

```
<srp:path>
  <srp:action>
      http://schemas.microsoft.com/hs/2001/10/core#request</srp:action>
  <srp:to>http://this.cluster.myContacts.msn.com/danm@wrox.com/</srp:to>
  <srp:fwd>
    <srp:via/>
  </srp:fwd>
  <srp:rev>
    <srp:via/>
  </srp:rev>
  <srp:id>uuid:764CBFB8-A9FF-46D0-BAEC-3D11F9AA44A8</srp:id>
  <srp:relatesTo/>
</srp:path>
```

The constituent sub-elements of `<path>` are described in the table below.

Element	Mandatory?	Description
`<action>`	Yes	Absolute URI of the form http://schemas.microsoft.com/hs/2001/10/core#*xxxx*, where *xxxx* is the purpose of the message – request, response, notification, or fault. Note that if a request is transmitted by HTTP, the SOAPAction HTTP header field **must** contain this URI.
`<to>`	Yes in requests No in responses	Absolute URI of the form *protocol*://[*cluster*.]*service*.*domain*/[*instance*], which represents the ultimate destination of the message. It is mandatory for requests, optional for responses should there be a need to send it to an arbitrary URI, and must not be modified along the message path, once the message has been sent.
`<fwd>`	No	Holds a list of `<via>` sub-elements that detail the route the request message should take to its ultimate destination.
`<rev>`	No	Holds as a list of `<via>` sub-element that detail the route the reply to the message should take to its ultimate destination, the last element in the list. Omitting the `<rev>` element from the header indicates that no response is necessary.
`<via>`	Yes if `<fwd>` or `<rev>` elements are present, else no	Contains one element of an ordered list of absolute URIs representing the intermediary endpoints that the message will pass through to get to its ultimate destination. An empty list would indicate that the message should return the way it came. Most commonly, this would mean on top of the HTTP response corresponding to the HTTP request that the message came in on.
`vid`	No	Attribute of `<via>`. A unique ID that identifies a pre-defined route. Intermediate endpoints might not know the whole route but know where to send the message next based on the vid.
`<id>`	Yes	Universally unique identifier for a message generated by the sender. Cannot be shared by any two messages.
`<relatesTo>`	No in requests Yes in responses	Specifies the UUID of the request to which the message is a response.

The route from endpoint to server and back can involve several intermediaries that know how to receive and send on SOAP messages as required. It might also make use of several transport protocols as well. SOAP-RP currently allows us to define a path over the synchronous messaging protocols HTTP, UDP, and TCP only, but the need to support asynchronous messaging over SMTP as given in the SOAP specification should mean that SMTP will also be supported soon. Other messaging systems like Microsoft's MSMQ, IBM's MQSeries, .NET Remoting, and the Java Message Service (JMS) also have the capacity to send and receive SOAP messages as either intermediaries or endpoints.

Synchronous Messaging via HTTP

The HTTP request/response model mirrors that of SOAP almost perfectly and is the protocol of choice for synchronous messaging using SOAP. If a secure connection is required, HTTPS (HTTP + SSL) can be used in exactly the same fashion. It's generally recommended to use the HTTP POST request to send your SOAP message, as this will keep it hidden, as opposed to HTTP GET, which will attempt to append it to the destination URI. Indeed, the SOAP 1.1 specification provides details for binding SOAP to HTTP POST. It's all in the header.

```
POST /MyContacts HTTP/1.1
Content-Type: text/xml; charset="utf-8"
Content-Length: yyyy
SOAPAction : " http://schemas.microsoft.com/hs/2001/10/core#request "

<s:Envelope xmlns:s="http://schemas.xmlsoap.org/soap/envelope/"
...
```

The key lines of the HTTP header, specifying that the request contains an XML document using the utf-8 character set (HailStorm uses only **utf-8** encoding) and that it is a HailStorm request are highlighted. In response, a SOAP message with the header:

```
HTTP/1.1 200 OK
Content-Type: text/xml; charset="utf-8"
Content-Length: zzzz
```

is returned if the query worked and the SOAP message following the header contains a response indicating success. If, however, something went wrong on the server and an attempt to processing your query generated a SOAP fault, the response header will always take this form:

```
HTTP/1.1 500 Internal Server Error
Content-Type: text/xml; charset="utf-8"
Content-Length: zzzz
```

There are several different scenarios using HTTP we can hypothesize now, which should be working when HailStorm becomes a reality next year.

Scenario 1: No Response Necessary

The first and simplest is the minimal case where the SOAP request is sent over HTTP and doesn't require a response (indicated by not including the <rev> element).

```
<srp:path>
  <srp:action>
    http://schemas.microsoft.com/hs/2001/10/core#request
  </srp:action>
```

```
      <srp:to>http://this.cluster.myContacts.msn.com/danm@wrox.com/</srp:to>
      <srp:id>uuid:764CBFB8-A9FF-46D0-BAEC-3D11F9AA44A8</srp:id>
    </srp:path>
```

With all the optional elements taken out it's not too difficult to see how this all fits together.

Scenario 2: Response Needed from Sender

If we add in an empty `<rev>` element to this `<path>`, as below, we effectively add in that we would like a response and that it should be returned as an HTTP response to the original POST request.

```
<srp:path>
  <srp:action>
    http://schemas.microsoft.com/hs/2001/10/core#request</srp:action>
  <srp:to>http://this.cluster.myContacts.msn.com/danm@wrox.com/</srp:to>
  <srp:rev>
    <srp:via/>
  </srp:rev>
  <srp:id>uuid:764CBFB8-A9FF-46D0-BAEC-3D11F9AA44A8</srp:id>
</srp:path>
```

This is the most common way to instigate a synchronous request/response from the HailStorm server.

Scenario 3: Response Required Somewhere Else

If we needed to send the response to an endpoint other than the origin of the request, we would just add that as a value to the `<via>` element inside `<rev>`.

```
<srp:rev>
  <srp:via>http://send.response.here.com</srp:via>
</srp:rev>
```

Scenario 4: Working through a Proxy

For those behind firewalls, the fear that your SOAP messages won't go anywhere should be allayed with the knowledge that ports 80 and 443 (the defaults for HTTP and HTTPS respectively) are open on practically every firewall today. All that's required is for you to incorporate your firewall into your `<fwd>`/`<via>` and `<rev>`/`<via>` lists so the SOAP message knows how to find its way out and back in.

```
<srp:path>
  <srp:action>
    http://schemas.microsoft.com/hs/2001/10/core#request</srp:action>
  <srp:to>http://this.cluster.myContacts.msn.com/danm@wrox.com/</srp:to>
  <srp:fwd>
    <srp:via>http://internal_firewall_name:80</srp:via>
  </srp:fwd>

  <srp:rev>
    <srp:via>http://external_firewall_name</srp:via>
  </srp:rev>
  <srp:id>uuid:764CBFB8-A9FF-46D0-BAEC-3D11F9AA44A8</srp:id>
</srp:path>
```

Of course, HTTP isn't the only transport protocol capable of synchronous messaging, but it is the simplest. It's also the only one whose binding with SOAP has been finalized. The TCP and UDP bindings in SOAP-RP are still in the preliminary stages.

Asynchronous Messaging via SMTP

Sending SOAP messages via e-mail over SMTP or via some other asynchronous protocol is theoretically possible, in that the binding of SOAP to the SMTP protocol has been defined, but has yet to be implemented or documented. It should be only a matter of time before theory becomes practice though as SOAP-RP defines a binding to SMTP, allowing us to send our messages to HailStorm at least partly over e-mail. We might perhaps see intelligent lyris-like servers as intermediary endpoints that know how to read and react to the contents of a HailStorm message, forwarding it to the next endpoint in the <via> list or storing it for your final consumption later. *Theoretically then*, we might one day be able to send messages that went via SMTP for some of the journey and not for the rest of it:

```
<srp:fwd>
  <srp:via>smtp://192.168.0.1:25</srp:via>
  <srp:via>http://firewall_at_other_end:80/</srp:via>
</srp:fwd>
```

For the time being however, we must content ourselves with purposely embedding our SOAP message inside a MIME document and sending it on a one-leg journey to the server. MIME (Multipart Internet Mail Extensions) is a multipart mechanism for the bundling of several items within the same message. In this case, we would create a MIME document that held the SOAP message and any other files associated with it. For example, you could send a message to the myDocuments service saying 'Store the documents I have attached to this message', or perhaps send an electronic card to myContacts saying 'Read this card and store the information within.'

You can find the specification that describes how to bind SOAP 1.1 to MIME at http://www.w3c.org/TR/SOAP-attachments. In brief, it states that while the MIME envelope is aware of the SOAP message within (its `content-type` is set to `text/xml`), the SOAP message is unaware that it is being held inside a larger message. However, it does contain links to the other files attached in the MIME message within its <body> element. For example:

```
MIME-Version: 1.0
Content-Type: Multipart/Related; boundary=MIME_boundary; type=text/xml;
        start="<InsertDocument.xml@wrox.com>"
Content-Description: Document Storage Request

--MIME_boundary
Content-Type: text/xml; charset=UTF-8
Content-Transfer-Encoding: 8bit
Content-ID: <InsertDocument.xml@wrox.com>

<?xml version='1.0' ?>
<s:Envelope xmlns:s="http://schemas.xmlsoap.org/soap/envelope/"
...
>

  <s:Header>
    ...
  </s:Header>

  <s:Body>
      <insertRequest select="/myDocuments">
         <Document href="cid: <DocumentToStore.doc@wrox.com"/>
           ...
      </insertRequest>
  </s:Body>
```

```
        </s:Envelope>

        --MIME_boundary
        Content-Type: application/msword
        Content-Transfer-Encoding: ascii
        Content-ID:   <DocumentToStore.doc@wrox.com>

        ... Word document here ...

        --MIME_boundary--
```

The actual insert request for the myDocuments service is left out because the schema for the content document of that service hasn't been released yet.

The top of the document declares the version of MIME the document conforms to and that it contains separate files, which are related (`Multipart/related`) to a root document – our SOAP message, whose content type is given next (`text/xml`). The SOAP message follows in its usual form; the only difference is that the documents attached to the message are referred to in `href` links. In the message above then, we've included a reference to the Word document we want HailStorm to store for us. The document itself follows immediately after in the MIME message, an ASCII attachment with a content type of `application/msword`.

SOAP messages bound into a MIME document with or without any attachments they may have can be carried over any transport mechanisms – HTTP, messaging servers, etc – but the parsing of the MIME message itself is not very efficient. For this reason, Microsoft are developing an alternative to MIME encoding – DIME.

DIME, not MIME?

The reasoning behind the creation of DIME (Direct Internet Message Encapsulation) as MS sees it is twofold:

❑ SOAP isn't very good at storing certain types of files (for instance binary image files or other XML files with different character encoding) within a message.

❑ The speed of processing the SOAP message: SOAP message delimiters are only found once the whole message has been parsed. This adds to the overhead incurred in processing the message. Parsing a MIME multipart message can also take long time while trying to determine the various sub-parts of the MIME message.

DIME then is a 'leaner, meaner' binary encapsulation format for multipart documents with the media type `'application/dime'`. Like MIME, it doesn't worry about how it will be transported from endpoint to endpoint – just how the components of the message are put together and taken apart. It's SOAP-RP that takes care of this; using DIME is mandatory over UDP and TCP. Unlike MIME, it's very new; Microsoft only released specification document on May 23, 2001. You can view the DIME specification at http://www.gotdotnet.com/team/xml_wsspecs/dime/default.htm.

\<Header>/\<licenses> – Adding Some Authentication

Returning to our original SOAP message, the next part of the \<Header> to look at is the \<licenses> element. Like the \<path>, this too is a mandatory element for a SOAP message targeting a HailStorm service.

```
<ss:licenses>
  <hs:identity>
    <hs:kerberos>0123456789ACBDEF</hs:kerberos>
  </hs:identity>
  <hs:authorizedRole/>
</ss:licenses>
```

The `<licenses>` element itself is defined by the SOAP-SEC schema extension to SOAP that caters for the embedding of digital signatures inside messages. In our particular case, we're using it to store two things:

❑ The Kerberos ticket that was generated for us when we logged into Passport. This ticket must be present inside a SOAP request to HailStorm for it to be valid, in a nested `<hs:identity>`/`<hs:kerberos>` element.

❑ The `authorizedRole` of the current client application with respect to the web service it's talking to – for example, owner, friend, or associate. Typically, this element is empty on first contact with the web service, which then grants it a role license to be used in any subsequent communication. Using this element allows the service to determine whether or not the user has the right privileges to process the request much faster than if the license was not available. Note that a role license is valid only for the duration of the session during which it was created. A new one must be created for each new session with the service.

Note that with the Kerberos authentication system not yet built into Passport, this version of HailStorm at least, must use the artificial ID generated when you provisioned the services for the user. Running the hspost –p at the command prompt, can retrieve this ID.

```
<hs:kerberos>Insert artificial id here</hs:kerberos>
```

Two more elements you might find here in future releases of HailStorm are `<ss:integrity>` and `<ss:confidentiality>`. The former is used to hold any digital signatures that may need to be used and the latter to hold the `<encryptedData>` element specified by the XML Encryption initiative. Both also understand the SOAP `mustUnderstand` attribute that can be set to make sure that the recipient understands the whole message or else returns an error message.

You can find out more about the SOAP Security Extension at http://www.w3c.org/TR/SOAP-dsig/.

<Header>/<request> – The Request Header

The `<request>` header element contains all the request information HailStorm requires bar the location of the information to be queried and the actual XMI instruction to be carried out.

```
<hs:request service="myContacts" document="content" method="replace"
    genResponse="always">
  <hs:key puid="4D36E96A-E325-11CE-BFC1-08002BE10318"
      instance="danm@wrox.com" cluster="this.cluster"/>
</hs:request>
```

There are four attributes for the `<request>` element itself:

❑ The `service` attribute contains the name of the HailStorm service you are querying.

❑ The `document` attribute specifies which of the three documents – content, roleList, or system – associated with the service you are trying to access.

❏ The `method` attribute contains the name of the HSDL method you are attempting to call against the web service. For example, insert, delete, or update. For more information on HSDL, see Chapter 5.

❏ The `genResponse` attribute tells the service whether to create a response to the query and send it back to the address given in or implied by the `<rev>`/`<via>` element. This can have three values – `always`, `never`, and `faultOnly` – indicating that a response should always be generated, never be generated, or be generated only if an error occurred.

The `<key>` element meanwhile locates the exact XML document that is carrying the information you need to access. The `cluster` attribute states which server cluster the document is stored on while the `instance` attribute distinguishes which instance of the document owned by the entity with the given `puid` is being addressed. It is quite possible for one user/entity to have two sets of information stored within a service. For example, you could prefer to keep a list of business contacts separate from your personal contacts. In this case, the instance attribute could be all that differentiates the two sets of data from each other.

The `puid` attribute meanwhile is filled automatically with the Passport ID of the entity that logged on and was authenticated by Kerberos. Like the Kerberos license however, while this is what will happen when HailStorm is finally released, for now it must be filled in with the artificial ID that you can retrieve by running `hspost -p` at the command prompt.

`<Body>`/`<xxxxRequest>` – The Request Body

Last but by no means least, the body of the SOAP message contains the actual instructions to the service.

```
<s:Body>
  <hs:replaceRequest select="/hs:/myContacts/contact[@id='33']/lastName">
    <m:lastName>Simon</m:lastName>
  </hs:replaceRequest>
</s:Body>
```

Each instruction is expressed in HailStorm's own data-manipulation language (HSDL), which we look at in Chapter 5. The top-level element represents the instruction given by the `method` attribute of the `<request>` element in the header, and its `select` attribute holds the route to the node in the XML document containing the data to be accessed, given as an XPath string (see Chapter 4 for more on forming these). Any XML nested inside the request is new information which the user wishes to update or to insert into their DSDB.

Although it has taken a little while to work through it all, the individual elements of a HailStorm request message are pretty easy to take on board and as we'll see later, we won't even need to generate a great deal of the header when the HailStorm runtime libraries become available. For now though, let's take a look at the typical structure of SOAP response message we might get from HailStorm.

The Response from HailStorm

As you might expect, the format for a HailStorm response message doesn't differ greatly from that of a request. Of course, this time we need to know its construction in order to parse it rather than build it.

The namespace declarations for the response are the same as those for the request.

```
<s:Envelope xmlns:s="http://schemas.xmlsoap.org/soap/envelope/"
            xmlns:srp="http://schemas.xmlsoap.org/srp"
            xmlns:m="http://schemas.microsoft.com/hs/2001/10/myContacts"
```

```
            xmlns:hs="http://schemas.microsoft.com/hs/2001/10/core"
            xmlns:ss="http://schemas.xmlsoap.org/soap/security/2000-12"
            >

   <s:Header>
     <srp:path>
       <srp:action>
         http://schemas.microsoft.com/hs/2001/10/core#response</srp:action>
```

The path element, however, contains significantly less then before and the `<relatesTo>` element now contains the UUID for the request message to which this is the response.

```
       <srp:id>uuid:764CBFB8-AA00-46D0-BAEC-3D11F9AA44A8</srp:id>
       <srp:relatesTo>
               uuid:764CBFB8-A9FF-46D0-BAEC-3D11F9AA44A8</srp:relatesTo>
     </srp:path>
```

As we noted earlier, the `licenses` element in the response also includes the `authorizedRole` element that we can include with subsequent messages – in this session only. Using this means that HailStorm doesn't need to re-evaluate the user's role and permissions before executing the request.

```
       <ss:licenses>
         <hs:identity>
           <hs:kerberos>0123456789ABCDEF</hs:kerberos>
         </hs:identity>
         <hs:authorizedRole>6jS527ww</hs:authorizedRole>
       </ss:licenses>
```

The `<response>` header returns the role assigned by HailStorm to the entity associated to the PUID given in the request header. Even if it can't do this for some reason, the response header will always be present in the message. In this case, `"rt0"` indicates that the client has full read-write access to myContacts. We'll take a more detailed look at roles in Chapter 5.

```
       <h:response role="rt0"/>
     </s:Header>
```

Last but not least, the body of the request message contains either a success message or a SOAP fault. If it's a success, the body may also contain:

❑   The results of the query, if one was made

❑   The reference IDs for any new information added to the safe-deposit box, if any was added

```
     <s:Body>
         <h:replaceResponse status="success"/>
     </s:Body>
   </s:Envelope>
```

Interpreting SOAPFaults

Of course, it's unlikely that we won't create a few errors here and there, so it's useful to know what to look for when HailStorm returns a fault. SOAPFaults can look quite messy, especially if the lines wrap around to the next line. On reflection though, they can be quite easy to interpret. Like SOAP envelopes, there are two parts to a SOAP Fault:

❑ The overview, comprising the `<faultcode>` and `<faultstring>` elements

❑ The details of the errors generated, found in the `<faultChain>` element

Let's take an example. This is the error returned from the query above if we misspell myContacts, which is case-sensitive, with a lower case 'c':

```
<s:Fault>
  <s:faultcode>Client</s:faultcode>
  <s:faultstring>Syntax error</s:faultstring>
```

`<faultcode>` can return one of four values: `Client` and `Server` indicate that the client malformed the SOAP message or that the server was unable to process the message internally. The other two, `VersionMismatch` and `MustUnderstand` are SOAP-specific. The former indicates that HailStorm found the SOAP envelope defined by an invalid namespace and the latter that HailStorm failed to fully understand the semantics of a message for which the SOAP `mustUnderstand` attribute was set.

The `<faultstring>` element meanwhile holds a short description of the error.

```
    <hs:detail>
      <hs:faultResponseAction>Correct</hs:faultResponseAction>
      <hs:faultChain>

        <hs:fault>
            <hs:code>0x70004</hs:code>
            <hs:shortDescription>
              Syntax error
            </hs:shortDescription>
            <hs:longDescription>
              Undefined name 'mycontacts'.
            </hs:longDescription>
        </hs:fault>

      </hs:faultChain>
    </hs:detail>
</s:Fault>
```

The most useful information is found inside the `<faultChain>` element, with a long and short description of each error. Sure enough, in the `<longDescription>` field, the message informs us that we have spelled the service name incorrectly.

This example is perhaps a bit too simple, generating as it does only one error. As we all know, one error often leads to another and another. The key is just to read what's in front of you. Misspelling a closing tag for example throws three errors back at you, the misspelling first and then two consequences of that.

```
<s:Fault>
  <hs:faultcode>Client</hs:faultcode>
  <hs:faultstring>
    The end tag found or its namespace does not match the last open tag
  </hs:faultstring>
  <hs:detail>
    <hs:faultResponseAction>Correct</hs:faultResponseAction>
    <hs:faultChain>

      <hs:fault>
```

```
        <hs:code>0x20006</hs:code>
        <hs:shortDescription>
          The end tag found or its namespace does not match the last open
          tag</hs:shortDescription>
        <hs:longDescription>
          Tag name does not match queryRequest :
          Tag name mismatch on end tag Line: 4 Column: 17
        </hs:longDescription>
      </hs:fault>

      <hs:fault>
        <hs:code>0x20006</hs:code>
        <hs:shortDescription>
          The end tag found or its namespace does not match the last open
          tag  </hs:shortDescription>
        <hs:longDescription>
          XmlEndElement call returned an error code Line: 4 Column: 17
        </hs:longDescription>
      </hs:fault>

      <hs:fault>
        <hs:code>0x20006</hs:code>
        <hs:shortDescription>
          The end tag found or its namespace does not match the last open
          tag </hs:shortDescription>
        <hs:longDescription>
          Error parsing the body of the request
        </hs:longDescription>
      </hs:fault>
    </hs:faultChain>
  </hs:detail>
</s:Fault>
```

Of course, there's only one mistake rather than three. I think it could be because 'The end tag found or its namespace does not match the last open tag'. Hmm.

It's never going to be as trivial as this all the time, but you should at least know now how to read a SOAP fault if that's all you have to go by. On the other hand, if you're using an XML IDE, or perhaps even the HailStorm extension for Visual Studio .NET that is in the works, the raw SOAP fault message will probably be parsed for you first – lucky you.

Generating the SOAP Packets

With the theory out of the way, it's time to make use of our newfound knowledge of SOAP messages for HailStorm. We've still to cover exactly what we can do with the data stored in the XML documents the services govern and how to identify particular nodes in the documents, so unless you've skipped ahead and read Chapters 4 and 5, for the time being we're going to start adding some data to our services and leave it at that. Specifically, we're going to start adding some URLs to the myFavoriteWebSites content document.

At this stage of the game, sending SOAP messages to an installation of HailStorm in a Box is still limited. We can:

- ❏ Type out the instruction body of the SOAP message and send the XML fragment to HailStorm in a Box as raw text using the `hspost` executable provide with the SDK

- ❏ Create and send the whole SOAP message using a SOAP API like Microsoft's SOAP Toolkit v2.0

- ❏ Create the message through calls to functions in the HailStorm client runtime library

The third is a bit awkward at time of writing for reasons you'll see later (the trials of alpha software) but the first two are more than adequate to get you started experimenting with the services.

Raw XML

If the thought of writing out raw XML is a bit daunting, there are alternatives, but it really is the simplest way to start working with HailStorm. All we'll see here is a very simple HSDL request that adds a web site to the myFavoriteWebSites content document. The XML is simple to follow and we can concentrate on the responses, to formulate more complicated requests, just refer to Chapters 4 and 5, and the XMI manual. We've used Notepad to write these requests, but you can of course use whatever text editor or XML tool you prefer.

So then, our request to HailStorm looks like this:

```
<hs:insertRequest
  xmlns:hs="http://schemas.microsoft.com/hs/2001/10/core"
  xmlns:m="http://schemas.microsoft.com/hs/2001/10/myFavoriteWebSites"
  hs:select="m:myFavoriteWebSites">
  <m:favoriteWebSite>
    <m:title xml:lang="en-us">Wrox Press</m:title>
    <m:url>http://www.wrox.com</m:url>
  </m:favoriteWebSite>
</hs:insertRequest>
```

We're going to insert the URI for the Wrox Press home page just under the root of the myFavoriteWebSites content document, as denoted by the XPath location marked by the `select` attribute of the `request` element. That done, we'll save this fragment as `InsertWroxUrl.xml` and send it to HailStorm using the `hspost` command:

```
C:\>hspost -d content -s myFavoriteWebSites -f InsertWroxUrl.xml
```

You'll find `hspost` in the `bin` subdirectory of the HailStorm SDK installation. Indeed, we've already used it once this chapter to discover the temporary PUID you were assigned when you provisioned the services for your user account. In that instance we used the `-p` switch; here the `-d` switch tells `hspost` that we are going to work with the content document of a service (as opposed to the `roleList` or `system` documents) and `-s` states which service we're going to work with. Lastly, `-f` names the XML file containing the instructions to be carried out.

Note that the service names must be spelled correctly and in the right case. For example, MyFavoriteWebsites doesn't work, but myFavoriteWebSites will do. Mispelling (sic) the service name in the call to `hspost` will result in the not particularly helpful message:

Error 5 returned from HsGetServiceLocation()

In fact, this particular message is returned for a variety of errors, all based around forming either the call to `hspost` or the XML file. It will also be produced if you try to return the contents of an empty document.

Assuming then, that our XMI request is properly formed and our call to `hspost` goes smoothly, we should see something similar to this, as HailStorm echoes its response back to the command prompt.

```
C:\> hspost -d content -s myFavoriteWebSites -f InsertWroxUrl.xml
<?xml version='1.0'?>

<s:Envelope xmlns:s="http://schemas.xmlsoap.org/soap/envelope/"
            xmlns:hs="http://schemas.microsoft.com/hs/2001/10/core">
    <s:Header>
        <path xmlns="http://schemas.xmlsoap.org/rp">
            <action>
                http://schemas.microsoft.com/hs/2001/10/core#response
            </action>
            <from>http://jaws</from>
            <rev></rev>
            <id>3e4ef092-b1b0-11d5-8c86-00a0c94515ad</id>
            <relatesTo>5e66a091-b1b0-11d5-95ec-00b0d0d40fc1</relatesTo>
        </path>
        <hs:response>
        </hs:response>
    </s:Header>
    <s:Body>
        <hs:insertResponse
            xmlns:hs="http://schemas.microsoft.com/hs/2001/10/core"
            status="success" selectedNodeCount="1" newChangeNumber="274">
            <hs:newBlueId id="3e4ef091-b1b0-11d5-8c86-00a0c94515ad"/>
        </hs:insertResponse>
    </s:Body>
</s:Envelope>
```

The key we're looking for is the word `success` located in the body of the response. If your installation of HailStorm in a Box is working, that's exactly what you'll get, along with a reference number for the change just made to your document and the number of nodes affected by the request. The new ID for the `<favoriteWebSite>` element we've just inserted can be found in contents of the `<insertResponse>` element. As to why it's in a `<newBlueId>` element, we'll get to that in the next chapter.

We've been told that the URI is stored safely in the service's content document, but we can check quickly using a query.

```
<hs:queryRequest
  xmlns:hs="http://schemas.microsoft.com/hs/2001/10/core"
  xmlns:m="http://schemas.microsoft.com/hs/2001/10/myFavoriteWebSites">
  <hs:xpQuery select="m:myFavoriteWebSites" />
</hs:queryRequest>
```

This query will return all the contents of the `<myFavoriteWebSites>` element (the root element). Saving it to a file `query.xml` and sending it to the `myFavoriteWebSites` service via `hspost` will tell us what we need to know. Indeed, we get the (abridged) response:

```
C:\HailStorm\Bin>hspost -d content -s myFavoriteWebSites -f query.xml
<?xml version='1.0'?>

<s:Envelope xmlns:s="http://schemas.xmlsoap.org/soap/envelope/"
xmlns:hs="http://schemas.microsoft.com/hs/2001/10/core">
    <s:Header>
```

```
...
    </s:Header>
    <s:Body>

<hs:queryResponse xmlns:hs="http://schemas.microsoft.com/hs/2001/10/core"
xmlns:m="http://schemas.microsoft.com/hs/2001
10/myFavoriteWebSites">
<hs:xpQueryResponse status="success">
<m:myFavoriteWebSites>
<m:favoriteWebSite id="27246f18-b1a4-11d5-8c86-00a0c94515ad">
<m:title xml:lang="en-us">Wrox Press</m:title>
<m:url>http://www.wrox.com</m:url>
</m:favoriteWebSite>
</m:myFavoriteWebSites>
</hs:xpQueryResponse>
</hs:queryResponse>        </s:Body>
</s:Envelope>
```

There in the body of the `<xpQueryResponse>` tag, as expected, is the Wrox URI. Another success!

Using a SOAP API

If you don't fancy writing raw XML, then you can use a SOAP API to generate it for you. It does take several more lines of code, but the advantage is that you can generate your messages programmatically rather than writing them from scratch all the time. Check out http://www.soapware.org/directory/4/implementations for a comprehensive list of those currently available. You should find one to suit your taste what ever your favorite programming language.

If you do decide to use an API, you'll need to make sure that it has objects that can:

- ❏   Build and store the SOAP request you need to send to the service
- ❏   Bind that message to an HTTP stream and send it to the server
- ❏   Read in the response from your web service once you have sent it

Any mature API will have these three things, and most likely, a few other objects to deal with the RPC side of SOAP that we don't really need to worry about. In keeping with the Microsoft theme of the book, plus the fact that you actually need to install Windows Script Host as a prerequisite for HailStorm in a Box, we'll use Microsoft's SOAP Toolkit 2.0, downloadable from http://msdn.microsoft.com/soap in this section, and use VBScript to access the objects it provides. Just as our shopping list of functionality says the MS SOAP toolkit provides:

- ❏   A `SoapSerializer` object with which we can build our messages
- ❏   A `HttpConnector` object to bind to and send messages over HTTP to the server
- ❏   A `SoapReader` object which can read SOAP messages into a buffer for further processing

With that settled, let's get to work towards the objective of putting another entry into the `myFavoriteWebSites` content document. The first thing to do is create an instance of the `HttpConnector` object as it's this that sets the properties for the SOAP message as a whole as well as delimiting its beginning and end.

```
'' AddNewURI.vbs
Option Explicit

Dim Serializer
Dim Reader
Dim Connector

'' Create the Connector object, set message properties, and
'' start creating the message

Set Connector = CreateObject("MSSOAP.HttpConnector")

Connector.Property("EndPointURL") = "http://jaws/myFavoriteWebSites"
Connector.Property("SoapAction") =
    "http://schemas.microsoft.com/hs/2001/10/core#response"
Connector.BeginMessage
```

With the `Connector` object ready to send a message, we need now to create an instance of the `SoapSerializer` object that can create the elements and contents we want in our message and then stream them into the `Connector`.

```
'' Create Serializer Object and start streaming into the Connector
Set Serializer = CreateObject("MSSOAP.SoapSerializer")
Serializer.Init Connector.InputStream
```

One of the handier points of the raw XML and `hspost` method covered in the previous section is the absence of need to construct a header for your SOAP message. Provided your SRVLOCATOR environment variable is set up, `hspost` does the job for you. Not so with a SOAP API approach – the API's connector object does the sending, so headers must be constructed in script as well as the payload.

First the SOAP envelope and header elements:

```
'' Start Building SOAP Message
Serializer.startEnvelope "s",
    "http://schemas.xmlsoap.org/soap/encoding/", "UTF-8"
Serializer.startHeader
```

Every XML element inside the header and body are created using the serializer's `startElement` and `endElement` methods. The former takes four arguments – the name of the element, the URI of the namespace that governs the element, the value for the `encodingStyle` attribute of the element (which we've left blank, but could properly be en-US for example) and the namespace prefix that we have adopted.

```
'' Start building the path header element
Serializer.startElement "path", "http://schemas.xmlsoap.org/rp", , "srp"
Serializer.startElement "action", "http://schemas.xmlsoap.org/rp", , "srp"
Serializer.writeString
    "http://schemas.microsoft.com/hs/2001/10/core#response"
Serializer.endElement

'' Use empty rev element so response comes back the way it came and
'' into the reader stream we've set up for it.
Serializer.startElement "rev", "http://schemas.xmlsoap.org/rp", , "srp"
Serializer.startElement "via", "http://schemas.xmlsoap.org/rp", , "srp"
Serializer.endElement
Serializer.endElement
```

```
Serializer.startElement "to", "http://schemas.xmlsoap.org/rp", , "srp"
Serializer.writeString "http://jaws"
Serializer.endElement
```

It's important to remember when setting the <path>/<id> element that this needs to be a unique value each time the script is run. If you have access to a utility like Visual Studio's guidgen, which generates unique GUIDs on request, then use that. If not, you could try a self-incrementing counter:

```
Serializer.startElement "id", "http://schemas.xmlsoap.org/rp", , "srp"
Serializer.writeString "177c8982-a133-11d5-8c76-00a0c94515ad"
Serializer.endElement
Serializer.endElement
```

Again, don't forget to add in the temporary PUID assigned to you (run hspost -p to discover it) in the <kerberos> element of the licenses header.

```
'' Start building the licenses header element.

Serializer.startElement "licenses",
    "http://schemas.xmlsoap.org/soap/security/2000-12/", , "ss"
Serializer.startElement "identity",
    "http://schemas.microsoft.com/hs/2001/10/core", , "hs"
Serializer.startElement "kerberos",
    "http://schemas.microsoft.com/hs/2001/10/core", , "hs"

'' Add your temporary puid here
Serializer.writeString "7275"
Serializer.endElement
Serializer.endElement
Serializer.endElement
```

Likewise, when setting the puid attribute of the <request>/<key> element:

```
Serializer.startElement "request",
    "http://schemas.microsoft.com/hs/2001/10/core", , "hs"
Serializer.SoapAttribute "service", ,"myFavoriteWebSites"
Serializer.SoapAttribute "document", ,"content"
Serializer.SoapAttribute "method", ,"insert"
  Serializer.SoapAttribute "genResponse", ,"always"

Serializer.startElement "key",
        "http://schemas.microsoft.com/hs/2001/10/core", , "hs"
Serializer.SoapAttribute "instance", ,"0"
Serializer.SoapAttribute "cluster", ,"0"
Serializer.SoapAttribute "puid", ,"7275"
Serializer.endElement
Serializer.endElement
Serializer.endHeader
```

With the hard part over, there's just the business of building the actual insert request to myFavoriteWebSites and telling it what to add.

```
Serializer.startBody
Serializer.startElement "insertRequest",
    "http://schemas.microsoft.com/hs/2001/10/core", , "hs"
Serializer.SoapAttribute "xmlns:m", ,
    "http://schemas.microsoft.com/hs/2001/10/myFavoriteWebSites"
Serializer.SoapAttribute "select",
    "http://schemas.microsoft.com/hs/2001/10/core",
    "/m:myFavoriteWebSites", "hs"

Serializer.startElement "favoriteWebSite",
    "http://schemas.microsoft.com/hs/2001/10/myFavoriteWebSites", , "m"
Serializer.startElement "title",
    "http://schemas.microsoft.com/hs/2001/10/myFavoriteWebSites", , "m"
Serializer.SoapAttribute "xml:lang", ,"en-us"
Serializer.writeString "ASPToday"
Serializer.endElement
Serializer.startElement "url",
    "http://schemas.microsoft.com/hs/2001/10/myFavoriteWebSites", , "m"
Serializer.writeString "http://www.asptoday.com"
Serializer.endElement
Serializer.endElement
Serializer.endElement
Serializer.endBody
Serializer.endEnvelope
```

With the last of the calls to the Serializer finished (hooray!), the whole of the message has now been sent to HailStorm and we need only tell the Connector object that we have finished (with a call to its EndMessage method) for our request to HailStorm to be over.

```
Connector.EndMessage
```

Collecting the response from HailStorm is a matter of retrieving it from the Connector's ObjectStream. Using the SOAP Toolkit, the easiest way to do that for the purpose of parsing the message and making it easier to read, is by Loading it into an instance of the SoapReader object.

```
'' Read in SOAP Response from HailStorm
Set Reader = CreateObject("MSSOAP.SoapReader")
Reader.Load Connector.OutputStream
```

To keep the example short, we're not going to do anything fancy with the response – just check if there's an error and print it if there is. If not, then we'll print the response to the screen.

```
'' Display XML (or errors)
If Not Reader.Fault Is Nothing Then
  WScript.Echo "FAULT: " & Reader.faultstring.Text
Else
  WScript.Echo Reader.Envelope.xml
End If
```

▸▸ More Examples

Please note that the various values in this example were **deliberately** hardwired into calls to keep it short and easier to follow, especially for those not familiar with either VBScript or the SOAP Toolkit. A couple of more elegant solutions addressing roughly the same task can be found in the `samples\wsh` directory of the SDK. More on the objects in the SOAP Toolkit can be found in the documentation (the User Guide) installed with the Toolkit.

■

And that's it. Having saved the script as `AddNewURI.vbs`, we just need to run it. All being well, we get another nice response telling us the request was successful.

```
C:\HailStorm\Ch3>wscript AddNewURI.vbs
```

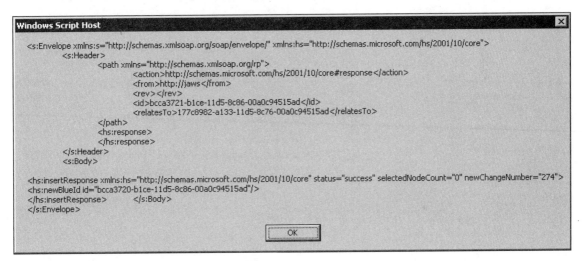

HailStorm Runtime Library

The third one is actually a lot trickier than it sounds – to write about at least. While the runtime library is planned to ship as a C API in time for the first release of HailStorm in a Box during October 2001, it hadn't appeared when this book went to press in September 2001. Sorry.

Summary

In this chapter, we have worked through a typical conversation between HailStorm endpoint and server. We have seen that:

❑ Once a user is authenticated by the Kerberos system in Passport, the Passport ID and Kerberos ticket given the user are then embedded in the request sent to the server to continue the authentication process.

❑ Each piece of conversation between endpoint and server is encapsulated in a SOAP message.

❑　　Each SOAP message includes routing information to the server and back, authentication info, and the request itself.

❑　　The request is in two parts – an instruction in HSDL (HailStorm Data-manipulation Language) and an XPath expression to identify the part of document the instruction is to be carried out on. We'll cover the formulation of XPath expressions in the next chapter and a description of each HSDL instruction in Chapter 5.

❑　　SOAP messages can be sent as raw XML, using a SOAP API, or using one of the HailStorm runtime libraries that will eventually become available.

In next chapter, we'll be taking at look at the structure of the XML documents that we've been querying and how to navigate about them using XPath.

early adopter

4

Picking One's Nodes with XPath

In Chapter 3 we covered the structure of the messages we will send to and receive back from HailStorm in a Box, leaving us with three things to check out:

❑   How to target the information already stored by the service

❑   The HSDL instructions we can send to each web service

❑   The structure of the XML payload

In this chapter then we'll look in depth at the first of these questions and discover XPath, the W3C Standard that Microsoft has chosen to use for this purpose.

A subset of XPath is implemented by HailStorm to cater to its needs. However, as Microsoft has not fully defined that subset, the tutorial herein will cover the core XPath functionality it would seem most prudent for HailStorm to support. You'll find a mark for whether or not each path works with the version of HailStorm we were able to test at the time of writing on or near each one for clarity.

The HailStorm Documents

Before we start on our tour of XPath, let's remind ourselves of the three documents that each service gives us access to.

❑   The content document. This is the main document, empty at first, which contains the information a user wants to store in this particular part of his/her digital safe-deposit box. The shape of the content document is governed by the relevant schema for the content document of that service.

❑   The roleList document. This contains the list of people and sites that have access to the information in the context document for the service. It also covers what level of access those users have to the information.

❑   The system document. This contains service-specific data like the role map and cache map for the service. It is essentially a read-only document to the user. Only the service itself can modify this document.

The roleList and system document we'll leave until Chapter 5. With the structures of both changing widely between each drop of HailStorm in a Box, the only sensible thing to do is cover those pieces that seem stable. For now, it's worth noting that you can manipulate these documents in the same way as the content document. You target elements within the document with the same XPath expressions as well.

And so to the content documents for each service; each one contains a different set of information to be stored, so each one is governed by a different schema. The myContacts content document is overseen by the .NET Contacts Document schema, myProfile by the .NET Profile Document schema, and so on. With a good knowledge of how the content documents are structured, we can easily find the place in the document we want, whether or not we know the specific information we are querying.

In this chapter, we are going to carry on using the myFavoriteWebSites service to demonstrate the various ways to navigate through its content document. It's not as complex as some of the others, but the concepts are easily translated to all the other services. We'll be using other services in the case studies featured in Chapters 6 and 7. If you want to refer to a different content document while looking through this chapter, you can find out its structure from Chapter 5.

XPath – What is it?

XPath was designed to provide a logical path notation for navigating through the hierarchical structure of an XML document, much akin to that of a URL. It became a W3C standard in November 1999, and is now an integral part of the forthcoming XML Query 1.0 and DOM Level 3 standards. You can find the full specification for XPath at http//www.w3c.org/TR/xpath and further coverage of XPath at http://www.zvon.org/xxl/XPathTutorial/General/exmples.html if you want to know more.

XPath works by treating every XML document as a tree, which contains up to seven different types of nodes:

❑   A root node

❑   Element nodes

❑   Attribute nodes

❑   Text nodes

❑   Namespace nodes

❑   Processing instruction nodes

❑   Comment nodes

As HailStorm developers, we only need to worry about the first three of these seven, due to the fact that HailStorm allows us only to target certain nodes within the documents. If we target anything else, we get a polite message saying that particular target 'can not be used in XPath select expressions'. We'll see exactly which nodes, why, and how this is enforced later on.

A Document to Query

All our XPath examples will be set against the following **abridged** myFavoriteWebSites document which holds just two web sites and a subscription.

```
<myFavoriteWebSites
    xmlns:hs="http://schemas.microsoft.com/hs/2001/10/core"
    xmlns="http://schemas.microsoft.com/hs/2001/10/myFavoriteWebSites">
    <favoriteWebSite id="1">
        <url>http://www.wrox.com</url>
    </favoriteWebSite>
    <favoriteWebSite id="2">
        <url>http://www.asptoday.com</url>
    </favoriteWebSite>
    <subscription id="3" creator="danm">
        <hs:trigger select="/myFavoriteWebSites/favoriteWebSite"
                    mode="includeData" />
        <hs:context uri="http://www.wrox.com" />
    </subscription>
</myFavoriteWebSites>
```

The majority of this tutorial remains theoretical as Microsoft has yet to complete its XPath support so I've:

❑   Set the default namespace to that of the myFavoriteWebSites content document schema

❑   Left out the changeNumber attributes for each web site and the subscription that should be (*but aren't currently* – somewhat of a large bug this) automatically generated by HailStorm when you add these entries

❑   Simplified the value of the creator attribute for the <subscription> element and the GUIDs which would live in the three id attributes to 1, 2, and 3

This should enable you to follow the paths without losing yourself in the complexity of the document. Note that if you do try to create this document as is, HailStorm will silently ignore the id values you supply and add its own generated GUIDs.

If you do want to follow the examples over the next few pages, or indeed check your own XPath selections against this simple document, you can find a file called InsertControlSet.xml in the code download for this book, which you can hspost to an empty myFavoriteWebSites content document to get it setup. It's then a matter of running the simple query below against the document to check out if your XPath works and does what you think it should do:

```
<hs:queryRequest
    xmlns:hs="http://schemas.microsoft.com/hs/2001/10/core"
    xmlns="http://schemas.microsoft.com/hs/2001/10/myFavoriteWebSites">

    <hs:xpQuery select="insert_your_XPath_here" />
</hs:queryRequest>
```

Just insert your XPath string into the select attribute, save the query and hspost it against myFavoriteWebSites:

```
C:\HailStorm\Bin>hspost -d content -s myFavoriteWebSites -f query_file.xml
```

Basic Syntax

The basic syntax for all XPath expressions assumes you know the actual structure of the XML document you are querying and in some cases which is the particular instance of a node you are navigating to.

Moving to Elements and Attributes

Writing a simple XPath expression is exactly the same as writing the location of a directory in a file hierarchy (a UNIX one anyway). An XPath selecting the element node "subscription" would take the form:

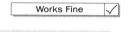

```
/myFavoriteWebSites/subscription
```

and would return us the following from HailStorm:

```
<m:subscription id="bc2ea283-b28b-11d5-8c86-00a0c94515ad" creator="danm">
    <hs:trigger select="/myFavoriteWebSites/favoriteWebSite" mode="includeData"/>
    <hs:context uri="http://www.wrox.com"/>
</m:subscription>
```

Note that regardless of the prefix we give the elements of our query, the response uses the HailStorm defaults.

In the case where there is more than one instance of the targeted element, each node that matches the expression is returned. So, for example, HailStorm would return the whole of both web site entries if we queried our document with the following XPath.

```
/myFavoriteWebSites/favoriteWebSite
```

Sure enough, we get a '**node-set**' containing two nodes.

```
<m:favoriteWebSite id="1">
    <m:url>http://www.wrox.com</m:url>
</m:favoriteWebSite>
<m:favoriteWebSite id="2">
    <m:url>http://www.asptoday.com</m:url>
</m:favoriteWebSite>
```

It's equally simple to access an element's attributes to retrieve its single value. By prefixing the attribute name with an @ symbol, we can treat it just like any other child element in the element hierarchy. To return the value of the <subscription>'s creator attribute then, we query:

```
/myFavoriteWebSites/subscription/@creator
```

and get the attribute and its value returned to us as the attribute and value of an <attributes> node. Any attributes returned by HailStorm are presented thus. You can use the same syntax to insert or update certain attributes in the documents as well without the need to change the associated element as a whole.

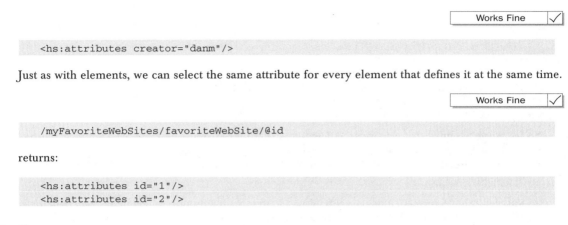

Works Fine ✓

```
<hs:attributes creator="danm"/>
```

Just as with elements, we can select the same attribute for every element that defines it at the same time.

Works Fine ✓

```
/myFavoriteWebSites/favoriteWebSite/@id
```

returns:

```
<hs:attributes id="1"/>
<hs:attributes id="2"/>
```

Indices

It all seems quite arbitrary. If there are multiple instances of an element in a document, they'll all be returned if our XPath points just at the element. However, we can be much more specific if we add an index value to the XPath. Indices work very much like those used to identify the individual elements of an array, with the top-most instance of an element in the document being given the index value 1, the next instance the value 2 and so on down the document. Eagle-eyed readers will have noticed already, that XPath indices are not zero-based as array indices usually are, but start from 1.

So then, to return just the details of the first website in the document, we can use:

Not Implemented X

```
/myFavoriteWebSites/favoriteWebSite[1]
```

which should return:

```
<m:favoriteWebSite id="1">
  <m:url>http://www.wrox.com</m:url>
</m:favoriteWebSite>
```

except that HSiaB hasn't implemented this yet. Note that there's no restriction on where in an XPath you can use indices. For example, to get just the second url stored in the document, you should be able to use:

Not Implemented X

```
/myFavoriteWebSites/favoriteWebSite[2]/url
```

as our XPath statment. This should return us:

```
<m:url>http://www.asptoday.com</m:url>
```

but of course doesn't work. Note that the use of just a number inside the square brackets is an abbreviation for a comparison against XPath's `position()` function that returns the index of the current element in the document. We could rewrite the first XPath index example above as:

Not Implemented	X

```
/myFavoriteWebSites/favoriteWebSite[position()=1]
```

and have the same information returned. Unfortunately, HailStorm in a Box does not support the use of position() yet, which is a shame.

count() and last()

So far, we've assumed that we already knew the position index of the element we wanted to return. In reality though, we're quite unlikely to know the exact location in the document of the particular element we're looking for. Two more XPath functions we can use to assist with this problem (until we look at contextual queries anyway) are count() and last().

As you might have guessed, a query using count() returns the number of elements matching the given XPath in that document – how many web sites are stored in HailStorm, how many categories you're using to classify them, or how many web sites have a subscription set up against them. For example:

Not Implemented	X

```
count(/myFavoriteWebSites/favoriteWebSite)
```

should return a value of 2.

A query using last() meanwhile returns the position of the last matching element in that document. When put inside the square brackets, it has the effect of returning the position of the last matching element in the document matching the XPath, which, thanks to HailStorm, is also the last element of that type added to the document.

Not Implemented	X

```
/myFavoriteWebSites/favoriteWebSite[last()]
```

should return:

```
<m:favoriteWebSite id="2">
    <m:url>http://www.asptoday.com</m:url>
</m:favoriteWebSite>
```

but unfortunately, last() is still undefined in HailStorm's XPath implementation.

Arbitrary Selection with *

We've already seen how to select multiple instances of the 'same' element, but quite often it's necessary to select instances of 'different' nodes at the same time, when selecting all the children of another element for instance. To do this, we use the wildcard character * (an asterisk).

So the following XPath will return all the children of the root node, <myFavoriteWebSites>, but not the node itself:

Works Fine	✓

```
/myFavoriteWebSites/*
```

We can use the same syntax to select all the attributes of an element as well:

| Works Fine | X |

```
/myFavoriteWebSites/subscription/@*
```

Sure enough, we are sent back:

```
<hs:attributes id="3"/>
<hs:attributes creator="danm"/>
```

! – changeNumber missing

As noted earlier, a `changeNumber` attribute should be generated automatically by HailStorm when we insert or update either `<subscription>` or `<favoriteWebSite>` elements in the content document. However, it looks like the current build has lost this functionality. When it returns, `changeNumber` will also have been returned by the previous XPath.

Getting the Text Contents

If we want to return the text contents of an element or attribute, we can make use of the XPath function, `text()`. If, for example, we want to return the string `"http://www.wrox.com"` we can use the following expression:

| Unexpected Results | X |

```
/myFavoriteWebSites/favoriteWebSite[1]/url/text()
```

! - text() Ignored

The current version of HailStorm in a Box appears to support `text()` in that it does not return a SOAP fault saying that it doesn't recognize `text()`, but also seems to ignore it returning the whole node rather than just its text elements.

The Union Operator

If we want XPath to return us two unrelated node-sets from the same document, we can either make two queries or use the union operator |. Thus:

| Not Implemented | X |

```
/myFavoriteWebSites/favoriteWebSite | /myFavoriteWebSites/subscription
```

So "`//AAA | //BBB`" returns a node-set whose members are all "`AAA`" and "`BBB`" elements of the document. Or would do if HailStorm implemented the union operator, which currently it doesn't.

▶▶ - node()

There is also an expression combining `"*"` and `"text()"`. It is written as `"node()"` and it is equal to `"* | text() | processing-instruction() | comment()"`. The `"|"` character means an union of node-sets returned by individual parts of the expression, `"processing-instruction()"` returns processing-instructions nodes and `"comment()"` the comments. HailStorm doesn't support it, but it's handy to know.

■

Using Axes

So far the concepts are rather obvious and easy to understand. The next one, the concept of axes, is a bit more difficult to grasp; not because of its complexity, but just because people tend to think about a XML document as a marked-up document, and not in terms of what it really conveys.

We have to realize that XML is a notation that enables us to describe a tree structure without using pictures. If you get used to building a tree in your head from the XML source you are working with, then your thinking in XPath becomes very natural and axes become very valuable friends.

If we have a tree, we can talk about children, descendants, siblings, parents, and ancestors. To be able to express these relations, XPath introduces axes, usually denoted in XPaths by a double colon between it and the element.

The Child and Attribute Axes

The first thing to realize when working with axes is that when using XPath, we are always using some axis or another. In every example so far, we have been using the default, **child** axis, going one level deeper into the XML document tree with each forward slash. When no axis is specified, it is this axis that the XPath parser automatically assumes is being used.

The first example in this tutorial then could be rewritten as follow with the same response from the HailStorm server:

Works Fine ✓

```
/child::myFavoriteWebSites/child::subscription
```

Similarly, we have actually been using the abbreviated form of the **attribute** axis, denoted by the @ symbol, to return the values of an element's attributes. We could rewrite a couple of examples like so:

Works Fine ✓

```
/myFavoriteWebSites/favoriteWebSite/attribute::id
```

this still returns the `id` attributes from both `<favoriteWebSite>` elements and likewise:

Works Fine ✓

```
/myFavoriteWebSites/subscription/attribute::*
```

returns all the available attributes of the `subscription` element.

The Parent and Self Axes

In a notation borrowed from file system navigation, XPath also defines the **parent** (or "`..`") and **self** (or "`.`") axes. The parent axis reverses the direction of travel through the document hierarchy against that of the child axis, working its way towards the root node instead of the elements with no children. In a very roundabout way then, we can select the root node like so:

Not Implemented	X

```
/myFavoriteWebSites/favoriteWebSite/url/parent::favoriteWebSite/parent::myFavorite
WebSites
```

or in the abbreviated version:

Not Implemented	X

```
/myFavoriteWebSites/favoriteWebSite/url/../..
```

Each element can have only one parent so to select in this way the first `<favoriteWebSite>` element we can also write:

Not Implemented	X

```
/myFavoriteWebSites/favoriteWebSite[1]/url/parent::*
```

The problem here however is that HailStorm doesn't support the parent axis in either form at the moment.

In contrast to child and parent axes, the self axis only ever has the one member – the currently selected node. In an unnecessarily complex way then, we could select the URL of the second `<favoriteWebSite>` element thus:

Not Implemented	X

```
/myFavoriteWebSites/favoriteWebSite[2]/self::favoriteWebSite/self::favoriteWebSite
/url/self::url
```

This too can be written as an abbreviation:

Works Fine	✓

```
/myFavoriteWebSites/favoriteWebSite[2]/././url/.
```

Strangely, although HailStorm does understand the abbreviated form of the self axis, an error is returned saying that the axis isn't supported when the axis is written out in full.

Ancestors and Descendants

Both child and parent axes deal only with elements in the level below and above the current node. If we need to address all the elements that are below or above the specific node in the tree, we need to use the descendant and ancestor axes, respectively. Thus:

Unexpected Results X

```
/myFavoriteWebSites/descendant::*
```

should return any descendants of the `<favoriteWebSite>` elements and:

Unexpected Results X

```
/*/descendant::*
```

should return all the elements in the document except the root one ordered by level like this:

```
<m:favoriteWebSite id="1">
    <m:url>http://www.wrox.com</m:url>
</m:favoriteWebSite>

<m:favoriteWebSite id="2">
    <m:url>http://www.asptoday.com</m:url>
</m:favoriteWebSite>

<m:subscription id="3" creator="danm">
    <hs:trigger select="/myFavoriteWebSites/favoriteWebSite" mode="includeData"/>
    <hs:context uri="http://www.wrox.com"/>
</m:subscription>

<m:url>http://www.wrox.com</m:url>
<m:url>http://www.asptoday.com</m:url>
```

Notice that only the `<url>` nodes are returned as level two elements, another indication that HailStorm will return only certain elements of the documents we create. There's a full explanation of what's going on here at the end of the chapter in the section *'Red, Blue, and Black Tags'*.

> A bug has crept into this build of HailStorm to the extent that these queries, which used to work, now return an error saying that the `favoriteWebSite/cat` element cannot be targeted by a query. But we haven't defined that element...

Working up the tree rather than down it, the ancestor axis complements the descendant axis (or would if HailStorm implemented it). For example:

Not Implemented X

```
/myFavoriteWebSites/favoriteWebSite[2]/url/ancestor::*
```

selects the root node and the (second) `<favoriteWebSite>` element above the URL node we want the ancestors of. We can actually qualify which ancestor we want to select using indices. In this case, the indices start from 1 with the element's parent and work up towards the root node. Thus both the following expressions would select only the root node.

```
/myFavoriteWebSites/favoriteWebSite[2]/url/ancestor::*[2]
/myFavoriteWebSites/favoriteWebSite[2]/url/ancestor::*[last()]
```

Note that the ancestor and descendant axes do not include the current node in the returned node-set. If we need to include them as well we can use the **ancestor-or-self** or **descendant-or-self** axes which combine together these axes with the self axis. A useful abbreviation to know is:

```
//*
```

This expression selects all the elements in the document including the root node and returns them all with contents in full ordered by level. "`//`" is short for "`/`**descendant-or-self**`::node()/`" and combined with the star it selects every element in the document. Unfortunately, it also seems to suffer from the same bug as noted in the glitch box above.

! – //@* and //text()

According to the XPath specification, `//@*` should likewise select and return every attribute in the document and `//text()` all text nodes. Instead, HailStorm goes slightly AWOL on standards, with the former usually returning all selectable attributes **plus** the entire document in full, as follows:

```
<myFavoriteWebSites>
    ...    - full listing of the content document
</myFavoriteWebSites>
<attributes changeNumber="1"/>        - for root
<attributes id="1"/>                  |
<attributes creator="danm"/>                    |- for catDef
<attributes changeNumber="1"/>                  |
<attributes changeNumber="1"/>                  - for website 1
<attributes changeNumber="1"/>        - for website 2
<attributes id="2"/>                  - for website 1
<attributes id="3"/>                  - for website 2
```

Note the attributes for the web sites are returned in a grouped and sorted order, rather than returned per element as one would expect. At the moment however, it produces an error if it comes across any attribute which it can't select, rather than ignoring it and returning those attributes it is allowed to select.

As we noted earlier, `text()` seems to be a valid call in HailStorm but is currently ignored to the extent that `//text()` is read as `//`, or `/descendant-or-self::node()/` and returns just the root node in full.

■

The Sibling Axes

Every axis so far has allowed us to go up and down in the hierarchy, but there are two others that allow us to iterate through the elements at the same level in the hierarchy, much as if we were iterating over the items in a collection object or, to a lesser extent, over a range.

The **following-sibling** axis allows you access to the next node at the same level in the hierarchy and the previous-sibling axis, the previous node at the same level. Thus:

Not Implemented	X

```
/myFavoriteWebSites/favoriteWebSite[2]/preceding-sibling::*
```

should return you the `favoriteWebSite` element that precedes it:

```
<m:favoriteWebSite id="1">
    <m:url>http://www.wrox.com</m:url>
</m:favoriteWebSite>
```

and:

Not Implemented	X

```
/myFavoriteWebSite/favoriteWebSite[2]/following-sibling::*
```

should return the subscription node in full.

```
<m:subscription id="3" creator="danm">
    <hs:trigger select="/myFavoriteWebSites/favoriteWebSite" mode="includeData"/>
    <hs:context uri="http://www.wrox.com"/>
</m:subscription>
```

This could come in particularly handy if your HailStorm endpoint offered some sort of browse functionality through a document. For example, if a user wanted to review the different payment methods s/he had stored in myWallet.

Putting Things into Context

One thing we can always assume is that we will have to *find* the specific node in the content document to alter rather than *know* exactly which node it is and just supply the path. The retrieval of data must be transparent to the user and not rely on him to provide any more direction to the target node than some key piece of information that relates to it – perhaps the URL of a web site, a contact's first name, a type of credit card, etc. It could be just as likely that the user is querying a service to recall a piece of information s/he can't remember all the details of – "the guy's last name was Maharry I think," or "have I put any Amex card details in myWallet yet?"

In either case, it's up to us to translate the query and find out if the service does in fact contain a node bearing a resemblance to the description s/he has given. Assuming the query isn't something unrealistic like "What's the name of that contact my dad gave me last week?", XPath has a small set of contextual functions that can go a long way to finding answers to the questions posed in an `<xpQuery>`.

Indeed, the first we've seen already when using indices. By appending a pair of square brackets containing a condition to an element, we add a conditional clause to the XPath – the equivalent of a `where` clause in a SQL query – called a **predicate**. A node will only be selected if it fulfils the predicate. In the case of indices, this is, 'where' `position()=index`' or where '`position() = last()`' as appropriate.

►► – From Basic SQL Queries to XPaths

Let's take the analogy one step further. Suppose the user wants to pull up the whole entry for www.wrox.com. If we were writing a SQL query against myFavoriteWebSites as a database table, it would probably look like this:

```
SELECT favoriteWebSite FROM myFavoriteWebSites WHERE url =
"http://www.wrox.com"
```

The root node (and any other parent nodes) sits in the `from` clause, the node you require follows the `select` keyword and the `where` clause houses the predicate that you'd put in square brackets. In the general case then, a SQL `SELECT` statement takes the form:

```
SELECT field_name FROM database_table WHERE condition
```

This translates into an XPath of the form:

```
/database_table/other_parent_nodes/field_name[condition]
```

More often than not, we'll be looking to return the node, one of whose child elements has a given value or a piece of a given value. In the former case, the predicate takes the condition `subelement=value`. For example, if we wanted to select the web site entry that contains `http://www.wrox.com` as its URL, we would use:

| Works Fine | ✓ |

```
/myFavoriteWebSites/favoriteWebSite[url='http://www.wrox.com']
```

If the node we wish to select is not the immediate parent of the element being compared in the predicate, we can set a path to the element in the predicate, instead of just the element itself. Our web site document doesn't have enough levels in its hierarchy for a useful example, so let's answer one of the questions above, "The guy's last name was Maharry I think." Looking at the document skeleton for the myContacts content document in Chapter 5, we can see that the correct XPath for this query is:

| Works Fine | ✓ |

```
/myContacts/contact[name/lastName='Maharry']
```

Predicate Functions

We're not limited to checking if an element is equal to a value either. As indicated earlier, we can query against a substring of the contents of an element thanks to some text-based predicate functions that XPath supports.

Again however, HailStorm doesn't supports these functions yet, but hopefully will in time for v1.0.

contains()

The first function, `contains()`, takes two strings as arguments, returning `true` if the first string contains the second. When used as a predicate then, if an element or attribute contained the string then that node would be returned. For example, we would use:

Not Implemented | X

```
/myFavoriteWebSites/favoriteWebSite/url[contains(.,'ftp://')]
```

to return all the FTP addresses stored in a user's safe deposit box. In our example document of course this would return nothing at all, but should we replace `ftp://` with `http://`, both URLs would be returned. Note that we use the abbreviated form of the self axis to make the contents of the URL the first argument in the predicate.

▸▸ – Casting Node Objects to Other Types

One problem you may come across while using predicate functions are the errors caused because XPath returns a node object rather than a string or number etc., to compare against a given value. Fortunately, XPath does define a group of functions that cast these objects into primitive types. They are `string()`, `boolean()`, `date()`, `time()`, and `date-time()`. Each takes an object as an argument and returns a value of the appropriate type. For example, the previous XPath demonstrating contains could have been written:

```
/myFavoriteWebSites/favoriteWebSite/url[contains(string(.),'ftp://')]
```

■

substring(), substring-before(), and substring-after()

Unlike `contains()`, which returns a Boolean value based on whether or not one string is a substring of another, the three other substring functions actually return a string. It's this string that we'll use in one half of the predicate to return a Boolean value and thus select a node or not. This gives us a little more control than we had using `contains()`.

The first function, `substring()`, takes three arguments – a string to be sliced into, the `startIndex` of the slice (the numbering starts at 1), and the `sliceLength`, returning a slice of the original string. Thus

Not Implemented | X

```
/myFavoriteWebSites/favoriteWebSite/url[substring(string(.),1,4)='http']
```

should return both URL nodes. The last argument – the length of the slice – can be omitted, in which case `substring()` returns a slice starting from the index position to the end of the original string. For example:

Not Implemented | X

```
/myFavoriteWebSites/favoriteWebSite/url[substring(string(.),17)="com"]
```

also returns both URL nodes. The `substring()` function works well if you know where the slice should be in your target node, but if you don't, the `– before()` and `– after()` variations come in handy. The `substring-before()` function then takes two string arguments, returning that part of the first which precedes the second. We could rewrite the `contains()` example above using this function as follows:

Not Implemented | X

```
/myFavoriteWebSites/favoriteWebSite/url[substring-before(.,"://")="ftp"]
```

Not surprisingly, the `substring-after()` function works in exactly the same way as the `substring-before()` function, but returns the part of the first string that comes after the second.

| Not Implemented | X |

```
/myFavoriteWebSites/favoriteWebSite/url[substring-after(.,"press.")="com"]
```

string-length()

A fifth text function, `string-length()` returns the length of the string you've selected. Again, this can be used as the left hand side of a predicate in an XPath. For example:

| Not Implemented | X |

```
/myFavoriteWebSites/favoriteWebSite/url[string-length(.)=19]
```

will return the Wrox Press homepage URL, but not that for ASPToday.

Operators

Up to this point we've used only the equality operator = inside our predicates, but XPath actually defines most of the basic operators we would find in a programming language, as follows.

Type of Operator	Operator
Comparison	=, !=, <, >, <=, >=
Boolean	and, or, not
Concatenation		
Arithmetical	+, -, *, div, mod

We've already seen the concatenation operator, so we'll not go over it again.

Comparison Operators

Beyond the equality operator, we have at our disposal the not equals operator != and the numerical greater and less than operators, <=, <, >=, and >. These work in the usual way once the operands either side of the operator are of the same type. Like any programming language that must deal with incompatible types, XPath has several rules for the implicit casting of one operand from one type to another.

There are three basic possibilities, either both operands are node-sets, one of them is a node-set, or none of them is a node-set. If neither operand is a node-set, then both are converted to the same type:

❑ If one of the operands is Boolean for example "true()", "false()", "1=1", then both operands are converted to Boolean type. A number is converted to "true" if it is not equal to "0" or "NaN", and string is "true" if it contains at least one character.

❑ If one of the operands is a number and the second is a string, then the string is converted to a number as well. Basically it means with some simplification that if the string looks like number, it is converted to the relevant number, if not, it is converted to "NaN" (Not a Number).

Operators "=" (equal) and "!=" (not equal) are then used in usual way. Operators "<=", "<", ">=" and ">" are defined only for numbers. Strings are automatically transformed to numbers when using these operators and so their usage on strings not representing numbers always results in "false".

❑ When one of the operands is a node-set and other is a string or a number then the value of each node from the node-set is compared with it. If at least one comparison returns "true" then the whole expression returns "true".

❑ If both operands are node-sets, all possible combination of nodes from the first node-set and the second one are evaluated. If any of these comparisons returns "true", the whole expression returns "true" as well.

The net result of this is that we can now select groups of nodes based on something other than equality. We could select the credit card node that hasn't expired yet when we need to pay for something online. We could cycle through our list of web sites ten at a time based on their index in the XML document, or return a list of contacts whose birthdays haven't occurred yet this year.

Boolean Operators

The predicate we create in our XPath returns a Boolean value based on a condition. If this value is true for a node, then that node is returned as part of the selection from the document we've targeted. We can extend our predicate to include more than one condition with the use of the Boolean operators, "or" and "and", which work in the usual way. For example:

```
Works Fine    ✓
```

```
/myFavoriteWebSites/favoriteWebSite[@id>'1' and @id<'3']
```

returns only the second favoriteWebSite node in our document, and the concept here is easily extended to the idea of returning subsets of content from a document of equal size. Don't forget to use the real values for ID rather than the simple ones if you're running the queries.

XPath also caters for the use of the unary "not" operator, which negates a given Boolean expression as you would expect. If we took the previous example and added not to it:

```
Works Fine    ✓
```

```
/myFavoriteWebSites/favoriteWebSite[not(@id>'1' and @id<'3')]
```

we'd be returned the first favoriteWebSite node. Note that XPath is case-sensitive and so these operators must be written in lowercase. Also, there are no abbreviated Boolean operators like "&&" or "||".

Mathematical Operators

Addition, subtraction, and multiplication are supported in XPath using the standard operators +, -, and * respectively, while standard division is supported using "div" as the more usual operator / is already taken in XPath. There is also a modulus operator, "mod", which returns the remainder after both operands are cast to integers and the first divided by the second.

Three of these five operators should be surrounded by whitespace for an error not to occur. The operators -, div and mod all contain characters allowed in the name of an element, so while "foo - bar" would indeed subtract the value of element "bar" from the value of element "foo", "foo-bar" would just return the value of element foo-bar. The same is true for mod and div.

The characters * and + meanwhile are not permitted in element names and so if a processor encounters "foo+bar" or "foo*bar", it knows that it should add or multiply the value of element foo with the value of element bar, respectively, but it's easier to remember one convention.

It's somewhat less obvious how we can use the mathematical operators to aid our selection although an application may become apparent with the addition of services yet to appear in HailStorm. For now we can pseudo-randomly select elements using the modulus operator, picking every second, third, fourth node etc. To select every element in the myFavoriteWebSites content document whose value is an odd number we would use the following query statement:

Not Implemented	X

```
//*[position(.) mod 2 = 1]
```

Note that as HailStorm doesn't support position() this search pattern doesn't actually work at the moment.

This draws to a close our look at XPath itself, to the extent that we've covered the subset of XPath that HailStorm supports and he remainder of the basic XPath functionality that it doesn't support yet, but hopefully will. In the second half of this chapter, we take a look at the pieces of the HailStorm that affect the way we'll form our XPath select statements.

> **Don't forget that each element of your XPath must be prefixed with the correct identifier if the default namespace is not defined by the schema of the document you are querying. For example:**
>
> ```
> <hs:queryRequest
>     xmlns:hs="http://schemas.microsoft.com/hs/2001/10/core"
>     xmlns:m="http://schemas.microsoft.com/hs/2001/10/myFavorite
>         WebSites">
>   <hs:xpQuery select="/m:myFavoriteWebSites/m:favoriteWebSite"/>
> </hs:queryRequest>
> ```

Refining Query Results

The one problem with the tutorial above is that the document it works against is grossly simplified to make it easier to introduce the concepts of XPath as simply as possible. In practice, it's quite feasible to imagine content documents with several hundred entries to be searched through, even thousands. Retrieving a large amount of this data with a single xpQuery could be troublesome if returned in the random order in which it was added to the service. Fortunately, xpQuery includes a number of options (expressed as subelements) which allow us to shape and refine our returned dataset into something more manageable. All we need to do is add a few lines to our original query XML file, as shown.

```
<hs:queryRequest>
    <hs:xpQuery select="//m:widget">
        <hs:options>
            ... add your options here ...
        </hs:options>
    </hs:xpQuery>
</hs:queryRequest>
```

There are two possible options with which to complete the query above, plus a third whose format is still 'to be decided'. They can be used on their own or in combination.

`<hs:sort>` specifies that the returned nodes should be sorted into either ascending or descending order based on the value of an attribute or subelement within those nodes. It takes two attributes: `key` gives the location of the sort key within the node and `direction` takes one of two values, 'ascending' or 'descending' and determines the sort order.

`<hs:range>` allows us to specify the number of nodes returned and, to a lesser degree, which nodes they are. It also takes two attributes, both mandatory: `first` allows you to specify the index of the first node in the document to be part of the range and `count` the number of elements in the range.

Interestingly, the first attribute can take values which incorporate the `count()` and `position-of()` functions, which do the same thing as the XPath `count()` and `position()` functions. Thus we can specify the first node in the range with respect to the last node in the set using `count()` - x as the index, or with respect to a predicate given as the argument to `position-of()`. For example, `position-of(.[@id="2"])`.

`<hs:shape>` allows us to shape the data as you can in SQL Server and other RDBMSs. The exact call and attributes to this element however were still to be decided as we went to press.

To broach a complete example then, let's assume a user has already asked us to return the first ten web sites in their safe-deposit box and now wants the next ten, ordered alphabetically by title. The full query would look like this:

```
<hs:queryRequest
    xmlns:hs="http://schemas.microsoft.com/hs/2001/10/core"
    xmlns:m="http://schemas.microsoft.com/hs/2001/10/myFavoriteWebSites">
    <hs:xpQuery select="//m:favoriteWebSites">
        <hs:options>
            <hs:sort key="./title" direction="ascending" />
            <hs:range first="position-of(.[@id='10'])+1" count="10" />
        </hs:options>
    </hs:xpQuery>
</hs:queryRequest>
```

The HailStorm core schema also states that a fourth user-defined option could be used here provided it is qualified with a proper namespace and schema. It does this by placing an {any} element, which we look at in more details in the next section, inside the `<hs:options>` element.

Content Document Schemas

The world of HailStorm is a world of well-formed XML. As we noted in Chapter 3, there are five different schemas used in sending a SOAP request to a server to perform a task – each one adds a little more meaning to its construction. Every task is accomplished by changing the structure of one of the XML documents that sit behind the service being queried. Their structures are in turn defined by other schemas – one per document in fact. Recall that all a user's information is stored in just one document per service (the content document) and realize that if we are to develop applications effectively against HailStorm, we need a full and clear knowledge of the schemas that define the content documents; the .NET Contacts schema for the myContacts content document, the .NET Profile schema for the myProfile content document, and so on. If an endpoint is to offer its users a means to effectively secure their information, its developers also need access to the roleList schema as well.

Sure enough, Microsoft has made the schemas available in the documentation that comes with the HailStorm SDK (the XMI Manual) for you to peruse. To quote the same self documentation, however, "All HailStorm data is defined using heavily annotated XSD schema files. [These] accurately type the data, but since XSD is a verbose and complex language, [...] document structure is easier to comprehend using document skeletons", which are also available to read (and which sometimes disagree with the schemas too). Bearing this in mind, we'll use the skeleton approach here rather than the schema.

Red, Blue, and Black Tags

The first thing to note harks back to the top of the section on XPath where it was noted that HailStorm allows us to target only certain nodes with our select statements. It does so by 'color-coding' the elements in each HailStorm document, as follows:

- ❏ The root element (whose name matches that of the service) and the elements one level below that are **blue** elements. Or, rather they are marked in the schema with `<xdb:blue />` tags.

- ❏ Within each blue element there are one or more sub-elements or attributes that are key to the location (using XPath) and description of the blue elements marked out as **red** nodes. In the schemas, they are marked with `<xdb:red />` tags.

- ❏ The remaining elements and attributes that are neither blue nor red are officially uncolored (although I find it handy to call them **black** nodes, as that's the color they'll be in official Microsoft documentation).

When creating an XPath for your SOAP message, you may only target the red and blue elements in a document for retrieval and you may only use red elements as points of comparison inside a predicate. If you include any black elements within your XPath, the SOAP response will be a SOAP fault telling you politely that you can't target that particular element. For example, sending a query to retrieve the subelements of a subscription element, which are all black, won't work. Hence:

```
/myFavoriteWebSites/subscription/*
```

will get you the aforementioned message saying that you cannot target any of these nodes. Likewise, you cannot make a black tag the target of a comparison in a predicate. For example:

```
/myFavoriteWebSites/subscription/[to='hs:myAlerts']
```

returns a similar message saying that /myFavoriteWebSites/subscription/to can not be used in predicate expressions.

The red, blue, and black approach is there strictly to limit the number of nodes that an XPath can select, enforcing the need to operate on an item of information (for example a web site) as a whole rather than on the atomic items that comprise that item (URL, description, etc.). This not only makes it more straightforward for the endpoint developer (consider that the myWallet document skeleton has 79 elements, but only 21 red or blue elements – making those search pages simpler if nothing else) but also for HailStorm itself, as it can search for and retrieve the nodes in a much more stream-lined way, given the significantly reduced number of nodes it needs to index and be aware of.

*Of course, one thing that the color-coding of elements is not conducive to is its documentation in a black-and-white book! To this extent, we'll follow the convention that **blue** elements are written in **bold** when appropriate and <u>red</u> elements will be <u>underlined</u>.*

The {any} Tag

The sell and customize process has been one Microsoft has subscribed to for many years, and it's obvious that those using HailStorm as a platform may need to extend the schemas beyond their initial dataset to contain information specific to their own application. To this extent, every HailStorm content document skeleton contains several instances of the {any} tag to indicate that an endpoint can insert additional information there.

Any additional information you do decide to add in place of an {any} element should be well-formed XML properly qualified by a namespace. Note however that HailStorm will treat it as almost totally invisible. The root element of this additional information and its attributes will be treated as red elements of type xsd:string but its sub-elements are automatically black.

Say for example then, that we need to add some more information to the web site entries we have already in HailStorm. Our extended information might take the form:

```
<webext:moreInfo xyz:loggedby="danm">
    <webext:icon>favicon.ico</webext:icon>
    <webext:lastVisited>09/13/01</webext:lastVisited>
</webext:moreInfo>
```

We can use webext:moreInfo and webext:moreInfo/@webext:loggedby in XPaths and their predicates, but the rest remains unavailable except when retrieved as children of an ancestor element.

! – "{any} Problems"

One possible problem with leaving {any} elements inside the HailStorm schemas is the potential for namespace clashes. It's conceivable (although unlikely) that two or more endpoints could end up using the same namespace to store information at the same point in a HailStorm document. Currently, there seems to be nothing to prevent this occurring apart from employing common sense when naming namespaces.

myFavoriteWebSites in Full

Let's look at one document skeleton – that of the myFavoriteWebSites content document – in full regalia with <u>red</u>, **blue** and black pieces marked as appropriate. It isn't the simplest of the five available in the first release of HailStorm, but it does illustrate all the core concepts of the content schemas nicely. It also has one or two features in its skeleton worth a closer inspection without being as long as those documents in myProfile or myContacts.

First, let's take a look at a skeleton of just the **blue** tags to illustrate the large pieces of information that we can store inside this document and the elements we are most likely to be targeting in our XPaths.

```
<m:myFavoriteWebSites changeNumber="..." instanceId="..."
    xmlns:m="http://schemas.microsoft.com/hs/2001/10/myFavoriteWebSites"
    xmlns:hs="http://schemas.microsoft.com/hs/2001/10/core">
  <m:favoriteWebSite> ... </m:favoriteWebSite>
    <!-- Zero, one or more websites -->
  <m:subscription>  ...    </m:subscription>
    <!-- Zero, one or more subscriptions -->
  {any}
</m:myFavoriteWebSites>
```

The myFavoriteWebSites content document provides a subset of the functionality provided by the major browsers, defining blue elements for storing web sites and subscriptions to notify you when something concerning the web site has changed. Whether or not a user stores some, none, or just one instance of each blue tag is up to them. There's also an {any} tag at this level to let endpoints store any other information they think necessary.

The root node, <myFavoriteWebSites>, has two attributes, changeNumber and instanceId. The former is a read-only attribute that HailStorm increases when a change to that element occurs – much like a timestamp. The latter is used to identify the content document in the event that a user has created two or more documents to store, for example, his or her business favorites in one and his or her home-based favorites in the other. This attribute is also read-only and a value assigned when the service is provisioned for that service.

Web Sites

Unlike most blue elements, almost every child node of the <favoriteWebSite> element itself is a red tag – the URL of the website, its given title, and {any} other information we want to store about it for the user. We can also specify a category for the web site in the same way as we group our bookmarks in a web browser. The cat/@ref attribute stores the actual location of the category definition in one of three forms:

- ❑ 'system#category_name' if the category is defined in the system document of the myCategories service

- ❑ 'content#category_name' if the category is defined in the content document of the myCategories service

- ❑ 'URI#category_name' if the category is defined in a document (at the URI given) outside of the HailStorm environment

The blue element itself has three attributes, the pseudo-timestamp we saw previously, the GUID that HailStorm generates to uniquely identify that particular blue node and an entry for the creator of the node in the first place. Amusingly, the XMI manual describes this last attribute (creator) as identifying the creator of the node in terms of userId, appId, and platformId, but is currently user-definable so danm, for example, seems to work just fine.

```
<m:favoriteWebSite changeNumber="..." id="..." creator="...">
   <m:cat ref="..."> category_for_the_website </m:cat>
   <m:title xml:lang="..."> name_of_the_website </m:title>
   <m:url> URL_to_the_website </m:url>
   {any}
</m:favoriteWebSite>
```

The full list of XPaths to the red tags under the <favoriteWebSite> blue element that can be addressed in XPaths is:

- ❑ /**myFavoriteWebSites**/**favoriteWebSite**/@changeNumber

- ❑ /**myFavoriteWebSites**/**favoriteWebSite**/@id

- ❑ /**myFavoriteWebSites**/**favoriteWebSite**/@creator

- ❑ /**myFavoriteWebSites**/**favoriteWebSite**/cat/@ref

- ❑ /**myFavoriteWebSites**/**favoriteWebSite**/title

- ❑ /**myFavoriteWebSites**/**favoriteWebSite**/url

- ❑ /**myFavoriteWebSites**/**favoriteWebSite**/{any}

Subscriptions

The other blue element in the myFavoriteWebSites allows you to define a subscription/notification arrangement whereby HailStorm will send the user a notification – a subscriptionResponse message in fact – that something has been altered within a target set of elements in their safe deposit box. For example, you may set up a subscription to alert you when a company updates your details in myProfile at your request.

```
<m:subscription changeNumber="..." id="..." creator="...">
   <hs:trigger select="..." mode="..." baseChangeNumber="...">
      trigger_event
   </hs:trigger>
   <hs:expiresAt> time_of_subscription_expiry </hs:expiresAt>
   <hs:context uri="..."> {any} </hs:context>
   <hs:to> destination_of_subscription_message </hs:to>
</m:subscription>
```

The key in this subscription element is the trigger, which allows you to determine the set of elements HailStorm should keep an eye on and the contents of the notification when it is sent. Its select attribute holds an XPath to one or several **blue** (only) elements and the baseChangeNumber reflects the original state of the elements relative to which the changes should be recorded. The mode attribute meanwhile determines the content of the notification – whether or not it includes the new values of the element or just a note that it changed – with the values 'includeData' and 'excludeData' respectively.

Rounding off the information pertaining to a subscription, the `<expiresAt>` element specifies when the subscription should expire and be removed from the document, context contains a reference to the URI (usually a UUID) that the subscription is concerned with, and also holds the address to which the notification should be sent – either `<hs:myAlerts>`, which will cause it to be sent to the default myAlerts service of the creator (the default setting) or to an endpoint/other web service that knows how to read and process such HailStorm subscription messages.

The XPaths to the red nodes for you to select or check against the value of under this blue element are as follows:

❑   **/myFavoriteWebSites/subscription/@changeNumber**

❑   **/myFavoriteWebSites/subscription/@id**

❑   **/myFavoriteWebSites/subscription/@creator**

Note that there are no {any} elements inside the subscription element.

Common Attributes across Schemas

That's all there is to the myFavoriteWebSites content document, except to point out specifically a few elements (besides {any}) that are common across all the content schemas in HailStorm.

Blue Element IDs

Every blue element in a document contains an id attribute, which contains a GUID uniquely identifying this blue element from every other one. This GUID is generated by HailStorm when the element is added to the document and returned as part of the insert response message should the insert request be successful. It's also used internally as the anchor to a blue element when subscriptions or changes are being made to that element.

xml:lang

A number of sub-elements across the various content documents contain a mandatory xml:lang attribute to indicate the language type of their contents. The value of this attribute must be an ISO 639 language code or an ISO 3166 country code as described in RFC 1766. For example, en, US, or en-US.

changeNumber

We've looked at this briefly already, but it's worth reiterating the importance this particular attribute could have for certain types of endpoints that make use of information acquired from HailStorm and then cache it again for later use. The changeNumber attribute of an element makes a note of the number of times that element or its contents have been altered, increasing this value each time something within its scope is modified. If many elements are updated at once, they all receive the same new changeNumber. It is using this element then that endpoints should determine whether or not the user has updated that particular element and thus whether or not it should be reached.

It's also against this attribute that subscriptions compare the baseChangeNumber attribute in the trigger to determine whether or not a change has occurred and send notification if it has.

Summary

Even at this early stage in the development of HailStorm, it's obvious that its support for XPath will change over the coming months, first with the finalization and documentation of the subset of XPath that it will actually support in its first release version and then with the eventual support for XPath 2.0 when it is ratified.

In this chapter, we've seen how to create a well-formed XPath that selects one or more nodes in a HailStorm document, using the myFavoriteWebSites content document as an example. An XPath can either point directly at a specific node (or nodes) if its location within the document is known or can locate the node in question by referring to the value of one of its sub-nodes.

We've also seen that HailStorm categorizes the nodes in the documents it maintains for a user into red, blue, and uncolored (black) nodes and that XPaths may only refer to red or blue nodes, else an error will occur. Finally, we looked at the full structure of the myFavoriteWebSites content document, how it's colored and what information it can contain, highlighting the elements common across other HailStorm schemas.

Of the five standard HSDL request messages, four of them allow an XPath to select zero or more nodes in a document upon which to act. An <updateRequest> works in a slightly different way, using its own XPath to define a global set of elements from which its atomic requests can use their own XPaths to pick their nodes from. But that's really for Chapter 5 to demonstrate.

early adopter

HailStorm XMI Messaging

What is XMI?

In the last two chapters we covered two technologies that are fundamental to HailStorm – SOAP messaging and the current HailStorm querying language, XPath. We are now ready to discuss the heart of HailStorm: its **XML Messaging Interface** (**XMI**). We will cover the **HailStorm Data-manipulation Language** (**HSDL**), the various services, and their schemas. By the end of this chapter, you will know how to manipulate the HailStorm services and understand the data and functional aspects of the HailStorm schemas.

One statement that you always hear at Microsoft presentations is that XML is the key to .NET. The more you learn about HailStorm, the more you'll see how very true that is. In fact, every aspect of HailStorm is based on XML:

- ❑   SOAP is used for accessing services

- ❑   XPath is used for querying documents

- ❑   HSDL is used for performing data manipulation on services

- ❑   XML schemas describe each service and a lot of the functionality

- ❑   The content and other documents that form the basis of each service are XML documents`

Because HailStorm is a set of identity-bound XML documents that are accessed by XML messages or SOAP, and manipulated with HSDL (another XML-based language), the entire product can be summed up as an XML message interface.

This chapter contains two sections: the first describes the HSDL language and the six common operations it exposes. The second section describes the schema for each of the currently available services.

HSDL

HSDL is the data manipulation language for HailStorm; it used to build statements that interact with HailStorm. These messages can be stored as an XML file and sent using the hspost utility, programmed into an ASP page (or any other programming language), or generated in part or full with a tool like Visual Studio .NET. Let's look at a typical hspost call and the sample HSDL message used in the call:

```
C:\HailStorm\Bin>hspost -d content - s myContacts -f file.xml
```

The HSDL statement must be passed to the services as the payload of a SOAP message. Using the hspost utility, we only need to pass it the name of the file containing the HSDL statement and some other parameters and it will do the rest. As you should already know from Chapter 4, the -d content specifies that we want to modify the content document, -s myContacts specifies the myContacts service, and -f file.xml specifies the name of the file containing the HSDL statement.

The body of the SOAP message and most of what is required to communicate with HailStorm is derived from the HSDL statement. The purpose of the sample below is to demonstrate where HSDL fits into the picture. See Chapter 3 on SOAP for details on the messaging.

Contents of file.xml:

```
<hs:insertRequest select="/myProfile"
    xmlns:hs="http://schemas.microsoft.com/hs/2001/10/core"
    xmlns="http://schemas.microsoft.com/hs/2001/10/myProfile">
  <name>
    <givenName xml:lang="en">John</givenName>
  </name>
</hs:insertRequest>
```

As you can see, this is a request to insert a new contact with the given name John in to the myContacts service. The response statement sent back would include an <insertResponse> element that contains information on the node that was added or a SOAPFault if the operation was not successful. The above request would produce the following statement in the SOAP body:

```
<hs:insertResponse xmlns:hs="http://schemas.microsoft.com/hs/2001/10/core"
status="success" selectedNodeCount="1" newChangeNumber="902">
```

As mentioned in Chapter 1, programmers familiar with XML processing, node selection, and node manipulation will feel at home with HailStorm. Those that are not will have to learn the syntax of XML querying languages, which is straightforward in this case. However, learning to work with the hierarchical nature of XML documents, and not always being able to select the precise data element you want may take some time to get used to. For example, in XPath you have to ensure that you do not get the same contact name multiple times. In some cases, you may have to bring an entire element of data down and then manipulate it with the DOM or XSLT.

The Standard Operations

Each HailStorm service supports six standard operations, and some services have custom operations as well. The standard operations form the base of HailStorm's HSDL language and provide a consistent interface to the services. These operations are insert, delete, replace, update, query, and subscription response. Providing six common operations for each service enables endpoints accessing the service a guaranteed contract to perform the basic operations necessary on the service. The six operations are briefly described below:

- ❑ Insert – Inserts red or blue elements into a selected blue element.

- ❑ Delete – Deletes a red or a blue element from a selected blue element.

- ❑ Replace – Replace the contents of a red or blue node with the contents of the `<replaceRequest>` message.

- ❑ Update – Shell operation to store multiple operations and run them at the same time; this method supports `<updateBlocks>` and an `error` attribute.

- ❑ Query – Selects blue nodes or receives information on status of changes for caching.

- ❑ Subscription Response – This message is generated in response to a subscription firing within a service. A subscription is based on an XML node inside a service document. The subscription node is created, modified, and canceled by the insert, replace, and delete methods.

Custom Operations

Custom operations can be used to add new functionality or to streamline one of the standard operations. For example, querying the myCalendar service with XPath or any other querying language would be difficult because you would not know the specific business rules of the service. A custom operation could be designed to provide an efficient method to query the myCalendar service for open appointments this month on workdays. At the time of writing, no custom operations are available, so only the six common operations are covered in this chapter, as a result, you will be limited by the flexibility of XPath.

Consistent Items across the Operations

The core set of operations share a lot of standard attributes and functionality. Before diving into some of the services in detail, let's cover some of the common elements across the operations, and some items that are important to the messages and working with HailStorm.

Each HailStorm request statement must be well formed XML; for instance, the insert operation begins with `<insertRequest>` and ends with `</insertRequest>`. Each pair of these tags contains XML elements specific to that operation, and the XPath query statement necessary for the query section of that operation. The most common attributes are listed below:

- ❑ `Select="..."` – This attribute allows you to select the part of the HailStorm document the operation will be carried out on. Note that it must select a blue or red element(s). At the time of writing, the select statement supported a subset of XPath and xmQuery (according to Microsoft), but only XPath was documented, so it is the de facto querying method used throughout the book.

❑ useClientIds="..." – IDs are generally created by HailStorm. However, if this tag is used, the ID can be passed to HailStorm during an insert or replace operation performed on a blue element. When set to true, it will prevent HailStorm auto-generating IDs; this permits the application or service to assign their own IDs. This should only be done in rare cases and the application needs to validate the uniqueness of the ID, when doing this manually.

❑ minOccurs="..." – this specifies the minimum number of nodes that should be selected in order for this operation to succeed. This optional attribute's default is 0, and with this setting no error is returned even if no nodes are selected. Set it to 1, and an error will be returned if no nodes are selected.

❑ maxOccurs="..." – this specifies the maximum number of nodes returned by a select operation before an error is returned. Setting this value to 1 is very useful when querying for a unique ID where only one node should be returned. The default value is unbounded. Setting this to an upper limit can be useful in many cases, including to ensure that the amounts of data are returned to small devices does not exceed its capabilities, to decrease network traffic, and for preventing runaway queries. This operation will return an error if the number of nodes selected is larger than the specified value.

All messages operate on data relative to the "current context". For all messages except update, the "current context" is "/", which specifies the root of the current document.

Insert

The Insert statement allows you to insert red and blue elements into selected blue elements. It is one of the more basic operations; however, its functionality extends beyond just a simple insert. When properly used, it can control the generation of IDs as well as accommodate inserts that are more complex.

Request Definition

This uses the basic attributes common to all operations as well as an <options> and <attributes> element to control the <insertRequest>. However, the <options> element was not fully supported at the time of writing. Even with its robust functionality, the insert statements are still small. Below is a schema fragment that shows the format of an insert message:

```
<hs:insertRequest select="..." useClientIDs="..." minOccurs="..."
    maxOccurs="..."
    xmlns:hs="http://schemas.microsoft.com/hs/2001/10/core">
  <hs:options>0...1{any}</hs:options>
  <hs:attributes {any}="...">0...unbounded</hs:attributes>
  {any}
</hs:insertRequest>
```

The <insertRequest> element has the four standard attributes and two subelements that affect its operation.

There are a couple of important things to mention about these attributes. The useClientIDs attribute only shows up in insert and replace, so if you want to insert your own IDs, do so now. For more information on using clientIDs, see the general section earlier in this chapter. You should also take note of the importance of minOccurs when it is used with insert. If your minOccurs is set to 0, the default value, it will say the insert was successful even if the select statement did not make any matches and thus nothing was inserted.

> To force HailStorm to throw an error when no nodes are inserted, set `minOccurs=1`.
> If a select has zero matches, nothing will be inserted and an error will be thrown.

The `<options>` and `<attributes>` elements were not completely documented at the time of writing, so a complete picture is unavailable. However, there is a general description of the elements below:

Name	minOccurs	maxOccurs	Description
`<options>`	0	1	This element is an optional element that will add more functionality to the insert
`<attributes>`	0	unbounded	This element allows you to insert attributes into the element you selected with the select statement
`{any}`			This isn't actually an element; it's simply a placeholder for the element(s) that you will be inserting

Response Definition

Assuming your XML was well formed and there were no delivery problems, you will get back an `<insertResponse>` that will look like the template below:

```
<hs:insertResponse newChangeNumber="..." selectedNodeCount="..."
  status="..."
  xmlns:hs="http://schemas.microsoft.com/hs/2001/10/core">
  <hs:newBlueId id="...">0...unbounded</hs:newBlueID>
</hs:insertResponse>
```

The `<insertResponse>` element has three attributes and one element. The three attributes are described below:

Name	Description
newChangeNumber	This attribute is the new changeNumber
selectedNodeCount	This attribute tells you how many items were selected with the select statement.
Status	For inserts, the status can be success, failure, or not attempted

In addition to those attributes, a successful `<insertResponse>` will also contain the `<newBlueID>` element. That element has one attribute, id, which is the ID of the newly created blue elements.

Example

To help tie things together, let's look at a sample insert request. This example demonstrates a basic insert operation that adds a contact into the myContacts service. It will set its own `clientID`. However, the current version of HailStorm does not actually use the IDs, so it is more a simulation of what HailStorm is supposed to do. Below is the `<insertRequest>` for this sample:

```
<hs:insertRequest select="/myContacts" useClientIDs="true"
    xmlns:hs="http://schemas.microsoft.com/hs/2001/10/core"
    xmlns="http://schemas.microsoft.com/hs/2001/10/myContacts"
    xmlns:mp="http://schemas.microsoft.com/hs/2001/10/myProfile">
  <contact id="1253">
    <name id="12531">
      <mp:givenName xml:lang="en">John</mp:givenName>
    </name>
    <emailAddress id="12532">
      <mp:email>jdoe11562@hotmail.com</mp:email>
    </emailAddress>
  </contact>
</hs:insertRequest>
```

Here are snapshots of the document:

Before

```
<m:myContacts
id="4823832842834"
changeNumber="1">
<m:contact id="423ewr2r2r">
...
</m:contact>
</m:myContacts>
```

After

```
<m:myContacts
  id="4823832842834"
    changeNumber="2">
  <m:contact id="423ewr2r2r">
    ...
  </m:contact>
  <m:contact id="1253">
    ...
  </m:contact>
</m:myContacts>
```

This is the response message for this example:

```
<hs:insertResponse xmlns:hs="http://schemas.microsoft.com/hs/2001/10/core"
status="success" selectedNodeCount="1" newChangeNumber="2">
  <hs:newBlueID id="1253"/>
  <hs:newBlueID id="1253"/>
  <hs:newBlueID id="1253"/>
</hs:insertResponse>
```

You will notice that once added, the inserted contact retains the ID it was inserted with instead of taking on an auto-generated ID. Since the select statement was pointing to myContacts, there was only one place to insert at, so `selectedNodeCount` is 1. Finally, as expected with a simple command such as this, the `status` is "success".

Delete

Delete allows the deletion of multiple blue or red items. It will not limit your delete, so you should take care to make sure you do not delete too many items.

Request Definition

A delete operation will have the following general format:

```
<hs:deleteRequest select="..." minOccurs="..." maxOccurs="..."
  xmlns:hs="http://schemas.microsoft.com/hs/2001/10/core">
  <hs:options>0...1{any}</options>
</hs:deleteRequest>
```

The only subelement of `<deleteRequest>` is options, which has not yet been documented, so we cannot detail its functionality.

> Use the **maxOccurs** attribute to avoid deleting to many nodes in a runaway query.

Response Definition

The `<deleteResponse>` is also simple; it only lists the basic information about how the operation went. Here is a template for a `<deleteResponse>`:

```
<hs:deleteResponse newChangeNumber="..." selectedNodeCount="..."
    status="..."
    xmlns:hs="http://schemas.microsoft.com/hs/2001/10/core"/>
```

The attributes for a `<deleteResponse>` are as follows:

Name	Description
newChangeNumber	This attribute is the new changeNumber
selectedNodeCount	This attribute tells you how many items were selected with the select statement
status	For deletes, the status can be success, failure, or not attempted

The attributes for a `<deleteResponse>` have the same purpose as the attributes for an `<insertResponse>`, so we will skip straight to some examples.

Example 1

In the first example, let's delete a credit card that was recently canceled from the myWallet service. Here is the request for our sample:

```
<hs:deleteRequest select="/myWallet/card[networkBrand='VISA']"
    xmlns:hs="http://schemas.microsoft.com/hs/2001/10/core"
    xmlns="http://schemas.microsoft.com/hs/2001/10/myWallet"/>
```

Here is the service document:

Before	After
| ```
<m:myWallet changeNumber="1">
    <m:card id="…">
        . . .
        <m:networkBrand>VISA
        </m:networkBrand>
        . . .
    </m:card>
    <m:card id="…">
        . . .

<m:networkBrand>MasterCard
        </m:networkBrand>
        . . .
    </m:card>
</m:myWallet>
``` | ```
<m:myWallet
changeNumber="2">
    <m:card id="…">
        . . .
        <m:networkBrand>
        MasterCard
        </m:networkBrand>
        . . .
    </m:card>
</m:myWallet>
``` |

The response is:

```
<hs:deleteResponse xmlns:hs="http://schemas.microsoft.com/hs/2001/10/core"
    newChangeNumber="2" selectedNodeCount="1" status="success"/>
```

This was a simple delete, so it should be easy to see how it works. If you look at the document, you will notice that the Visa card has been removed. Since there was only one card removed, the selectedNodeCount is 1. As with any successful operation, the changeNumber was indexed up one, and the status is equal to "success".

Example 2

The next delete will illustrate how to use maxOccurs to avoid deleting too many nodes. The request is:

```
<hs:deleteRequest select="/myContacts/contact[name/mp:givenName='John']"
    maxOccurs="1" xmlns:hs="http://schemas.microsoft.com/hs/2001/10/core"
    xmlns="http://schemas.microsoft.com/hs/2001/10/myContacts"
    xmlns:mp="http://schemas.microsoft.com/hs/2001/10/myProfile"/>
```

The service document before request:

```
<m:myContacts>
    <m:contact id="…">
        <m:name id="…">
            <mp:givenName xml:lang="en">John</mp:givenName>
            <mp:surName xml:lang="en">A</mp:surName>
        </m:name>
```

```
    </m:contact>
    <m:contact id="…">
      <m:name id="…">
        <mp:givenName xml:lang="en">John</mp:givenName>
        <mp:surName xml:lang="en">B</mp:surName>
      </m:name>
    </m:contact>
    <m:contact id="…">
      <m:name id="…">
        <mp:givenName
    xml:lang="en">John</mp:givenName>
        <mp:surName xml:lang="en">C</mp:surName>
      </m:name>
    </m:contact>
  </m:myContacts>
```

The response is:

```
<hs:deleteResponse xmlns:hs="http://schemas.microsoft.com/hs/2001/10/core"
    status="failure" selectedNodeCount="3"/>
```

Since we really only wanted to delete one John and had forgotten that there were three in myContacts, using maxOccurs kept us from deleting all three. After receiving the failure, we can check selectedNodeCount and find out that we had selected too many nodes.

Replace

The replace operation is like executing a delete and then an insert on a blue or red element. The item, no matter what element it is (even the root), will be completely replaced by the new data.

> **If you try to replace one part of element, and make the `<replaceRequest>` select the whole element, you need to include the rest of that element's data, or it will be deleted. In other words, if replacing a contact in order to change its `<name>` element make sure you include the other elements, such as `<emailAddresss>`, `<address>`, etc.**

Request Definition

Here is a template for the `<replaceRequest>`:

```
<hs:replaceRequest select="..." useClientIDs="..." minOccurs="..."
    maxOccurs="..." xmlns:hs="http://schemas.microsoft.com/hs/2001/10/core">
  <hs:options>0...1</hs:options>
  <hs:attributes {any}="...">0...unbounded</hs:attributes>
  {any}
</hs:replaceRequest>
```

The `<replaceRequest>` uses the four standard attributes, the `<options>` element (not yet supported) and `<attributes>` element like the insert. A `<replaceRequest>` is very similar to an insert. However, the select statement points to the element to be replaced, whereas in an insert it points to the parent of the element being inserted.

> **The replace and insert operations are the only operations that allow you to set clientIDs.**

Response Definition

The <replaceResponse> has attributes and subelements that are the same as an <insertResponse>. Here's a template of the response just to remind you of what it looks like:

```
<hs:replaceResponse xmlns:hs="http://schemas.microsoft.com/hs/2001/10/core"
    newChangeNumber="..." selectedNodeCount="..." status="...">
  <hs:newBlueId id="...">0...unbounded</hs:newBlueId>
</hs:replaceResponse>
```

The <replaceResponse> also has the same <newBlueID> subelement as the <insertResponse>. You should still pay attention to the selectedNodeCount, because like an insert or a delete, you may get an error due to a select that did not meet the max and min requirements, and the selectedNodeCount could indicate what happened.

Example

Now on to an example that replaces an address in myProfile and sets a new client-based ID.

Here is the request:

```
<hs:replaceRequest select="/myProfile/address" useClientIDs="true"
    xmlns:hs="http://schemas.microsoft.com/hs/2001/10/core"
    xmlns="http://schemas.microsoft.com/hs/2001/10/myProfile" >
  <address id="46556">
    <primaryCity xml:lang="en">Fremont</primaryCity>
  </address>
</hs:replaceRequest>
```

Here is the document:

Before	After

``
<m:myProfile>
  ...
 <m:address id="65287">
  <m:primaryCity
xml:lang="en">
    Newark
  </primaryCity>
 </m:address>
  ...
</m:myProfile>
``
	``
	<m:myProfile>
	  ...
	 <m:address id="46556">
	  <m:primaryCity
	xml:lang="en">
	    Fremont
	  <primaryCity>
	 </m:address>
	  ...
	</m:myProfile>
	``

Finally the response:

```
<hs:replaceResponse xmlns:hs="http://schemas.microsoft.com/hs/2001/10/core"
    status="success" selectedNodeCount="1" newChangeNumber="2">
  <hs:newBlueId id="46556"/>
</hs:replaceResponse>
```

The most interesting thing to note about this operation is that the blue item that was replaced has the client-based ID. Since a replace is very similar to an insert or a delete, you can look back at the examples of more complicated inserts or deletes to get an idea of what a complex replace would be like.

Update

The update method combines the functionality of an insert, delete, and replace, making it rather complex, yet very useful. It allows you to run batches of operations with controllable failure logic to ensure that you get the results you want. You can roll back the actions of a batch if one of the operations in a batch fails. If you have multiple batches, you can specify what to do if one of the batches rolls back. All this functionality is used to make a robust system for managing caches or large amounts of data. It is useful for tasks such as synchronizing a PDA to HailStorm, which may have access to HailStorm only when docked to a computer.

Request Definition

To get a quick glimpse of update, here is a template of an updateRequest:

```
<hs:updateRequest xmlns:hs="http://schemas.microsoft.com/hs/2001/10/core">
  <hs:updateBlock select="..." onError="...">
    <hs:insertRequest select="..." useClientIDs="..." minOccurs="..."
      maxOccurs="...">
    <hs:options>0...1</hs:options>
      <hs:attributes {any}="...">0...unbounded</hs:attributes>
      {any}
    </hs:insertRequest>
    <hs:deleteRequest select="..." minOccurs="..." maxOccurs="...">
      <hs:options>0...1</hs:options>
    </hs:deleteRequest>
    <hs:replaceRequest select="..." useClientIds="..." minOccurs="..."
      maxOccurs="...">
      <hs:options>0...1</hs:options>
      <hs:attributes {any}="...">0...unbounded</hs:attributes>
      {any}
    </hs:replaceRequest>
  </hs:updateBlock>
</hs:updateRequest>
```

The key element of the <updateRequest> is the <updateBlock>. The <updateBlock> is the container for a batch of operations. You can have multiple update blocks in one updateRequest. It has two attributes, which are as follows:

- ❑ select – this attribute sets the scope of the operations contained within this update. It would be useful if you wanted to make multiple changes to a contact, since you could set the select of the <updateBlock> to that contact, and have the elements for the insert, delete, and replace point to the subelements to change.

- ❑ onError – this tells HailStorm what to do when an error occurs.

There are three potential values that you can assign to onError, which will greatly affect what it will do when an error occurs. The options are as follows:

- ❑ rollbackBlockAndFail – the service is brought back to the state it was in previous to running this block, and the updateRequest ends in failure

- ❑ rollbackBlockAndContinue – this block is rolled back, but the following blocks are still executed

- ❑ Ignore – execution of the current block is ended, there is no rollback, and execution carries on to the next blocks

Proper usage of onError and upDateBlock is important. Just as with commit and rollback operations in database applications, you have to understand your application and your data thoroughly to use upDateBlock and onError in HailStorm. It is possible for any single operation to fail, with an adverse effect on subsequent operations that were expecting the changes requested by the first operation to occur. These commands should also be trapped to ensure they are run again if they do not succeed and if that is necessary. Choose your updateBlocks carefully, and trap all errors returned.

> When using update, you should make logical clean breaks between your update blocks, for example, if you are updating myContacts after going to a conference, you may want to allocate an **updateBlock** for each contact.

Response Definition

The response to an update, like the request, uses its own element to encapsulate the responses from the various subelements. Here is a template of an updateResponse:

```
<hs:updateResponse newChangeNumber="..."
    xmlns:hs="http://schemas.microsoft.com/hs/2001/10/core" >
  <hs:updateBlockStatus selectedNodeCount="..." status="...">
    <hs:insertResponse selectedNodeCount="..." status="...">
      <hs:newBlueId id="..."/>
    </hs:insertResponse>
    <hs:deleteResponse selectedNodeCount="..." status="..."/>
    <hs:replaceResponse selectedNodeCount="..." status="...">
      <hs:newBlueId id="..."/>
    </hs:replaceResponse>
  </hs:updateBlockStatus>
</hs:updateResponse>
```

First off, there is one important thing to note that isn't obvious when looking in the XMI manual:

> By their own definition, the **insertResponse, deleteResponse,** and **replaceResponse** return the new **changeNumber.** However, when encapsulated in an **updateBlockStatus** they will not return the **newChangeNumber.** Although multiple operations are executed with an update, there is only one **newChangeNumber,** which is an attribute of **updateResponse.**

For each <updateBlock> in the <updateRequest>, there is an updateBlockStatus in the <updateResponse>. The updateBlockStatus has the following attributes:

❑ selectedNodeCount – the number of nodes matched by the select statement in the <updateBlock>

❑ status – the status of the execution of that block as a whole

The possible values for status are as follows:

Value	Description
success	The entire block completed successfully
failure	The block failed to complete
rollback	The block had a failure and the document was rolled back to its state prior to execution of this block
notAttempted	This block was not attempted, probably because rollbackBlockAndFail was used in a previous block

Within each <updateBlockStatus> element there is a response for each of the insert, delete, and replace requests sent. When running the commands before, you would have only received a status of success or failure. However, now that they are encapsulated within an <updateBlock>, it is possible that a previous request had an error and the block was rolled back, leaving some of the requests not attempted. Probably the best way to understand update fully, is to see some examples and play around with it yourself.

Example

The following example will show how useful the onError option can be. This sample is an update of multiple contacts; a user might do this when connecting their mobile phone to the computer in order to synchronize their contacts.

Here is the request:

```
<hs:updateRequest xmlns:hs="http://schemas.microsoft.com/hs/2001/10/core"
  xmlns="http://schemas.microsoft.com/hs/2001/10/myContacts"
xmlns:mp="http://schemas.microsoft.com/hs/2001/10/myProfile">
   <hs:updateBlock
        select="/myContacts/contact[name/mp:surName='Plank']"
        onError="rollbackBlockAndContinue">
     <hs:deleteRequest select="name/mp:givenName" minOccurs="1"/>
     <hs:insertRequest select=".">
     <emailAddress>
```

109

```
      <mp:email>
         ben@hotmail.com
      </mp:email>
    </emailAddress>
  </hs:insertRequest>
</hs:updateBlock>
<hs:updateBlock select="/myContacts" onError="rollbackBlockAndContinue">
<hs:insertRequest select=".">
<contact>
    <name>
       <mp:givenName xml:lang="en">Ben</mp:givenName>
       <mp:surName xml:lang="en">Eisenberg</mp:surName>
    </name>
    </contact>
  </hs:insertRequest>
  </hs:updateBlock>
</hs:updateRequest>
```

Here is the service document before execution of the request:

```
<m:myContacts>
  <m:contact id="…">
    <m:name id="…">
       <mp:givenName xml:lang="en">Ben</mp:givenName>
       <mp:surName xml:lang="en">Fuller</mp:surName>
    </m:name>
  </m:contact>
</m:myContacts>
```

Here is the service document after execution of the request:

```
<m:myContacts>
  <m:contact id="…">
    <m:name id="…">
       <mp:givenName xml:lang="en">Ben</mp:givenName>
       <mp:surName xml:lang="en">Fuller</mp:surName>
    </m:name>
    <m:name id="…">
       <mp:givenName xml:lang="en">Rob</mp:givenName>
       <mp:surName xml:lang="en">Eisenberg</mp:surName>
    </m:name>
    </m:contact>
</m:myContacts>
```

Here is the <updateResponse>:

```
<hs:updateResponse newChangeNumber="7">
  <hs:updateBlockStatus selectedNodeCount="1" status="rollback">
    <hs:deleteResponse selectedNodeCount="0" status="failure"/>
       <hs:insertResponse selectedNodeCount="" status="notAttempted"/>
  </hs:updateBlockStatus>
  <hs:updateBlockStatus>
    <hs:insertResponse selectedNodeCount="1" status="success">
       <hs:newBlueId id="234324234234"/>
```

```
          <hs:newBlueId id="234324234234"/>
        </hs:insertResponse>
      </hs:updateBlockStatus>
    </hs:updateResponse>
```

There are a few important things to notice in this example. The first big thing is the effect of a rollback. Since there was an error with the `deleteRequest` in the first `<updateBlock>`, the whole block was rolled back, so even though the `insertRequest` could have run fine, it still didn't run. The next big thing to notice is that since we used roll back and continue, the next `<updateBlock>` was still executed, and it has changed the document by inserting the new contact. The update had one successful operation and as a result, we still have a new `changeNumber` and in this case a new `BlueId` as well.

Query

Although the query method is described as being one method, it has two distinct pieces of functionality. The first one, `xpQuery`, is a basic query that displays the selected data from a service. The second, `changeQuery`, is a much more robust query that lists how the selected node(s) have been changed. This includes not only the nodes that have been inserted and replaced, but also the nodes that have been deleted. The `xpQuery` is used for creating queries when searching for certain data, whereas the `changeQuery` is mostly used to help maintain caching systems.

Request Definition

The basic setup for a query is as follows:

```
<hs:queryRequest xmlns:hs="http://schemas.microsoft.com/hs/2001/10/core">
  <hs:xpQuery select="..." minOccurs="..." maxOccurs="...">
    <hs:options>
      <hs:sort direction="..." key="..."/>
        <hs:range first="..." count="...">
          <hs:shape base="...">
            <hs:include select="...">...</hs:include>
            <hs:exclude select="...">...</hs:exclude>
          </hs:shape>
          {any}
    </hs:options>
  </hs:xpQuery>
  <hs:changeQuery select="..." baseChangeNumber="...">
    <hs:options>
      <hs:sort direction="..." key="..."/>
      <hs:range first="..." count="..."/>
      <hs:shape base="...">
        <hs:include select="...">...</hs:include>
        <hs:exclude select="...">...</hs:exclude>
      </hs:shape>
      {any}
    </hs:options>
  </hs:changeQuery>
</hs:queryRequest>
```

The query method bears some similarities to the update method. Since each query is contained within its own subelement of the <queryRequest>, you can have multiple queries. However, it does not have any rollback functionality, because the queries aren't changing the document. As a result, if there is an error in one xpQuery or changeQuery, the others will still be executed. The attributes that make up the core functionality for xpQuery are as follows:

❑ select – this attribute selects the nodes you would like to receive details on

❑ minOccurs – this attribute sets the lower boundary for what the select is expected to return

❑ maxOccurs – this attribute sets the upper boundary for what the select is expected to return

Inside the <xpQuery> element, you can use the <options> element along with any of its subelements to fine-tune your results. Since the <options> element was not fully defined at the time of writing this book, we will only give an overview of how they are used; for a more complete explanation, please review the latest version of the XMI manual.

❑ sort – used to apply sorts to the returned results based on some element or attribute

❑ range – forces a certain range of results to be returned; for example, results 5 through 10

❑ shape – using this with any combination of the <include> and <exclude> subelements, you can control what data is returned. For example, making a search for contacts return the contacts with only their name and e-mail address

None of the concepts in an xpQuery should be new. The main difference is now you are selecting what you would like to view, not what you want to change.

> The **minOccurs** and **maxOccurs** attributes could be useful here when doing queries over a low bandwidth connection where you may want to limit the amount of data being returned. However, it is important to remember that a **maxOccurs** of 5 will not force only the first 5 elements to be returned; it will throw an error if more than 5 are returned.

Here are the attributes for a changeQuery:

❑ select –this attribute selects the nodes you would like to receive

❑ baseChangeNumber – this attribute sets the change number that is used to locate a particular version of the data

> At the time of writing this book, HailStorm did not support changeQuery; however, it should be working with the first full release.

Like an xpQuery, the select statement will select the nodes you want information on; however, you will probably only be making simple selects because you are trying to update a cache, not find a specific piece of information. The way it computes the changes is by comparing the changeNumber you pass it to the changeNumber of the element you selected, as well as its subelements. It will then return a list of changes that have been made. If the baseChangeNumber is so out of date that HailStorm no longer has a log of changes from that long ago, the query will return a value telling the client to refresh their cache (using xpQuery).

Response Definition

To get an idea of what will be returned from an xpQuery or a changeQuery, here is a template for a <queryResponse>:

```
<hs:queryResponse xmlns:hs="http://schemas.microsoft.com/hs/2001/10/core">
  <hs:xpQueryResponse status="...">...{any}</hs:xpQueryResponse>
  <hs:changeQueryResponse baseChangeNumber="..." status="...">
   <hs:changedBlue>...{any}</hs:changedBlue>
   <hs:deletedBlue id="..."/>
  </hs:changeQueryResponse>
</hs:queryResponse>
```

The only attribute for an <xpQueryResponse> is status, which can have a value of success of failure. Since an error on a previous query will not stop execution of a later one, there is no potential for a status of "not attempted". The {any} element in the <xpQueryResponse> is simply a placeholder for the content of the response, which is whatever you specified with your select statement. The changeQueryResponse request has the following two attributes:

❑ baseChangeNumber – this attribute selects the nodes you would like to receive

❑ status – the status of the changeQuery; can be success, failure, or refresh

The baseChangeNumber attribute of the change <QueryResponse> is the value of the current changeNumber of the element(s) specified in the select statement of the query. It is important for caches to update their changeNumber with the new one. If the current changeNumber is much higher than the one specified in the query, the status will have a value of refresh. <changeQuery> has two subelements, which are as follows:

❑ <changedBlue> – this element shows the contents of any blue elements that have been changed or replaced.

❑ <deletedBlue> – this element returns the ID of a blue element that was deleted. However, it does not contain the contents of the item that has been deleted.

> One of the awkward aspects of the **<changeQuery>** is that inserted and changed items are both returned within the **<changedBlue>** element. As a result, you should query your cache to see if the **<changedBlue>** element you are moving into the cache should simply be inserted, or if it is replacing something else.

Example 1

For the first example, let's take a simple xpQuery and a simple changeQuery. Keep in mind that at the time of writing this book, changeQuery was not functioning, so this example is simulating what the results should be:

```
<hs:queryRequest xmlns:hs="http://schemas.microsoft.com/hs/2001/10/core"
    xmlns="http://schemas.microsoft.com/hs/2001/10/myContacts"
    xmlns:mp="http://schemas.microsoft.com/hs/2001/10/myProfile">
  <hs:xpQuery select="/myContacts/contact[name/mp:givenName='Joe']"/>
```

```
   <hs:changeQuery
     select="/myContacts/m:contact[name/mp:surName='Eisenberg']"
     baseChangeNumber="2"/>
 </hs:queryRequest>
```

The xpQuery will find the contact information of for Joe. The second query should find out if any changes have been made to the contact information for people in the Eisenberg family.

Here's the service document that we are querying:

```
<m:myContacts changeNumber="5">
  <m:contact changeNumber="2">
    <m:name changeNumber="2">
      <mp:givenName>Joe</mp:givenName>
      <mp:surName>Hagerty</mp:surName>
    </m:name>
    <m:emailAddress changeNumber="2">
      <mp:email>joe@hotmail.com</mp:email>
    </m:emailAddress>
  </m:contact>
  <m:contact changeNumber="3">
    <m:name changeNumber="1">
      <mp:givenName xml:lang="en">Jan</mp:givenName>
      <mp:surName xml:lang="en">Eisenberg</mp:surName>
    </m:name>
    <m:address changeNumber="3">
      <hs:primaryCity xml:lang="en">San Diego</hs:primaryCity>
      </m:address>
    </m:contact>
  <m:contact changeNumber="5">
    <m:name changeNumber="1">
      <mp:givenName xml:lang="en">Mark</mp:givenName>
      <mp:surName xml:lang="en">Eisenberg</mp:surName>
    </m:name>
    <m:emailAddress changeNumber="3">
      <mp:email>joe@hotmail.com</mp:email>
    </m:emailAddress>
  </m:contact>
</m:myContacts>
```

Here is the body of the response returned:

```
<hs:queryResponse xmlns:hs="http://schemas.microsoft.com/hs/2001/10/core"
    xmlns:m="http://schemas.microsoft.com/hs/2001/10/myContacts"
    xmlns:mp="http://schemas.microsoft.com/hs/2001/10/myProfile">
  <hs:xpQueryResponse status="success">
    <m:contact changeNumber="2">
      <m:name changeNumber="2">
        <mp:givenName xml:lang="en">Joe</mp:givenName>
        <mp:surName xml:lang="en">Hagerty</mp:surName>
      </m:name>
      <m:emailAddress changeNumber="2">
        <mp:email>joe@hotmail.com</mp:email>
```

```
            </m:emailAddress>
         </m:contact>
      </hs:xpQueryResponse>
      <hs:changeQueryResponse baseChangeNumber="5" status="success">
         <hs:changedBlue>
            <m:address>
               <hs:primaryCity>San Diego</hs:primayCity>
            </m:address>
         </hs:changedBlue>
         <hs:deletedBlue Id="23423423423423"/>
         <hs:changedBlue>
            <m:emailAddress>
               <mp:email>joe@hotmail.com</mp:email>
            </m:emailAddress>
         </hs:changedBlue>
      </hs:changeQueryRequest>
   </hs:queryResponse>
```

This was a relatively simple example. As expected, the xpQuery returned the contact entry for Joe. In addition, the <changeQueryResponse> returned everything one would expect. However, besides just having the changed blue elements that you could see has a recent change number in the service document, it also returned a deletedBlue that was no longer in the service document.

Example 2

This next example will show some of the more complex functionality of the query method. Here is the request for this example:

```
<hs:queryRequest xmlns:hs="http://schemas.microsoft.com/hs/2001/10/core"
    xmlns="http://schemas.microsoft.com/hs/2001/10/myProfile">
  <hs:changeQuery select="/myProfile" baseChangeNumber="1"/>
  <hs:xpQuery select="myProfile/memberInformation" minOccurs="1"/>
  <hs:xpQuery select="/myProfile/myName"/>
</hs:queryRequest>
```

Here is the service document being used for this example:

```
<m:myProfile changeNumber="514">
  <m:name changeNumber="514">
    <m:givenName xml:lang="en">rob</m:givenName>
  </m:name>
</m:myProfile>
```

Here is the response:

```
<hs:queryReponse xmlns:hs="http://schemas.microsoft.com/hs/2001/10/core">
  <hs:changeQueryResponse baseChangeNumber="514" status="refresh"/>
  <hs:xpQueryResponse status="failure"/>
  <hs:xpQueryResponse status="success">
    <m:name changeNumber="514">
      <m:givenName xml:lang="en">rob</m:givenName>
    </m:name>
  </hs:xpQueryResponse>
</hs:queryResponse>
```

There are a few important things to notice in this response. The first is that the changeQuery was out of date, so it has a status of refresh. The first queryResponse returned a status of failure due to a simply minOccurs error. Finally, it is important to notice that although there was a refresh and an error prior to the last xpQuery, it was still executed and returned the expected results.

Subscription

The <subscription> element permits applications to subscribe to receive a notification when changes occur. This notification can be sent to any application or web service capable of receiving SOAP, or the myAlerts service.

Subscription Definition

Subscription elements are triggers within the schemas that send messages to the <to> element described below when data covered by the subscription changes.

```
<subscription changeNumber="..." id = "..." creator="..."
    xmlns:hs="http://schemas.microsoft.com/hs/2001/10/core">
  trigger select="..." mode="..." baseChangeNumber="..."</trigger>
  <expiresAt> </expiresAt>
  <context uri="..."> {any}</context>
  <to/>
</subscription>
```

The subscription attributes are described below:

Attribute	Description
changeNumber	This tells HailStorm whether it should create new IDs for all new blue items, or use the ones specified by the client
id	ID of the blue element
Creator	Identifies the creator of the element

The subelements and their attributes for a subscription are as follows:

Subelement	MinOccurs	MaxOccurs	Description
<trigger>	1	1	This element is used to specify what nodes to watch for changes and what to do when they do change.
trigger/@select	1	1	This is where the XPath selection is specified to select the blue nodes required.

Subelement	MinOccurs	MaxOccurs	Description
trigger/@mode	0	1	The valid modes are includeData, which will send the data that changed with the message, and excludeData, which will only send the message.
trigger/@basechangeNumber	0	1	This synchronizes the trigger with the changeNumber attribute.
<expiresAt>	0	1	This provides a way of subscribing to an element for a period. After the time expires, the subscription node is removed. The default is not to expire.
<context>	0	1	This element is the only element used to correlate a subcriptionResponse to the subscription entry.
context/@uri	0	1	The URI that the subscriber chooses to identify this subscription
context/{any}	0	1	Place holder for user-defined elements.
<to>	1	1	The valid options are myAlerts, which will route it through the creator's notification services, or protocol://, which will route it through the creator's domain ID. The default is the myAlerts service.

Because the subscription statement is an element within the schema, it is created and/or edited with an insert, replace, or delete operation, and not sent as a standard operation.

Response Definition

Once in the schema, the trigger will fire when the requisite data changes. Here is a sample subscription response message:

```
<hs:subscriptionResponse
    xmlns:hs="http://schemas.microsoft.com/hs/2001/10/core" >
    <hs:triggerData>
```

117

```
        <hs:changedBlue> {any}</hs:changedBlue>
        <hs:deletedBlue id="..."> </hs:deletedBlue>
    </hs:triggerData>
    <hs:context uri="..."> {any}</context>
</hs:subscriptionResponse>
```

The `<subscriptionResponse>` element has the following attributes:

Attribute	Description
triggerData	This element contains the changed and deleted blue nodes
triggerData/changedBlue	This item is found in the body of an HSDL response message, it contains the server-generated ID, the related local tag, and the change number for inserts and replaces
triggerData/changedBlue/{any}	Place holder for any user-defined elements
triggerData/deletedBlue	This item is found in the body of an HSDL response message and contains the server-generated ID, the related local tag, and the change number for deletes
triggerData/deletedBlue/@id	Specifies the ID of the deleted item
context	This references the subscription that triggered this message
context/@uri	The URI specified by the creator of this service to use as context
context/{any}	Place holder for any user defined elements

A successful `<subscriptionResponse>` will also contain the `<newBlueId>` element; it has one attribute, `id`, which is the ID of the newly created blue element.

Example

To help tie things together, here is a sample of the subscription service. It will be a basic example showing a subscription, its response, and the change in the document that triggered it.

> ! At the time of writing this book, the subscription service was not working. These samples are based on the current understanding of how it should work.

Here are the details of the subscription:

```
<subscription changeNumber="3" id = "17" creator=""
    xmlns:hs="http://schemas.microsoft.com/hs/2001/10/core"
    xmlns="http://schemas.microsoft.com/hs/2001/10/myContacts">
  <trigger
```

```
      select="/myContacts"
      mode="includeData"
      baseChangeNumber="1"
  </trigger>
  <context uri="uuid:32328738787"></context>
  <to>hs:myAlerts</to>
</subscription>
```

Here are snapshots of the document before and after the change occurred:

Before	After
```<m:myContacts id="4823832842" changeNumber="1"> <m:contact id="423ewr2r2r"> ... </m:contact> <m:subscription ...> ... </m:subscription></m:myContacts>```	```<m:myContactsid="4823832842" changeNumber="2"> <m:contactid="423ewr2r2r"> ... </m:contact> <m:contact id="1253"> ... </m:contact> <m:subscription ...> ... </m:subscription></m:myContacts>```

Finally, here is the `<subscriptionResponse>` that should be generated by the above operation:

```
<hs:subscriptionResponse
    xmlns:hs="http://schemas.microsoft.com/hs/2001/10/core" >
  <m:triggerData>
    <m:changedBlue>
      <m:contact id="1253">
        ...
      </m:contact>
    </m:changeBlue>
  </m:triggerData>
  <m:context uri="uuid:32328738787"/>
</hs:subscriptionResponse>
```

This was a simple example showing how the subscription will generate notifications of change.

Items Not Yet Described and/or Functioning Across Services

These items are described in more detail below, and are listed here to provide a quick reference. They were either not working or not documented at the time of writing the book. Although we were not able to work with these, the examples you will find that use these items are based on our interpretation of the XMI manual.

Item	Description
changeNumber	It is unclear to what degree this is functioning. Data returned by xpQueries always returns with a changeNumber of 1; however, after manipulation operations are run, the changeNumbers being returned have a changeNumber that is being incremented after each operation.
useClientIDs	This option does not currently work.
<options>	This element will provide additional functionality to the operations. It is not working or documented at the time of writing this book, so it will not be covered.
<options/any>	The purpose of this element is not clear because it is not documented.
Sorting	This is meant to be used with the query statement and would return the results in sorted order.
acl document type	This is the document view to manipulate the entities that can access the information the service holds.
Custom operations	There are no custom operations documented for any of the services.

Services Section

This section will cover the heart of HailStorm, the services. These services are based around XML schemas that are exposed as XML documents that are bound to an identity. These services are user-centric because they revolve around authentication and identity; however, user-centric does not mean they are limited to an individual. These services can be bound to an individual, a group, or an organization. These XML documents can be retrieved and processed by any authorized endpoint that is capable of sending and receiving SOAP messages, capable of manipulating XML documents, and capable of authentication through Passport.

This section will cover the HailStorm services in detail. At the end of this section, you will have seen:

❑   What functionality the services expose

❑   The methods and security roles of each service

❑   What data elements are contained in each schema

❑ What these data elements mean in general

❑ How the services interoperate

❑ How the notification, preferences, and the building block services interoperate with the other services and HailStorm in general

❑ The interrelations between the services

❑ The schema fragments and an analysis of them

The last bullet-point should not be underestimated. Understanding the schema fragments is critical if you want to understand the HailStorm services. The schemas contain all the data layouts and rules. The section on HSDL explains how to query, add, and delete data from the services, but it is the schemas that provide a conceptual understanding of what the services do. Investigating the schemas will provide some insight into Passport integration: how the services share data among themselves, how the notification service is integrated, and how a user profile will be built. This section will primarily focus on the services available at the time of writing, but will discuss some of the other services as they seem to be integrated into the schemas of the current services.

Common Components of Services

Each service exposes three views:

❑ content – this is the main, service-specific document. The schema for this document is the schema that is accessed when normally working with the service. Every service contains a content view and the content view contains the data for that service. For example, the content view of the myContacts service contains the name and address functionality normally associated with a contact. The content view of the myWallet service contains the payment and account information associated with the myWallet service.

❑ roleList – this document contains roleList information, information that governs access to the data, and methods exported by the service. This is the security view of the service. Each service contains this view and this view can be accessed and manipulated via standard HSDL commands. This is an amazing part of HailStorm. The component permits users the ultimate flexibility of doling out access to their data as promised in HailStorm. It is described in more detail below. It is a schema-based operation and almost a service itself.

❑ system – this is manipulated using the .NET My Services standard data manipulation mechanisms. The shape of this document is governed by the .NET My Services core schema's roleListType XML data type. This is a system-only view of the document, and is not covered in this chapter. Internal operations including changing cache size are processed in this view. These changes are performed by the HailStorm system itself and not by users or developers.

How Security is Handled in Services

Microsoft has consistently promised that it will provide a security system for HailStorm that will permit users to control their own data. It has insisted that users will be able to provide the precise web sites, web services, applications, and other users with access to the specific data they want to provide them access to and that users will even be able to place time limits on this access. This begs the question, how will Microsoft do it? The HailStorm roleListEditor, the tool that permits users to grant access is still not available at the time this book is being written. However, it does seem that a lot of the backend logic is here.

We will now look at setting up the standard <roleTemplate> elements and then mapping them to users when we cover <roleList> elements. This is the way security is set up in HailStorm.

Each service has a <roleMap>, which contains a set of <roleTemplate> elements. Each <roleTemplate> contains a name and a list of methods. The list of methods can contain scope information also. For example, two <roleTemplate> elements that both have access to the query operation may not be able to query the same data. One may be able to query all data and the other may only be able to see public data or just data for contacts that like to play baseball. Most HailStorm services contain three to five <roleTemplate> elements, which are virtually identical across the HailStorm services. Services will have their own domain specific <roleTemplate> elements as well. The standard <roleTemplate> elements are:

❑   rt0 – The purpose of this <roleTemplate> is to provide full access to all information.

❑   rt1 – The purpose of this <roleTemplate> is to provide full ability to read information with minimal ability to write. The caller can add information to the service, and can only delete information that it inserted or replaced.

❑   rt2 – read-only: query/subscribe, all information.

❑   rt3 – read-only: query/subscribe, public information only. HailStorm elements can be set to public or private by using the <catDef> element described below.

❑   rt99 – no access.

Currently, all the available services support all these roles.

The <roleList> is where we map <roleTemplate> privileges to users that we want to share our information with. You could grant rt0 rights to your secretary who needs full rights to your data, and grant rt3 rights to a colleague who needs to see some, but not all, of your contacts. For practical purposes the roleTemplates will be a good starting point, but we will create groups of users and assign them access based on <roleList> elements, which will be customized roleTemplates. In general the <roleList> elements will contain real access privileges, where the roleTemplates will contain very broad access restrictions. If we were providing access to salespeople across the country, we might only let them see accounts in their state.

The <roleListEditor> is the only tool authorized to manipulate a <roleList>. We can only imagine the level of thought going into creating a tool that permits individual, group, and organization-based identities to efficiently and securely provide access to their data. Below, we'll look at the schema fragments for the <roleMap> and <roleList> elements, which will give you some insight into how this will work. Because the tool is not available at the time this book is being written, it is not possible to provide details on how it will work from an interface standpoint.

General Schema Information

We've already seen that at the core of HailStorm are the schemas that describe the various services. One question you might have is why Microsoft took this approach. In this section, we'll spell out some of the advantages that schemas offer for this sort of application.

Striving for Scalability and Internationalism

As many of us know from experience, most of the work involved in creating large systems is spent on the fine details of the system. It takes time to ensure the system will be secure, reliable, scalable, and fast. With HailStorm, Microsoft is attempting to create a super application that supports all languages, stores all different date formats, stores all different addresses worldwide, or in summary can hold almost any type of data, for an unlimited number of people. A lot of the work that has gone into HailStorm is based on this.

Something worth noting is that most name and address fields contain an `xml:lang` attribute that permits the data contained within the element to be stored in any language. They also have a `dir` attribute to specify which way text should be read (right to left or left to right) that is necessary for a few countries, and extensibility elements contained throughout the schemas.

HailStorm is based on XML and the broad extensibility features in XML makes it more practical for Microsoft to attempt something like HailStorm. However, technology is only a tool; its usage determines its effectiveness. Microsoft is taking a lot of time designing the schemas for HailStorm, because if this is not done well, there is no way that HailStorm will scale or even succeed.

Striving for Synchronized Fresh Data

Currently, address and contact information is stored as separate islands of information. Every time this information changes, it sets off a chain reaction of changes. Friends, family, business associates, customers, and vendors all have to receive notification of the change and then update all of their systems and documents. Everybody using HailStorm can store their address information in the myProfile service. When the address information in the myProfile service changes, it will automatically propagate the changes to the myContacts service for all people who have your contact information, if they provide this access. This is specific to a couple of services, but it's worth mentioning it here because it is another example of the level of thought that is going into HailStorm. Just imagine in the future, if your contact information changes and all relevant documents, devices, services, and applications are all automatically updated with the new information.

Subscription Element

The `<subscription>` element is an element that stores triggers. When a trigger is inserted, it causes a subscription to be registered. When the data changes and the trigger is activated, a `subscriptionResponse` message is generated and sent to the specified destination address, possibly via the myAlerts service. The `<subscription>` element is also one of the six standard operations, and is explained in detail in the HSDL section below. This operation is different from the other operations in that the request message creates the element, and the response message is not generated until the trigger is activated.

Schemas

You may have noticed that we referred to **schema fragments** and not schemas. Schema fragments are template documents that provide a conceptual understanding of the schemas. Data type, element naming, and other information necessary for the schemas to function is removed to reduce clutter and enhance readability. There are comments below each schema that provide narrative on the elements and attributes contained within the schema. In most cases, this narrative combined with the schema fragment should provide a complete description of the schemas. When you need more detail, you should consult the XMI manual.

A couple of points that may not be obvious as you look through the schema fragments are:

❏ The xml:lang attribute that is used to track the language the element is stored in

❏ There are 0..0, 0..1, 0..unbounded, 1..1, and 1..unbounded notations throughout the schema fragment. These are the min/max attributes.

❏ As in Chapter 4 "**blue**" are shown in **bold** and "<u>red</u>" elements are <u>underlined</u>

Here is a brief description of each of the available services:

❏ myContacts – this is an electronic address book available to services, applications, and programs across the Internet. It is one of the key foundation building-block services of HailStorm.

❏ myFavorites – conatins a list of favorite web sites that can be categorized and subscribed to.

❏ myProfile – contains personal profile information. Similar to the information contained in myContacts for other people.

❏ myServices – holds the locations of the other web services looking after information in your digital safe-deposit box.

❏ myWallet – provides an electronic payment mechanism for Passport and HailStorm users. It can store credit/debit cards, bank accounts, and other accounts to process payment.

❏ myCalendar – an electronic calendar that can store calendar information and is a key component of the HailStorm notification appointment.

❏ myCategories – a very flexible service that provides all HailStorm services with extensive classification and categorization abilities

❏ myLists – can be used to create shopping lists, to-do lists, or any other type of lists. These lists can be categorized and accessed throughout HailStorm.

Now let's move on and examine each of these services in detail.

myContacts Service

The myContacts service is an electronic address book. It contains standard contact information and features including name, address, the ability to categorize contacts, phone number, e-mail address, and special dates, for example birthdays that are part of most contact-management systems. The myContacts service functionality and data are available to programs, services, devices, and applications across the Internet.

The combination of the data being accessible in the Internet cloud and the synchronization features built into HailStorm may provide for one set of live contact information being available to all programs, devices, and services that rely on the information. In the future, eCommerce and secretaries typing a word processing document will always have the most current address if HailStorm is successful.

Currently, most sites and associates have static copies of your contact information. When this information changes, if you do not notify them, their information is out of date. With HailStorm's addressing capabilities, the need to give updates to third parties is removed. Each contact may contain a **PUID (Pairwise Unique ID)**. The PUID is the key identifier in Passport and provides a way of synchronizing the myContacts service with the myProfile services. It is also the mechanism used to tie together all data belonging to an individual, group, or organization across all HailStorm service. One of the big challenges HailStorm faces is to successfully integrate and manipulate the data and functionality between all of these services.

As mentioned above, in general Microsoft is attempting to provide true international address support and is focusing a great deal of effort on that aspect of this service. Anyone who has ever tried to make a system support European and US addresses is aware of the challenges involved. Microsoft is attempting to support addresses all over the world, and Microsoft's challenge in the address element is ensuring that it is flexible enough to support this international requirement.

The myContacts service is needed by almost everyone and will be part of most HailStorm implementations. In order for HailStorm to succeed, it needs to be scalable and flexible enough to accomplish this.

Schema Fragments and Description

This is the root element of this service, and has the same name as the service. It encapsulates the content document for the service, and it contains a global cache scope for the service. It also contains a set of namespaces referring to the myContact, myProfile, myCalendar, and core namespaces. These are used to prefix the elements throughout the schema.

❑ `/myContacts/@changeNumber` contains a `changeNumber` attribute for tracking changes and making caching easier.

❑ `/myContacts/@instanceId` – this attribute is a unique identifier typically assigned to the root element of a service. It is a read-only element and assigned by the HailStorm system when a user is provisioned for a particular service.

Here is the schema fragment for the root element of the myContacts service:

```
<m:myContacts changeNumber="..." instanceId="..."
    xmlns:m="http://schemas.microsoft.com/hs/2001/10/myContacts"
    xmlns:mp="http://schemas.microsoft.com/hs/2001/10/myProfile"
    xmlns:mc="http://schemas.microsoft.com/hs/2001/10/myCalendar"
    xmlns:hs="http://schemas.microsoft.com/hs/2001/10/core">1..1
```

Several non-standard operations (`updateContactData`, `serviceOnLine`, and `serviceOffLine`) have been yet been documented.

It is now time to walk through the myContacts schema fragment. Each top-level-blue element and each major section of data will be explained. In the myContacts service, most of the data is contained under the `contact` element, so each element under the `contact` element will be explained.

myContacts/contact

```
<m:contact synchronize="..." changeNumber="..." id="..."
    creator="...">0..unbounded
    <m:cat ref="...">0..unbounded</m:cat>
```

This first-class-level element stores all data for an individual contact. The address information is stored in the `<address>` element. The `<contact>` element contains a `synchronize` attribute that attempts to keep this contact synchronized with the contact's myProfile service. If the `synchronize` attribute is set to `yes`, HailStorm will attempt to synchronize a contact with the contact's myProfile service. The PUID is used to match the contact with the contact's myProfile information. A value of `no` stipulates that the contact should not attempt to keep this contact in synch.

The contacts can be categorized because it contains a `cat ref` attribute.

myContacts/contact/name

```
<m:name changeNumber="..." id="..." creator="...">0..unbounded
   <mp:cat ref="...">0..unbounded</mp:cat>
   <mp:title xml:lang="..." dir="...">0..1</mp:title>
   <mp:givenName xml:lang="..." dir="...">0..1</mp:givenName>
   <mp:middleName xml:lang="..." dir="...">0..1</mp:middleName>
   <mp:surname xml:lang="..." dir="...">0..1</mp:surname>
   <mp:suffix xml:lang="..." dir="...">0..1</mp:suffix>
   <mp:fileAsName xml:lang="..." dir="...">0..1</mp:fileAsName>
   {any}
</m:name>
```

The <name> element is used to store an unlimited number of categorized names for each contact. Contacts may have 0 names, as in the case of contacts that are for customer service departments, or may contain multiple names when, for example, storing the names of the contacts children. It is surprising that this section does not contain a PUID to reference to other contact records. This would be a good way to reference additional contacts when the additional names being entered have their own contact records; this is common when storing contacts related companies. All of the elements in the name element are prefaced with mp:. This is because their attributes were defined in the myProfile service. This permits one set of definitions for common element like names that are used in many services and schemas.

> The optional **dir** attribute is used to determine if the data in the element should be read from right to left or from left to right. The required **xml:lang** attribute is used to specify the language type of the content within an element. The valid options are ISO 639 language codes or an ISO 3166 country codes. This is just a reminder of the amount of effort going into ensuring HailStorm can store all different types of data throughout the address and name elements within the services.

Most of the elements here are self-explanatory. The optional <fileAsName> element normally contains the combination of <title>, <givenName>, <middleName>, <surname>, and <suffix>. This permits a different order or preferred name to be stored for this contact. Another item to point out is that most of the name element is accessible to the HSDL language, with the exception of <middleName> and <suffix>. Neither of these elements seems like a common search element.

The {any} element is the way that HailStorm can be extended; it is a placeholder that supports well-formed XML extensions.

myContacts/contact/puid

```
<m:puid>0..1</m:puid>
```

The PUID contains a unique identifier for this contact. This element will be used to keep track of this contact throughout HailStorm. It is the field that is used to synchronize the contact element with the myProfile service and, in general, it is the key field in HailStorm. HailStorm is an identity-based system and the PUID is the element that stores the identities.

myContacts/contact/specialDates

```
<m:specialDate calendarType="...">0..unbounded
  <mp:cat ref="...">0..1</mp:cat>
  <mp:date>1..1</mp:date>
  {any}
</m:specialDate>
```

The `<specialDates>` element provides a place to store all of the dates related to a contact. This may include birthdays, anniversaries, and review dates. The `calendarType` attribute specifies the calendar type to use. See the XMI manual for a listing of the date types supported.

myContacts/contact/picture

```
<m:picture>0...unbounded
  <mp:cat ref="...">0...1</mp:cat>
  <mp:url>1...1</mp:url>
  {any}
</m:picture>
```

The `<picture>` element is used to store an unlimited number of categorized URLs that point to photographs of the individual.

myContacts/contact/gender

```
<m:gender>0...1</m:gender>
```

This `<gender>` element contains the gender of the individual.

myContacts/contact/notes

```
<m:notes xml:lang="..." dir="...">0..1</m:notes>
```

This `<notes>` element is used to store any additional notes that you want to associate with a contact.

myContacts/contact/address

```
<m:address changeNumber="..." id="..." creator="...">0..unbounded
  <hs:cat ref="...">0..unbounded</hs:cat>
  <hs:officialAddressLine xml:lang="..." dir="...">
      0..1
  </hs:officialAddressLine>
  <hs:internalAddressLine xml:lang="..." dir="...">
    0..1
  </hs:internalAddressLine>
  <hs:primaryCity xml:lang="..." dir="...">0..1</hs:primaryCity>
  <hs:secondaryCity xml:lang="..." dir="...">0..1</hs:secondaryCity>
  <hs:subdivision xml:lang="..." dir="...">0..1</hs:subdivision>
  <hs:postalCode>0..1</hs:postalCode>
  <hs:countryCode>0..1</hs:countryCode>
  <hs:latitude>0..1</hs:latitude>
  <hs:longitude>0..1</hs:longitude>
  <hs:elevation>0..1</hs:elevation>
  <hs:velocity>0..1
    <hs:speed>0..1</hs:speed>
```

```
        <hs:direction>0..1</hs:direction>
    </hs:velocity>
    <hs:confidence>0..1</hs:confidence>
    <hs:precision>0..1</hs:precision>
    {any}
</m:address>
```

The <address> element is used to store an unlimited number of categorized addresses for each contact. This element is a combination of the attempt to ensure that practically every address in the world can be stored within it and the location-based elements that add a little information beyond the normal address. The entire <address> element, with the exception of the cat ref attribute (make sure to categorize your addresses thoroughly if you want to search on them) and the {any} element, are black and, thus, are not searchable, which might be surprising as it is common to search for contacts based on city, zip, or street name. However, the owner is able to retrieve all the data and perform a search locally if they so wish – but to expect that search to be performed by the HailStorm server is asking a lot. Also making these addresses searchable is probably inviting misuse by services that make use of HailStorm on our behalf.

The <address> element contains two sections: the first contains the standard postal address in a format that supports international addresses. The <address> element is not as self-explanatory as the other parts of the schema, so here is a brief description of each element:

❑ officialAddressLine – this element contains the most precise, official line for the address. This element should store the street address or post office box.

❑ internalAddressLine – this element contains internal routing information like department or suite number.

❑ primaryCity – this element contains the city as expected.

❑ secondaryCity – this does not contain the second city, but rather the city district, city wards, postal towns, etc.

❑ subdivision – in the United States, this element will contain the two letter state abbreviation; in other countries it will contain the province, region, territory, or whatever is used in a similar capacity in a given country.

❑ postalCode – this element contains the official postal code. In the United States this would be the zip code

❑ countryCode – this element contains the 2 letter ISO-3166 ID of the country, dependency, or functionally equivalent region for this address.

❑ latitude – this element contains the latitude of this address in decimal degrees.

❑ longitude – this element contains the longitude of this address in decimal degrees.

❑ elevation – this element contains the elevation above sea level.

❑ velocity – this element is only used to track addresses that are not stationary like boats. This element specifies the last known velocity associated with this address. It will have a value of 0 or be empty for stationary addresses.

❑ speed – the last known speed of this address in meters per second.

❑ Direction – the last known direction of this address in units of degrees decimal.

❏ confidence – this element contains the percentage of confidence that the location information is correct within the specified precision.

❏ precision – this element specifies the spherical zone in meters that the location falls within.

❏ any – this element is the extensibility placeholder, as explained above.

myContacts/contact/emailAddress

```
<m:emailAddress changeNumber="..." id="..." creator="...">0..unbounded
  <mp:cat ref="...">0..unbounded</mp:cat>
  <mp:email>1..1</mp:email>
  <mp:name xml:lang="..." dir="...">0..1</mp:name>
  {any}
</m:emailAddress>
```

The <emailAddress> element is used to store an unlimited number of categorized e-mail addresses for each contact. Each <emailAddress> element can contain the e-mail address and a friendly name.

myContacts/contact/webSite

```
<m:webSite changeNumber="..." id="..." creator="...">0..unbounded
  <mp:cat ref="...">0..1</mp:cat>
  <mp:url>1..1</mp:url>
  {any}
</m:webSite>
```

The <webSite> element is used to store an unlimited number of categorized URLs for each contact, such as their company or personal web site. There is also a standalone service that can contain a list of web sites that are not specific to a contact:

myContacts/contact/screenName

```
<m:screenName>0..unbounded
  <mp:cat ref="...">0..1</mp:cat>
  <mp:name xml:lang="..." dir="...">1..1</mp:name>
  {any}
</m:screenName>
```

The <screenName> element is used to store an unlimited number of categorized screen names for each contact. This is important because many predict a big part of HailStorm will be a new form of commerce-based instant messaging.

myContacts/contact/telephoneNumber

```
<m:telephoneNumber changeNumber="..." id="..." creator="...">
  0..unbounded
  <hs:cat ref="...">0..unbounded</hs:cat>
  <hs:countryCode>0..1</hs:countryCode>
  <hs:nationalCode>1..1</hs:nationalCode>
  <hs:number>1..1</hs:number>
  <hs:numberExtension>0..1</hs:numberExtension>
  <hs:pin>0..1</hs:pin>
  {any}
</m:telephoneNumber>
```

The `<telephoneNumber>` element can be used to store an unlimited number of categorized telephone numbers. As with the `address` element, a great deal of work has been put into creating an element that can store all types of international phone numbers.

myContacts/contact/identificationNumber

```
<m:identificationNumber>0..unbounded
  <mp:cat ref="...">0..1</mp:cat>
  <mp:number>1..1</mp:number>
  {any}
</m:identificationNumber>
```

The `<identificationNumber>` is an optional element that is used to store an unlimited number of categorized identification numbers. These include social security numbers, driver license number, and employee numbers.

myContacts/contact/workInformation

```
<m:workInformation changeNumber="..." id="..." creator="...">
    0..unbounded
  <mp:cat ref="...">0..unbounded</mp:cat>
  <mp:profession xml:lang="..." dir="...">0..1</mp:profession>
  <mp:jobTitle xml:lang="..." dir="...">0..1</mp:jobTitle>
  <mp:officeLocation xml:lang="..." dir="...">0..1</mp:officeLocation>
  <mp:coworkerOrDepartment>0..unbounded
    <hs:name xml:lang="..." dir="...">0..1</hs:name>
    <hs:puid>0..1</hs:puid>
    <hs:email>0..1</hs:email>
    <hs:cat ref="...">1..1</hs:cat>
  </mp:coworkerOrDepartment>
  {any}
</m:workInformation>
```

The `<workInformation>` element is used to store an unlimited number of categorized coworkers PUIDS, names, e-mail addresses, job titles, and other information. It is not obvious why coworkers are unique. This is a great start and is very flexible but why aren't they categorized using the `<catDef>` element like any other contact? If the `<catDef>` element is not flexible enough to store your coworkers, how can it be flexible enough to store customer contacts from large companies? It seem like this will be integrated into the `<catDef>` logic or another service will be defined to track them. Remember this is alpha software and it is not set in stone; things change quickly in HailStorm.

myContacts/contact/workInformation

```
<m:userReference>0..unbounded
  <hs:name xml:lang="..." dir="...">0..1</hs:name>
  <hs:puid>0..1</hs:puid>
  <hs:email>0..1</hs:email>
  <hs:cat ref="...">1..1</hs:cat>
</m:userReference>
```

The `<userReference>` element is used to store an unlimited number of categorized contacts or referenced individuals. For each contact, the e-mail address and the PUID are stored. Again, this seems like an additional name related to a contact, and there is some streamlining to be done in this schema definition. Remember, version 1.0 will not be here for another year.

myContacts/contact/securityCertificate

```
<m:securityCertificate>0..unbounded
  <mp:cat ref="...">0..unbounded</mp:cat>
  <mp:certificate>1..1</mp:certificate>
</m:securityCertificate>
```

The `<securityCertificate>` element is used to store an unlimited number of categorized security certificates. This is obviously to provide support for some type of security certificates at the contact level but was not documented at the time of writing.

myContacts/contact/contactGroup

```
<m:contactGroup>0..1
  <m:emailAddress>0..1
    <mp:email>1..1</mp:email>
  </m:emailAddress>
  <m:enableDelivery>1..1</m:enableDelivery>
  <m:maxMessageSize>1..1</m:maxMessageSize>
  <m:restrictSubmitter>1..1</m:restrictSubmitter>
  <m:forwardAutoResponse>1..1</m:forwardAutoResponse>
  <m:subscribeOpen>1..1</m:subscribeOpen>
  <m:unsubscribeOpen>1..1</m:unsubscribeOpen>
  <m:hideDL>1..1</m:hideDL>
  <m:hideMembership>1..1</m:hideMembership>
  <m:submitters>0..1
    <m:emailAddress>0..unbounded
      <mp:email>1..1</mp:email>
    </m:emailAddress>
  </m:submitters>
</m:contactGroup>
{any}
</m:contact>
```

At first glance, it may seem that this supports the setting up of e-mail groups at the contact level but it can only occur 0 to 1 times per contact, so it seems like a robust set of parameters to filter, forward, and ensure size limitations are not exceeded for e-mail.

Notice the end `<contact>` tag. We are finally done with the `<contact>` element.

myContacts/subscription

```
<m:subscription changeNumber="..." id="..." creator="...">0..unbounded
  <hs:trigger select="..." mode="..." baseChangeNumber="...">
      1..1
  </hs:trigger>
  <hs:expiresAt>0..1</hs:expiresAt>
  <hs:context uri="...">1..1 {any}</hs:context>
  <hs:to>1..1</hs:to>
</m:subscription>
{any}
</m:myContacts>
```

The <subscription> element was described above. However, let's repeat the text for this one service, so you can compare it to the schema fragment.

The <subscription> element stores triggers. When a trigger is inserted, it causes a subscription to be registered. When the data changes and the trigger is activated, a subscriptionResponse message is generated and sent to the specified destination address and may be routed through the myAlerts service. The <subscription> element is also one of the six standard operations, and it is explained in detail in the HSDL section above. This operation is different from the other operations in that the request message creates the element, and the response message is not generated until the trigger is activated.

myProfile Service

The myProfile service provides an online profile for an individual. It stores an individual's name, address, work information, membership information, pointers to photographs, ID numbers, and other elements. The myProfile service will provide messages via the myAlerts service to notify other services, including the address service, of changes to address data that are also used by the address service.

The myProfile service functionality and data are available to programs, services, devices, and applications across the Internet. myAlerts, myCalendar, my Application Settings, and myDevices were not available at the time of writing. However, examining the myContacts and myProfile services offers some clues as to how HailStorm will be able to offer combined personal and professional preference storage and targeted notifications. As stated in the myContacts service, the myProfile service is one of the fundamental building block services of HailStorm. The preferences and notifications are going to be central to all applications, services, and individuals that will use HailStorm as the plumbing to deliver notifications and route them to the correct device.

Schema Fragment and Description

This is the root element of this service and has the same name as the service. It encapsulates the content document for the service, and it contains a global cache scope for the service. It also contains a set of namespaces referring to the myContact, myProfile, myCalendar, and core namespaces. These are used to prefix the elements throughout the schema.

- ❑ /myProfile/@changeNumber – This contains a changeNumber attribute for tracking changes and making caching easier.

- ❑ /myProfile/@instanceId – This attribute is a unique identifier typically assigned to the root element of a service. It is a read-only element and assigned by the HailStorm system when a user is provisioned for a particular service.

Here is the schema fragment for the root element of the myProfile service.

```
<m:myProfile changeNumber="..." instanceId="..."
    xmlns:m="http://schemas.microsoft.com/hs/2001/10/myProfile"
    xmlns:mc="http://schemas.microsoft.com/hs/2001/10/myCalendar"
    xmlns:hs="http://schemas.microsoft.com/hs/2001/10/core">1..1
```

This myProfile will have the the following custom operations: updateContactMaps, ServiceOnLine, ServiceOffLine but these were not documented at the time of writing.

The myProfile service contains many first-class-level elements, because most elements reside within the root element instead of within the contact element as they do in the myContacts service. There are also many of the same elements that are in the myContacts service, including address, name, and telephone number. This is because myProfile stores "your" address and myContacts stores addresses for many contacts. The synchronize attribute in the myContacts service provides a mechanism to automatically synchronize between the myProfile and myContacts service. Another minor difference is that some elements that are the same in both services contain different color-schemes. This is because the searching requirements of elements vary from service to service and because most elements are contained beneath the root element in the myProfile service and not under a shell element (the contact element) as in the myContacts service. The high-level of duplication and the varying use of categorization as mentioned in the myContacts service is an indicator that the structures of these services are not finalized at this stage.

With the exception of the languagePreference, memberInformation, and the timeZonePreference elements, the rest of the myProfile schema fragment was already described in the myContacts schema fragment. Most of the name and address elements in the myContacts service were prefixed with mp: because they originate in the myProfile namespace. This is obviously important to have one version of the truth when it comes to the data structures in a large system.

Here is the rest of the schema fragment with descriptions provided for the three new elements:

myProfile/name

```
<m:name changeNumber="..." id="..." creator="...">0..unbounded
  <m:cat ref="...">0..unbounded</m:cat>
  <m:title xml:lang="..." dir="...">0..1</m:title>
  <m:givenName xml:lang="..." dir="...">0..1</m:givenName>
  <m:middleName xml:lang="..." dir="...">0..1</m:middleName>
  <m:surname xml:lang="..." dir="...">0..1</m:surname>
  <m:suffix xml:lang="..." dir="...">0..1</m:suffix>
  <m:fileAsName xml:lang="..." dir="...">0..1</m:fileAsName>
  {any}
</m:name>
```

myProfile/memberInformation

```
<m:memberInformation changeNumber="..." id="..." creator="...">0..unbounded
  <m:memberNamePortion xml:lang="..." dir="...">1..1
  </m:memberNamePortion>
  <m:domainNamePortion>1..1</m:domainNamePortion>
</m:memberInformation>
```

This first-class-level element seems to store a list of people at a domain name like robert@wrox.com but it is not currently obvious exactly what it is for.

myProfile/languagePreference

```
<m:languagePreference level="..." changeNumber="..." id="..."
  creator="...">0..unbounded</m:languagePreference>
```

This element specifies the preferred language code of the identity encoded using ISO 639 language codes or ISO 3166 country codes as defined by RFC1766. Its purpose is to inform devices, services, and applications working with this profile what is the preferred language.

myProfile/timeZonePreference

```
<m:timeZonePreference changeNumber="..." id="..." creator="...">0..unbounded
  <m:cat ref="...">0..unbounded</m:cat>
  <m:timeZone>1..1</m:timeZone>
</m:timeZonePreference>
```

This element supplies the time-zone preference for this entity.

The rest of the schema for myProfile is the same as for myContacts so we won't examine this in any detail.

```
<m:specialDate calendarType="..." changeNumber="..." id="..."
    creator="...">0..unbounded
  <m:cat ref="...">0..1</m:cat>
  <m:date>1..1</m:date>
  {any}
</m:specialDate>
<m:userReference changeNumber="..." id="..." creator="...">0..unbounded
  <hs:name xml:lang="..." dir="...">0..1</hs:name>
  <hs:puid>0..1</hs:puid>
  <hs:email>0..1</hs:email>
  <hs:cat ref="...">1..1</hs:cat>
  {any}
</m:userReference>
<m:picture changeNumber="..." id="..." creator="...">0..unbounded
  <m:cat ref="...">0..1</m:cat>
  <m:url>1..1</m:url>
  {any}
</m:picture>
<m:gender changeNumber="..." id="..." creator="...">0..1</m:gender>
<m:identificationNumber changeNumber="..." id="..." creator="...">
    0..unbounded
  <m:cat ref="...">0..1</m:cat>
  <m:number>1..1</m:number>
  {any}
</m:identificationNumber>
<m:workInformation changeNumber="..." id="..."
    creator="...">0..unbounded
  <m:cat ref="...">0..unbounded</m:cat>
  <m:profession xml:lang="..." dir="...">0..1</m:profession>
  <m:jobTitle xml:lang="..." dir="...">0..1</m:jobTitle>
  <m:officeLocation xml:lang="..." dir="...">0..1</m:officeLocation>
  <m:coworkerOrDepartment>0..unbounded
  <hs:name xml:lang="..." dir="...">0..1</hs:name>
  <hs:puid>0..1</hs:puid>
  <hs:email>0..1</hs:email>
  <hs:cat ref="...">1..1</hs:cat>
  </m:coworkerOrDepartment>
  {any}
</m:workInformation>
<m:address changeNumber="..." id="..." creator="...">0..unbounded
  <hs:cat ref="...">0..unbounded</hs:cat>
  <hs:officialAddressLine xml:lang="..." dir="...">0..1
  </hs:officialAddressLine>
```

```
          <hs:internalAddressLine xml:lang="..." dir="...">0..1
          </hs:internalAddressLine>
          <hs:primaryCity xml:lang="..." dir="...">0..1</hs:primaryCity>
          <hs:secondaryCity xml:lang="..." dir="...">0..1</hs:secondaryCity>
          <hs:subdivision xml:lang="..." dir="...">0..1</hs:subdivision>
          <hs:postalCode>0..1</hs:postalCode>
          <hs:countryCode>0..1</hs:countryCode>
          <hs:latitude>0..1</hs:latitude>
          <hs:longitude>0..1</hs:longitude>
          <hs:elevation>0..1</hs:elevation>
          <hs:velocity>0..1
             <hs:speed>0..1</hs:speed>
             <hs:direction>0..1</hs:direction>
          </hs:velocity>
          <hs:confidence>0..1</hs:confidence>
          <hs:precision>0..1</hs:precision>
          {any}
       </m:address>
       <m:webSite changeNumber="..." id="..." creator="...">0..unbounded
          <m:cat ref="...">0..1</m:cat>
          <m:url>1..1</m:url>
          {any}
       </m:webSite>
       <m:emailAddress changeNumber="..." id="..." creator="...">0..unbounded
          <m:cat ref="...">0..unbounded</m:cat>
          <m:email>1..1</m:email>
          <m:name xml:lang="..." dir="...">0..1</m:name>
          {any}
       </m:emailAddress>
       <m:screenName changeNumber="..." id="..." creator="...">0..unbounded
          <m:cat ref="...">0..1</m:cat>
          <m:name xml:lang="..." dir="...">1..1</m:name>
          {any}
       </m:screenName>
       <m:telephoneNumber changeNumber="..." id="..." creator="...">0..unbounded
          <hs:cat ref="...">0..unbounded</hs:cat>
          <hs:countryCode>0..1</hs:countryCode>
          <hs:nationalCode>1..1</hs:nationalCode>
          <hs:number>1..1</hs:number>
          <hs:numberExtension>0..1</hs:numberExtension>
          <hs:pin>0..1</hs:pin>
          {any}
       </m:telephoneNumber>
       <m:subscription changeNumber="..." id="..." creator="...">0..unbounded
          <hs:trigger select="..." mode="..." baseChangeNumber="...">1..1
          </hs:trigger>
          <hs:expiresAt>0..1</hs:expiresAt>
          <hs:context uri="...">1..1 {any}</hs:context>
          <hs:to>1..1</hs:to>
       </m:subscription>
       <m:securityCertificate changeNumber="..." id="..." creator="...">
             0..unbounded
          <m:cat ref="...">0..unbounded</m:cat>
          <m:certificate>1..1</m:certificate>
```

135

```
   </m:securityCertificate>
   {any}
</m:myProfile>
```

myServices

This internal service supports the HailStorm services being accessed. Each time a user is provisioned, they are registered in the myServices service. It contains the PUID, cluster information, and service name information that are used when requesting a service.

Schema Fragment and Description

This is the root element of this service and has the same name as the service. It encapsulates the content document for the service, and it contains a global cache scope for the service. It also contains a couple of namespaces referring to the myServices and the core namespaces. These are used to prefix the elements throughout the schema.

❑   /myServices/@changeNumber – This contains a changeNumber attribute for tracking changes and making caching easier.

❑   /myServices/@instanceId – This attribute is a unique identifier typically assigned to the root element of a service. It is a read-only element and assigned by the HailStorm system when a user is provisioned for a particular service.

Here is the schema fragment for the root element of the myServices service:

```
<m:myServices changeNumber="..." instanceId="..."
    xmlns:m="http://schemas.microsoft.com/hs/2001/10/myServices"
    xmlns:hs="http://schemas.microsoft.com/hs/2001/10/core">1..1
```

Here is the rest of the schema fragment with descriptions provided at the end because it is so short:

myServices/service

```
    <m:service name="..." changeNumber="..." id="..." creator="...">
        0..unbounded
    <m:cat ref="...">0..unbounded</m:cat>
    <m:key puid="..." instance="..." cluster="...">0..1</m:key>
    <m:refer>0..1</m:refer>
    <m:to>1..1</m:to>
    <m:spn>1..1</m:spn>
    <m:realm>1..1</m:realm>
    {any}
    </m:service>
    {any}
</m:myServices>
```

This first-class-level element is used to store an unlimited number of categorized services. This element contains the name of the service being accessed. It is used in the SOAP message when requesting a service.

myServices/service/key

This element contains the PUID that owns the document, the instance ID of the document, and the cluster or partition key used to locate the machine resources that hold the document.

myFavoriteWebSites Service

The myFavoriteWebSites service provides a list of favorite web sites that can be accessed from any HailStorm-accessible device. There have been other systems that store favorite web sites so that they can be accessed from any computer. However, having them in HailStorm will provide more functionality, as the other services and the notification service can access this list, notify you of changes, and provide access from any HailStorm device.

Schema Fragment and Description

This is the root element of this service and has the same name as the service. It encapsulates the content document for the service, and it contains a global cache scope for the service. It also contains a couple of namespaces referring to the myFavoriteWebSites and the core namespaces. These are used to prefix the elements throughout the schema.

- ❏ `/myLists/@changeNumber` – This contains a `changeNumber` attribute for tracking changes and making caching easier.

- ❏ `/myLists/@instanceId` – This attribute is a unique identifier typically assigned to the root element of a service. It is a read-only element and assigned by the HailStorm system when a user is provisioned for a particular service.

Here is the schema fragment for the root element of the myFavouriteWebSites service:

```
<m:myFavoriteWebSites changeNumber="..." instanceId="..."
    xmlns:m="http://schemas.microsoft.com/hs/2001/10/myFavoriteWebSites"
    xmlns:hs="http://schemas.microsoft.com/hs/2001/10/core">1..1
```

Here is the rest of the schema fragment for the myFavoriteWebSites service:

myFavoriteWebSites/favoriteWebSite

```
<m:favoriteWebSite changeNumber="..." id="..." creator="...">0..unbounded
    <m:cat ref="...">0..unbounded</m:cat>
    <m:title xml:lang="..." dir="...">0..unbounded</m:title>
    <m:url>1..1</m:url>
    {any}
</m:favoriteWebSite>
```

The `<favoriteWebSite>` element permits an unlimited number of categorized URLs and titles that typically contain the HTML `<title>` element from the web site.

myFavoriteWebSites/subscription

```
<m:subscription changeNumber="..." id="..." creator="...">0..unbounded
    <hs:trigger select="..." mode="..." baseChangeNumber="...">1..1
    </hs:trigger>
        <hs:expiresAt>0..1</hs:expiresAt>
        <hs:context uri="...">1..1 {any}</hs:context>
        <hs:to>1..1</hs:to>
</m:subscription>
    {any}
</m:myFavoriteWebSites>
```

The `<subscription>` element was described in the myContacts service and in the header portion of the services section.

myWallet Service

The myWallet service is used to store the accounts that an identity uses to pay for items. These accounts or **Payment Instruments**, as Microsoft calls them, include credit/debit cards, bank accounts, and other types of accounts. The main reason for most of us to have myWallet is to support one-click shopping. The myWallet service and Passport are already used independently of HailStorm on many sites to provide this functionality. The myWallet service is actually supported by many more sites than Passport. See the Passport site for a list of sites that support it. As HailStorm and digital services become more common, services like myWallet will become more popular, as a way to pay for these services with little or no intervention. Paying for services this way also allows for notifications for backorders, delivery information, and new sale prices, though integration with the myAlerts service. The myWallet, myAlerts, and myDevices services will combine to create a new type of instant messaging-targeted commerce.

Schema Fragment and Description

This is the root element of this service and has the same name as the service. It encapsulates the content document for the service, and it contains a global cache scope for the service. It also contains a couple of namespaces referring to the myWallet and the core namespaces. These are used to prefix the elements throughout the schema.

- ❏ `/myWallet/@changeNumber` – This contains a `changeNumber` attribute for tracking changes and making caching easier.

- ❏ `/myWallet/@instanceId` – This attribute is a unique identifier typically assigned to the root element of a service. It is a read-only element and assigned by the HailStorm system when a user is provisioned for a particular service.

Here is the schema fragment for the root element of the myWallet service:

```
<m:myWallet changeNumber="..." instanceId="..."
    xmlns:m="http://schemas.microsoft.com/hs/2001/10/myWallet"
    xmlns:hs="http://schemas.microsoft.com/hs/2001/10/core">1..1
```

The first-class-level elements are `<card>`, `<account>`, and `<subscription>`. The myWallet schema contains one set of elements under the `<card>` element for card-type accounts and contains another set of elements under the `<account>` element for account-type transactions. Most of the structure under both of these elements is the same. The top section of the `<card>` element contains `typeOfCard`, `networkBrand`, `affiliateBrand`, `cardNumber`, `displayNumber`, and `nameOnCard`. The top section of the `<account>` element contains `typeOfAccount`, `accountRoutingNumber`, `accountNumber`, `displayNumber`, and `nameOnAccount`. The first line of elements is obviously tailored to a credit card company and the second line tailored to a bank. The rest of the schema fragment is duplicated for both types of accounts.

myWallet/card

```
<m:card changeNumber="..." id="..." creator="...">0..unbounded
    <m:cat ref="...">0..unbounded</m:cat>
    <m:typeOfCard>1..1</m:typeOfCard>
    <m:networkBrand>1..1</m:networkBrand>
```

```
    <m:affiliateBrand ref="...">0..1</m:affiliateBrand>
    <m:cardNumber>1..1</m:cardNumber>
    <m:displayNumber>1..1</m:displayNumber>
      <m:nameOnCard xml:lang="..." dir="...">1..1</m:nameOnCard>
      <m:description xml:lang="..." dir="...">1..1</m:description>
      <m:expirationDate>0..1</m:expirationDate>
      <m:issueDate>0..1</m:issueDate>
      <m:validFromDate>0..1</m:validFromDate>
      <m:issueNumber>0..1</m:issueNumber>
      <m:currency>1..1
        <m:currencyCode>1..1</m:currencyCode>
      </m:currency>
      <m:billingAddress>1..1
      <m:cat ref="...">0..unbounded</m:cat>
      <m:officialAddressLine xml:lang="..." dir="...">0..1
      </m:officialAddressLine>
      <m:internalAddressLine xml:lang="..." dir="...">0..1
      </m:internalAddressLine>
      <m:primaryCity xml:lang="..." dir="...">0..1</m:primaryCity>
      <m:secondaryCity xml:lang="..." dir="...">0..1</m:secondaryCity>
      <m:subdivision xml:lang="..." dir="...">0..1</m:subdivision>
      <m:postalCode>0..1</m:postalCode>
      <m:countryOrRegion xml:lang="..." dir="...">0..1</m:countryOrRegion>
      <m:geoLocation>0..1
        <m:reportingDevice>0..1
          <m:deviceId>0..1</m:deviceId>
          <m:deviceName>0..1</m:deviceName>
          {any}
        </m:reportingDevice>
        <m:latitude>0..1</m:latitude>
        <m:longitude>0..1</m:longitude>
        <m:elevation>0..1</m:elevation>
        <m:confidence>0..1</m:confidence>
        <m:precision>0..1</m:precision>
        {any}
      </m:geoLocation>
      {any}
    </m:billingAddress>
    <m:paymentInstrumentsIssuerPuid>0..1</m:paymentInstrumentsIssuerPuid>
    {any}
</m:card>
```

As mentioned above the <card> element contains the details necessary to charge a credit card account and the billing information of the credit card holder. The <address> element is slightly different from the one in the myContacts and myProfile services. It is the same as what was contained in a prior version for both of these, so presumably it will be changed for they myWallet service as well eventually.

Notice the PUID being used to identify the paymentInsturmentIssuer, or in this case, the credit card company.

myWallet/account

```
<m:account changeNumber="..." id="..." creator="...">0..unbounded
 <m:cat ref="...">0..unbounded</m:cat>
 <m:typeOfAccount>1..1</m:typeOfAccount>
 <m:accountRoutingNumber>0..1</m:accountRoutingNumber>
   <m:accountNumber xml:lang="..." dir="...">1..1</m:accountNumber>
   <m:displayNumber>1..1</m:displayNumber>
   <m:nameOnAccount xml:lang="..." dir="...">1..1</m:nameOnAccount>
   <m:description xml:lang="..." dir="...">1..1</m:description>
   <m:currency>1..1
     <m:currencyCode>1..1</m:currencyCode>
   </m:currency>
   <m:accountAddress>1..1
     <m:cat ref="...">0..unbounded</m:cat>
     <m:officialAddressLine xml:lang="..." dir="...">0..1
     </m:officialAddressLine>
     <m:internalAddressLine xml:lang="..." dir="...">0..1
     </m:internalAddressLine>
     <m:primaryCity xml:lang="..." dir="...">0..1</m:primaryCity>
     <m:secondaryCity xml:lang="..." dir="...">0..1</m:secondaryCity>
     <m:subdivision xml:lang="..." dir="...">0..1</m:subdivision>
     <m:postalCode>0..1</m:postalCode>
     <m:countryOrRegion xml:lang="..." dir="...">0..1</m:countryOrRegion>
     <m:geoLocation>0..1
       <m:reportingDevice>0..1
         <m:deviceId>0..1</m:deviceId>
         <m:deviceName>0..1</m:deviceName>
         {any}
       </m:reportingDevice>
       <m:latitude>0..1</m:latitude>
       <m:longitude>0..1</m:longitude>
       <m:elevation>0..1</m:elevation>
       <m:confidence>0..1</m:confidence>
       <m:precision>0..1</m:precision>
       {any}
     </m:geoLocation>
     {any}
   </m:accountAddress>
   <m:paymentInstrumentsIssuerPuid>0..1</m:paymentInstrumentsIssuerPuid>
   {any}
 </m:account>
 <m:subscription changeNumber="..." id="..." creator="...">0..unbounded
   <hs:trigger select="..." mode="..." baseChangeNumber="...">1..1
   </hs:trigger>
   <hs:expiresAt>0..1</hs:expiresAt>
   <hs:context uri="...">1..1 {any}</hs:context>
   <hs:to>1..1</hs:to>
 </m:subscription>
</m:myWallet>
```

As mentioned above, the account element contains the details necessary to charge an account (a bank account or other types of accounts) and the billing information of the credit card holder.

The information in the top section of the account element contains information including `accountNumber` and `accountRoutingNumber` required for processing a transaction against a bank and not a credit card company.

myLists Service

The myLists service permits the creation of to-do lists, shopping lists, and any other structured or unstructured lists. One neat aspect is that items can belong to multiple lists. The <cat> element is used to categorize the list. For example, to create a vacation list, set the `ref` attribute of the cat element to "`vacation list`". Items can also be categorized, assigned to individuals, prioritized, and assigned to a responsible person.

Schema Fragment and Description

This is the root element of this service and has the same name as the service. It encapsulates the content document for the service, and it contains a global cache scope for the service. It also contains a couple of namespaces referring to the myLists and the core namespaces. These are used to prefix the elements throughout the schema.

- ❑ `/myLists/@changeNumber` – This contains a `changeNumber` attribute for tracking changes and making caching easier.

- ❑ `/myLists/@instanceId` – This attribute is a unique identifier typically assigned to the root element of a service. It is a read-only element and assigned by the HailStorm system when a user is provisioned for a particular service.

Here is the schema fragment for the root element of the myLists service:

```
<m:myLists changeNumber="..." instanceId="..."
    xmlns:m="http://schemas.microsoft.com/hs/2001/10/myLists"
    xmlns:hs="http://schemas.microsoft.com/hs/2001/10/core">1..1
```

Here is the rest of the schema fragment for the myLists service.

myLists/list

```
<m:list changeNumber="..." id="..." creator="...">0..unbounded
 <m:cat ref="...">0..unbounded</m:cat>
 <m:title xml:lang="..." dir="...">0..unbounded</m:title>
 <m:description xml:lang="..." dir="...">0..unbounded</m:description>
 {any}
</m:list>
```

This element is used to create an unlimited number of structured lists. It contains the name of the list and a description of the list.

myLists/item

```
<m:item changeNumber="..." id="..." creator="...">0..unbounded
 <m:cat ref="...">0..unbounded</m:cat>
 <m:title xml:lang="..." dir="...">0..unbounded</m:title>
 <m:description xml:lang="..." dir="...">0..unbounded</m:description>
 <m:url>0..unbounded</m:url>
 <m:listRef ref="...">0..unbounded</m:listRef>
```

```
    <m:dueDate>0..1</m:dueDate>
    <m:status>0..1</m:status>
    <m:priority>0..1</m:priority>
    <m:assignedTo>0..unbounded
      <hs:name xml:lang="..." dir="...">0..1</hs:name>
      <hs:puid>0..1</hs:puid>
      <hs:email>0..1</hs:email>
    </m:assignedTo>
    {any}
  </m:item>
```

This element contains an **\<item>**. Items can be part of one or more lists, or can be freestanding and part of no list. The rest of the items element contains a URL to point to the item, priority information, and an `assignedTo` element that optionally uses a PUID to identify the person this item is assigned to. It seems powerful but there still seems to be some work need to bring the \<status> element and the \<priority> element under the \<catDef> functionality. As of now, the status is limited to `notStarted`, `inProgress`, and `completed`.

`myLists/subscription`

```
    <m:subscription changeNumber="..." id="..." creator="...">0..unbounded
      <hs:trigger select="..." mode="..." baseChangeNumber="...">1..1
      </hs:trigger>
        <hs:expiresAt>0..1</hs:expiresAt>
        <hs:context uri="...">1..1 {any}</hs:context>
        <hs:to>1..1</hs:to>
    </m:subscription>
    {any}
  </m:myLists>
```

The \<subscription> element was described in the myContacts service and in the header portion of the services section.

myCategories Service

The myCategories service provides a very powerful classification or categorization model in HailStorm. Categories are defined in the \<catDef> element of the myCategories service and referenced in other services in the \<cat> element. Any element that contains a \<cat> element can be referenced. Each category definition has a human readable name and description. The elements stored within the category can be located in XML document references by a qualified name.

Schema Fragment and Description

This is the root element of this service and has the same name as the service. It encapsulates the content document for the service, and it contains a global cache scope for the service. It also contains a couple of namespaces referring to the myCategories and the core namespaces. These are used to prefix the elements throughout the schema.

❑ `/myLists/@changeNumber` – This contains a `changeNumber` attribute for tracking changes and making caching easier.

❑ `/myLists/@instanceId` – This attribute is a unique identifier typically assigned to the root element of a service. It is a read-only element and assigned by the HailStorm system when a user is provisioned for a particular service.

Here is the schema fragment for the root element of the myCategories service:

```
<m:myCategories changeNumber="..." instanceId="..."
     xmlns:m="http://schemas.microsoft.com/hs/2001/10/myCategories"
     xmlns:hs="http://schemas.microsoft.com/hs/2001/10/core">1..1
```

Here is the rest of the schema fragment for the myCategories service:

myCategories/catDef

```
<m:catDef catDefId="..." changeNumber="..." id="..."
    creator="...">0..unbounded
    <hs:name xml:lang="..." dir="...">0..unbounded</hs:name>
    <hs:description xml:lang="..." dir="...">0..1</hs:description>
    <hs:implies ref="...">0..unbounded</hs:implies>
    <hs:cat ref="...">0..unbounded</hs:cat>
    {any}
</m:catDef>
```

As you can see, there is a place for the category name, description, and a couple of other elements used to store categories.

myCategories/subscription

```
<m:subscription changeNumber="..." id="..." creator="...">0..unbounded
    <hs:trigger select="..." mode="..." baseChangeNumber="...">1..1
    </hs:trigger>
    <hs:expiresAt>0..1</hs:expiresAt>
    <hs:context uri="...">1..1 {any}</hs:context>
    <hs:to>1..1</hs:to>
</m:subscription>
{any}
</m:myLists>
```

The <subscription> element was described in the myContacts service and in the header portion of the services section.

myCalendar Service

The myCalendar service is one of the services that will combine with others to trigger the myAlerts service. It is one of the most significant parts of HailStorm; the potential to deliver intelligent notifications. The myCalendar service is a very detailed schema that contains the information necessary to store appointments, reminders, attendees, and just about anything else related to a meeting.

Of course, the myCalendar service is available to other services, applications, and devices across the Internet and is PUID-based. This opens up all kinds of possibilities to creative developers and companies.

The myCalendar service is compatible with or can store information for Exchange, Microsoft Outlook, and MSN Calendar.

Schema Fragment and Description

This is the root element of this service and has the same name as the service. It encapsulates the content document for the service, and it contains a global cache scope for the service. It also contains a couple of namespaces referring to the myCalendar and the core namespaces. These are used to prefix the elements throughout the schema.

- ❏ /myLists/@changeNumber – This contains a changeNumber attribute for tracking changes and making caching easier.

- ❏ /myLists/@instanceId – This attribute is a unique identifier typically assigned to the root element of a service. It is a read-only element and assigned by the HailStorm system when a user is provisioned for a particular service.

Here is the schema fragment for the root element of the myProfile service.

```
<m:myCalendar changeNumber="..." instanceId="..."
    xmlns:m="http://schemas.microsoft.com/hs/2001/10/myCalendar"
    xmlns:hs="http://schemas.microsoft.com/hs/2001/10/core">1..1
```

Table of the non-standard methods:

Method	Description
getCalendarDays	This function that is aware of the calendar schema and business rules. It returns an XML stream of calendar appointments/events between two dates. If you have access to their data, multiple contacts can be accessed by providing multiple PUIDS. This method is very powerful and can access all parts of the calendar schema including calendar dates and appointment attendees, and has access to all of the calendar's business rules including holidays and appointment priorities.
getFreeBusyDays	This function returns a stream of XML fragments defining the user's freeBusy information between two dates. If you have access to their data, multiple people can be accessed by providing multiple PUIDS. The available options are Away (Off), Busy, Tentative, and Free.
getQuickView	This function provides an efficient way to select days that have 1 or more appointments or days that have 0 appointments.
meetingUpdate	This method permits a meeting organizer to invite and uninvite attendees to an event.
respond	This method permits invitees to respond to an invitation. Valid options are: accept, decline, accept tentatively, or counter propose.
updateReminder	Delegates function to myAlerts for creating or modifying calendar meeting reminders.

The calendar schema fragment is very long. It contains sections for the appointment body, attendees, attachments, reminders, attendees, and recurring appointments. As always with HailStorm, it is designed for ultimate flexibility, so it is very detailed.

The <event> element in the myCalendar schema contains all of the data and in order to avoid having multiple pages of schema fragment with no description, we'll analyze the myCalendar schema by its next level element. Here is the rest of the schema fragment for the myCalendar service:

myCalendar/event

```
<m:event calendarType="..." advanceHijriValue="..." changeNumber="..."
    id="..." creator="...">0..unbounded
```

The <event> is the myCalendar root element for events, appointments, and meetings.

There are two new attributes that are not that well documented but this much is known:

❏ The calendarType identifies an enumeration that determines the kind of calendar; HailStorm v1 will only support CAL_GREGORIAN_US

❏ The advanceHijruValue attribute is required for Hijri calendar support with an optional element

myCalendar/event/body

```
<m:body changeNumber="...">1..1
  <m:cat ref="...">0..unbounded</m:cat>
  <m:title xml:lang="..." dir="...">1..1</m:title>
  <m:fullDescription xml:lang="..." dir="...">0..1</m:fullDescription>
  <m:location xml:lang="..." dir="...">0..1</m:location>
  <m:recurrenceId>0..1</m:recurrenceId>
  <m:lastUpdateTime>0..1</m:lastUpdateTime>
  <m:startTime>1..1</m:startTime>
  <m:endTime>1..1</m:endTime>
  <m:allDay>0..1</m:allDay>
  <m:floating>0..1</m:floating>
  <m:travelTimeTo>0..1</m:travelTimeTo>
  <m:travelTimeFrom>0..1</m:travelTimeFrom>
  <m:freeBusyStatus>0..1</m:freeBusyStatus>
  <m:cuid>0..1</m:cuid>
  <m:organizer>0..1
    <hs:name xml:lang="..." dir="...">0..1</hs:name>
    <hs:puid>0..1</hs:puid>
    <hs:email>0..1</hs:email>
  </m:organizer>
  {any}
</m:body>
```

The <body> element contains a free-form description, the location, start time, end time, travel time, organizer's information (including their PUID), and a **CUID** (**Correlation Unique ID**). A CUID links an organizer's event to an attendee's event.

myCalendar/event/attendeeEventExtra

```
<m:attendeeEventExtra changeNumber="...">0..1
  <m:intendedFreeBusy>0..1</m:intendedFreeBusy>
  <m:delegateResponder>0..1
    <hs:name xml:lang="..." dir="...">0..1</hs:name>
```

```
        <hs:puid>0..1</hs:puid>
        <hs:email>0..1</hs:email>
    </m:delegateResponder>
    <m:responseTime>0..1</m:responseTime>
    <m:responseType>0..1</m:responseType>
    <m:counterProposeStartTime>0..1</m:counterProposeStartTime>
    <m:counterProposeEndTime>0..1</m:counterProposeEndTime>
    <m:counterProposeLocation>0..1</m:counterProposeLocation>
    {any}
</m:attendeeEventExtra>
```

The `<attendeEventExtra>` element contains additional information about an event, found only in an event invitee's schema. This information includes the `delagateResponder` information if a third party responds for an individual. The `<responseTime>` and `<responseType>` (accept, decline, tentative, or counter propose) are also stored. The last element is where the information for the `<counterResponse>` will go, if required.

myCalendar/event/attachment

```
<m:attachment changeNumber="..." id="..." creator="...">0..unbounded
    <m:name xml:lang="..." dir="...">1..1</m:name>
    <m:contentType>1..1</m:contentType>
    <m:contentTransferEncoding>1..1</m:contentTransferEncoding>
    <m:size>1..1</m:size>
    <m:attachmentBody>1..1</m:attachmentBody>
</m:attachment>
```

This element contains the attachment name, content-type, and may contain the attachment body, size, and the attachment encoding information. The attachment encoding information is necessary to decode the attachment.

myCalendar/event/reminder

```
<m:reminder changeNumber="..." id="..." creator="...">0..1
    <m:set>1..1</m:set>
    <m:to xml:lang="..." dir="...">1..1</m:to>
    <m:offset>1..1</m:offset>
    <m:interruptability>0..1</m:interruptability>
    <m:lastSentTime>1..1</m:lastSentTime>
    <m:nextTriggerTime>1..1</m:nextTriggerTime>
</m:reminder>
```

This element permits the setting of reminders for standard and recurring appointments. An importance attribute ranging from 1 to 10 can be set, with low numbers meaning that the appointment is important and should not be interrupted. This seems to be a flag that HailStorm utilizes to determine whether to interrupt you, or leave you a message. It is hard to comment on this without knowing the other factors that will be used when HailStorm makes these decisions.

myCalendar/event/attendee

```
<m:attendee changeNumber="..." id="..." creator="...">0..unbounded
    <hs:name xml:lang="..." dir="...">0..1</hs:name>
    <hs:puid>0..1</hs:puid>
```

```
      <hs:email>0..1</hs:email>
      <m:inviteType>1..1</m:inviteType>
      <m:invitationStatus>1..1</m:invitationStatus>
      <m:body xml:lang="..." dir="...">0..1</m:body>
      <m:responseTime>0..1</m:responseTime>
      <m:responseType>0..1</m:responseType>
      <m:counterProposeStartTime>0..1</m:counterProposeStartTime>
      <m:counterProposeEndTime>0..1</m:counterProposeEndTime>
      <m:counterProposeLocation>0..1</m:counterProposeLocation>
      {any}
   </m:attendee>
```

This element contains the attendee's PUID, e-mail address, invitation type (set by organizer to required, optional, or resource), invitation status (not sent, sent, or canceled), response time, and response type (accept, decline, tentative, or counter response). There are also elements to store the counter response data, if there is a counter response.

myCalendar/event/recurrence

```
  <m:recurrence changeNumber="...">0..1
     <m:rule changeNumber="...">1..1
        <m:firstDayOfWeek>1..1</m:firstDayOfWeek>
        <m:tzid>0..1</m:tzid>
        <m:repeat>1..1
           <m:daily dayFrequency="...">0..1</m:daily>
           <m:weekly su="..." mo="..." tu="..." we="..." th="..." fr="..."
               sa="..." weekFrequency="...">0..1
           </m:weekly>
           <m:monthlyByDay su="..." mo="..." tu="..." we="..." th="..."
               fr="..." sa="..." monthFrequency="..." weekdayOfMonth="...">
             0..1
           </m:monthlyByDay>
           <m:monthly monthFrequency="..." day="...">0..1</m:monthly>
           <m:yearlyByDay su="..." mo="..." tu="..." we="..." th="..."
               fr="..." sa="..." yearFrequency="..." weekdayOfMonth="..."
               month="...">0..1</m:yearlyByDay>
           <m:yearly yearFrequency="..." month="..." day="...">0..1
           </m:yearly>
           {any}
        </m:repeat>
        <m:windowStart isLeapYear="..." leapMonthValue="...">1..1
        </m:windowStart>
        <m:windowEnd>0..1</m:windowEnd>
        <m:repeatForever>0..1</m:repeatForever>
        <m:repeatInstances>0..1</m:repeatInstances>
        <m:deletedExceptionDate>0..unbounded</m:deletedExceptionDate>
        {any}
     </m:rule>
     <m:exception changeNumber="..." id="..." creator="...">0..unbounded
        <m:recurrenceId>1..1</m:recurrenceId>
        <m:body>0..1
           <m:title xml:lang="..." dir="...">0..1</m:title>
           <m:fullDescription xml:lang="..." dir="...">0..1
           </m:fullDescription>
```

```
            <m:location xml:lang="..." dir="...">0..1</m:location>
            <m:startTime>0..1</m:startTime>
            <m:endTime>0..1</m:endTime>
            <m:allDay>0..1</m:allDay>
            <m:travelTimeTo>0..1</m:travelTimeTo>
            <m:travelTimeFrom>0..1</m:travelTimeFrom>
            <m:freeBusyStatus>0..1</m:freeBusyStatus>
            <m:organizer>0..1
                <hs:name xml:lang="..." dir="...">0..1</hs:name>
                <hs:puid>0..1</hs:puid>
                <hs:email>0..1</hs:email>
            </m:organizer>
        </m:body>
        <m:attendeeEventExtra>0..1
            <m:intendedFreeBusy>0..1</m:intendedFreeBusy>
            <m:delegateResponder>0..1
                <hs:name xml:lang="..." dir="...">0..1</hs:name>
                <hs:puid>0..1</hs:puid>
                <hs:email>0..1</hs:email>
            </m:delegateResponder>
            <m:responseTime>0..1</m:responseTime>
            <m:responseType>0..1</m:responseType>
            <m:counterProposeStartTime>0..1</m:counterProposeStartTime>
            <m:counterProposeEndTime>0..1</m:counterProposeEndTime>
            <m:counterProposeLocation>0..1</m:counterProposeLocation>
            {any}
        </m:attendeeEventExtra>
        <m:deletedAttendee>0..unbounded</m:deletedAttendee>
        <m:deletedAttachment>0..unbounded</m:deletedAttachment>
        <m:attachment>0..unbounded
            <m:name xml:lang="..." dir="...">1..1</m:name>
            <m:contentType>1..1</m:contentType>
            <m:contentTransferEncoding>1..1</m:contentTransferEncoding>
            <m:size>1..1</m:size>
            <m:attachmentBody>1..1</m:attachmentBody>
        </m:attachment>
        <m:attendee>0..unbounded
            <hs:name xml:lang="..." dir="...">0..1</hs:name>
            <hs:puid>0..1</hs:puid>
            <hs:email>0..1</hs:email>
            <m:inviteType>1..1</m:inviteType>
            <m:invitationStatus>1..1</m:invitationStatus>
            <m:body xml:lang="..." dir="...">0..1</m:body>
            <m:responseTime>r</m:responseTime>
            <m:responseType>0..1</m:responseType>
            <m:counterProposeStartTime>0..1</m:counterProposeStartTime>
            <m:counterProposeEndTime>0..1</m:counterProposeEndTime>
            <m:counterProposeLocation>0..1</m:counterProposeLocation>
            {any}
        </m:attendee>
        <m:reminder>0..1
            <m:set>0..1</m:set>
            <m:offset>0..1</m:offset>
            <m:interruptability>0..1</m:interruptability>
```

```
            </m:reminder>
           {any}
         </m:exception>
        {any}
      </m:recurrence>
    </m:event>
```

This element contains the rules for recurring appointments in the first section under the rule element and exceptions in the <exception> element. The <exception> element is very long and covers what to do when recurring appointments have to be canceled because traffic is bad. This element also contains an element to replace the meeting organizer if they are not available. This is a very long section and is reasonably self-explanatory to look through.

myCalendar/subscription

```
      <m:subscription changeNumber="..." id="..." creator="...">0..unbounded
        <hs:trigger select="..." mode="..." baseChangeNumber="...">1..1
        </hs:trigger>
        <hs:expiresAt>0..1</hs:expiresAt>
        <hs:context uri="...">1..1 {any}</hs:context>
        <hs:to>1..1</hs:to>
      </m:subscription>
      {any}
    </m:myLists>
```

The <subscription> element was described in the myContacts service and in the header portion of the services section.

Summary

In this chapter, we've looked at HSDL and its six standard operations and backed this up with some examples. We've discussed the services schemas and their critical role within HailStorm and viewed the schema fragments in detail, examining their major elements. We went through examples of all of the six common operations. After all this you have got a taste of how massive HailStorm is or will become.

We also learned that, as mentioned in Chapter 2, this is pre-beta software and a fair amount does not work yet.

Knowledge of the schemas and the six standard operations will give you almost everything you'll need to start programming with HailStorm. The following chapters with show you how to put everything we've learned so far into practice with a couple of case studies.

early adopter

6

Case Study: An Auction Site

The Case Study

In this case study we're going to build the bare bones of an online auction site, and show how we can use HailStorm to enhance the user experience. We should stress that we really are talking about the bare bones of an auction site here – even with the power of HailStorm, there isn't *quite* enough space here to put together something that will compete with the likes of eBay.

Here's what our site is going to do. First, the user will have to log in; this part is somewhat specific to the current release of HailStorm, and in future, it will need modification to bring it under full Microsoft Passport/Kerberos control. Once we've accepted the log in, we fetch the user details and display them. The user will then have the opportunity to amend them if they want. Then we show the user a list of the available lots. The user can then select one of these and see what the current best bid is, if it happens to be theirs, and when the auction expires. If they wish, they can enter a bid at this point.

That's about it – almost. However, once we've set up this basic model, we'll take a look at what's coming soon in the area of notifications. This is an extremely exciting new development which promises to make possible a whole range of new functionality. For example, in this case, our user could elect to be notified when someone else trumped their bid – even if they had surfed off to somewhere entirely different in the meantime.

Our technology of choice is Microsoft Active Server Pages. We've chosen to do it this way, rather than with ASP.NET, in order to emphasize that you don't need .NET to do this sort of thing. In fact, because HailStorm is an entirely protocol-based technology, you don't even need a Windows client.

Preparation

We have to do a little preparation work before we launch into development. We'll assume that HailStorm is installed as described in Chapter 2

Provisioning

Next, we need to make sure that it is provisioned for the user we're going to be logging in as. Specifically, we need to have the myProfile service provisioned, as follows:

```
D:\Hailstorm\Bin>hsprov -l http://server_name -o username -s myProfile
```

to which we will see the following response, if successful:

```
myProfile service successfully provisioned
```

(The drive D: is mapped to our HailStorm installation directory.)

Populating Our Services

Now that our services are provisioned, we can populate them. There are currently two ways of doing this: either via SOAP or by using XMI and the hspost utility. In the future, the use of raw SOAP will be overtaken by the HailStorm client API. For setting things up, the latter is the more straightforward to do, so we'll use that to populate our myProfile service. Let's create a file called myProfile-insert.xml, as follows:

```xml
<hs:insertRequest hs:select="/myProfile"
                  xmlns:hs="http://schemas.microsoft.com/hs/2001/10/core"
                  xmlns="http://schemas.microsoft.com/hs/2001/10/myProfile">
   <name>
     <title xml:lang="en">Mr.</title>
     <givenName xml:lang="en">Jonathan</givenName>
     <middleName xml:lang="en">M.</middleName>
     <surName xml:lang="en">Pinnock</surName>
   </name>
   <address>
     <officialAddressLine xml:lang="en">Route 66</officialAddressLine>
     <primaryCity xml:lang="en">Nowheresville</primaryCity>
   </address>
</hs:insertRequest>
```

Note that the latest version of the XMI manual available at time of publication actually stated that the surName element should be all lower-case, but the actual schema required the upper-case N used here. Since the names of these elements have already changed from firstName and lastName to those used here as well, it is certainly possible they will change again.

A basic user name and address will suffice for our purposes, although there are, of course, many more elements in myProfile that we could populate if we so desired.

Here's our `hspost` command:

```
D:\Hailstorm\Bin>hspost -d content -s myProfile -f C:\myprofile-insert.xml
```

And here's the response:

```
<?xml version='1.0'?>

<s:Envelope xmlns:s="http://schemas.xmlsoap.org/soap/envelope/"
            xmlns:hs="http://schemas.microsoft.com/hs/2001/10/core">
    <s:Header>
        <path xmlns="http://schemas.xmlsoap.org/rp">
            <action>http://schemas.microsoft.com/hs/2001/10/core#response</action>
            <from>http://jaws</from>
            <rev></rev>
            <id>11ebfe07-b1a3-11d5-8c86-00a0c94515ad</id>
            <relatesTo>0899e491-b1a3-11d5-911d-0050da2df79d</relatesTo>
        </path>
        <hs:response>
        </hs:response>
    </s:Header>
    <s:Body>

<hs:insertResponse xmlns:hs="http://schemas.microsoft.com/hs/2001/10/core"
                   status="success" selectedNodeCount="1" newChangeNumber="582">
<hs:newBlueId id="11ebfe05-b1a3-11d5-8c86-00a0c94515ad"/>
<hs:newBlueId id="11ebfe06-b1a3-11d5-8c86-00a0c94515ad"/>
</hs:insertResponse>

    </s:Body>
</s:Envelope>
```

That looks like a success to me. But let's run a quick query just to check. Here's our XMI, in a file called `myProfile-query.xml`:

```
<hs:queryRequest xmlns:hs="http://schemas.microsoft.com/hs/2001/10/core"
xmlns="http://schemas.microsoft.com/hs/2001/10/myProfile">
  <hs:xpQuery hs:select="/myProfile" />
</hs:queryRequest>
```

Note the use of the XPath syntax to find our way to the head of `myProfile`. As it happens, the path `/` would also be adequate to retrieve the entire profile in this context. If, however, all we'd been interested in was the name, our path would be `//name`. However, a request for `//name/surName` would fail, as `surName` is not directly addressable, and we would have to go to the next highest `xdb:blue` node, `name`.

Here's the associated `hspost` command:

```
D:\Hailstorm\Bin>hspost -d content -s myProfile -f C:\myprofile-query.xml
```

And here's the interesting part of the response:

```
...
<hs:queryResponse xmlns:hs="http://schemas.microsoft.com/hs/2001/10/core"
                  xmlns:m="http://schemas.microsoft.com/hs/2001/10/myProfile">
<hs:xpQueryResponse status="success">
<m:myProfile>
<m:name id="11ebfe05-b1a3-11d5-8c86-00a0c94515ad">
<m:title xml:lang="en">Mr.</m:title>
```

153

```
<m:givenName xml:lang="en">Jonathan</m:givenName>

<m:middleName xml:lang="en">M.</m:middleName>
<m:surName xml:lang="en">Pinnock</m:surName>
</m:name>
<m:address id="11ebfe06-b1a3-11d5-8c86-00a0c94515ad">
<m:officialAddressLine xml:lang="en">Route 66</m:officialAddressLine>
<m:primaryCity xml:lang="en">Nowheresville</m:primaryCity>
</m:address>
</m:myProfile>
</hs:xpQueryResponse>
...
```

That's fine, as well. We'll need to bear this response structure in mind when we come to make our ASP queries later.

Who Am I?

Before we start development, we need to find out our PUID. The early releases of HailStorm use this identifier instead of a full-blown Kerberos ticket. In future releases, you will need to be logged in via Microsoft Passport before the sites that you are visiting can gain access to your HailStorm services. However, once logged in, you can use the same Kerberos ticket for whatever HailStorm-enabled site you go to in that session, so you won't have to keep logging in everywhere you go.

Finding out your PUID is very simple. All you do is issue the following command:

```
F:\Bin\SDK\Bin>hspost -p
```

And what you see in return is something like:

```
Your username is jon - PUID = 13971
```

Getting the Database Ready

We can't have an auction without somewhere to store the details of the lots and the bids. So we need a database. Seeing as SQL Server 2000 is a pre-requisite for HailStorm, we might as well use that (although there's no need for this database to be stored on the same SQL Server system as the HailStorm database). We create a database called "auction", containing a single table called "lot".

In case you're not familiar with SQL Server 2000, these are the steps you need to take:

1. From the Windows menu, start up SQL Server Enterprise Manager

2. Highlight Databases, right-click, and select the option New Database...

3. Enter "auction" as the name of the new database

4. Highlight Tables under auction, right-click, and select the option New Table...

5. Enter the columns as specified below save as the table lots

6. Highlight Users under auction, right-click, and select the option New Database User...

7. Select login name <new>; this will take you to the Login Properties dialog

8. On the General tab, enter the user name and choose whichever type of authentication suits you

9. Ignore the Server Roles tab

10. On the Database Access tab, ensure that Permit is checked against the database auction

In the table lots, we define the following columns:

- ❑ lot – this is the lot number, an integer. This should be set as the primary key for the table.

- ❑ description – this is a textual description of the lot. This is an 80 character text string.

- ❑ bid – this is the current best bid, and has a type of *money*.

- ❑ puid – this is the PUID of the current best bidder, and is an integer.

- ❑ enddate – this is the closing date of the auction, and is of type *datetime*.

None of these columns permits blanks

Having designed the table, we can populate it according to taste. All bids and PUIDs should initially be set to 0.

The AuctionDemo Site

We're ready to start coding now. We're going to have three pages to our site:

- ❑ The point of entry – index.htm

- ❑ The main auction page – AuctionDemo.asp

- ❑ The profile amendment page – ChangeProfile.asp

We'll use SOAP as our interface into HailStorm this time around, because XMI files are a somewhat inflexible tool for use from an ASP page.

The Entry Page

Let's get the entry page out of the way quickly. This is an absolutely standard HTML page, as follows:

```
<html>
<body>
<form action="AuctionDemo.asp" method="post" name="login">
<p><strong><font color=red size=5>Welcome to Wrox Wrecks Inc. - Junk, We Got
It!</strong></font>    </p>
<p>
<table>
```

```
    <tr>
      <td>Enter your HailStorm User ID:</td>
      <td><input id=text1 name=userID></td>
    </tr>
    <tr>
      <td>Enter your HailStorm Service Location:</td>
      <td><input id=text2 name=location value=http://></td>
    </tr>
    <tr>
      <td></td>
      <td><input id=submit1 name=submit1 type=submit value="Log in"></td>
    </tr>
  </table></P>
  </form>
  </body>
  </html>
```

As can be seen, it's a standard HTML form, which POSTs to our main ASP page when we click on the
Log in button (submit1). In this release of HailStorm, all we need in order to establish a connection is a
PUID and the name of the HailStorm server.

This is what the page looks like:

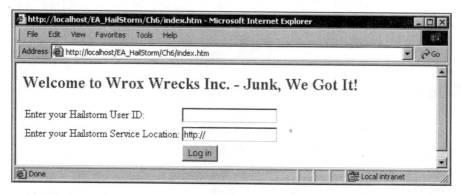

Like we said, eBay's can sleep easy in their beds for a while yet.

The Auction Page

Let's move on to something a little more interesting. There is a lot of code to this one, and we'll take it
one step at a time. Everything you see from now on until we say otherwise is contained in the one file,
AuctionDemo.asp.

We start off with the standard VBScript header, followed by a load of variable declarations.

```
<%@ Language=VBScript %>
<%

Option Explicit
```

We begin with the incoming data from the form in `Index.htm`:

```
Dim strUserID
Dim strLocation
```

Next, there's the identifier of our outgoing SOAP message. We'll be setting this up soon.

```
Dim strMessageID
```

Now for a few URIs:

```
Dim strSoapAction
Dim strSoapRPNamespace
Dim strHSCoreNamespace
Dim strSecNamespace
Dim strServiceNamespace
```

Next, we have our SOAP objects:

```
Dim Connector
Dim Serializer
Dim Reader
Dim Body
Dim Dom
```

Finally, here's where we store the data coming back from HailStorm:

```
Dim Title
Dim FirstName
Dim LastName
Dim Street
Dim City
```

Initialization

The code proper begins with us requesting the incoming data from the form on the entry page. The ASP page is re-entrant, calling back to itself a number of times in a single session, so the required values might not be there. If they're not, then they'll be in a couple of session variables. We know that they'll be there, because first time around, we save them there. We also need to initialize the session variable that we'll be using in the second pass through the page to blank.

```
strUserID = Request.Form("userID")
strLocation = Request.Form("location")

If strUserID = "" Then
  strUserID = Session("userID")
Else
  Session("userID") = strUserID
  Session("selectedLot") = ""
End If

If strLocation = "" Then
```

```
    strLocation = Session("location")
Else
    Session("location") = strLocation
End If
```

Next, we set up our message identifier. This is a GUID, and this brings us to one area where ASP.NET scores highly over standard ASP. This is because there's not way in standard ASP to generate a GUID on the fly (at least without developing a special COM object), whereas there is in ASP.NET. So for the purposes of this demo, we've generated a GUID using uuidgen and set it as a constant value:

```
strMessageID = "2741D0E0-A82C-11d5-8465-0040957713FA"
```

The final part of the initialization phase is to set up strings to refer to a number of URIs – one is the URI which defines the SOAP action for a HailStorm request, the others are XML namespaces. We'll need these in our SOAP message, and in analyzing the response:

```
strSoapAction          = "http://schemas.microsoft.com/hs/2001/10/core#request"
strSoapRPNamespace     = "http://schemas.xmlsoap.org/rp"
strHSCoreNamespace     = "http://schemas.microsoft.com/hs/2001/10/core"
strServiceNamespace    = "http://schemas.microsoft.com/hs/2001/10/myProfile"
strSecNamespace        = "http://schemas.xmlsoap.org/soap/security/2000-12/"
```

We're ready to get stuck into HailStorm now.

The SOAP Request

This is how we set up the SOAP connection and initialize the outgoing packet. We'll use HTTP as our SOAP transport here.

```
Set Connector = Server.CreateObject("MSSOAP.HttpConnector")
Connector.Property("EndPointURL") = strLocation & "/myProfile"
Connector.Property("SoapAction") = strSoapAction
Connector.BeginMessage()

Set Serializer = Server.CreateObject("MSSOAP.SoapSerializer")
Serializer.Init Connector.InputStream
```

We now come to the point where we have to set up the SOAP request. Here's the packet that we're going to have to send:

```
<?xml version="1.0" encoding="UTF-8" standalone="no"?>
<SOAP-ENV:Envelope encodingStyle="http://schemas.xmlsoap.org/soap/encoding/"
        xmlns:SOAP-ENV="http://schemas.xmlsoap.org/soap/envelope/"
        xmlns:ss="http://schemas.xmlsoap.org/soap/security/2000-12/"
        xmlns:h="http://schemas.microsoft.com/hs/2001/10/core"
        xmlns:srp="http://schemas.xmlsoap.org/rp"
        xmlns:m="http://schemas.microsoft.com/hs/2001/10/myProfile">
  <SOAP-ENV:Header>
    <srp:path>
    <srp:action>http://schemas.microsoft.com/hs/2001/10/core#request</srp:action>
      <srp:rev>
        <srp:via/>
      </srp:rev>
```

```
        <srp:to>http://jam</srp:to>
        <srp:id>2741D0E0-A82C-11d5-8465-0040957713FA</srp:id>
      </srp:path>
      <ss:licenses>
        <h:identity>
          <h:kerberos>5103</h:kerberos>
        </h:identity>
      </ss:licenses>
      <h:request service="myProfile" document="content"
                 method="query" genResponse="always">
        <h:key instance="0" cluster="0" puid="5103"/>
      </h:request>
    </SOAP-ENV:Header>
    <SOAP-ENV:Body>
      <queryRequest>
        <xpQuery select="/m:myProfile"/>
      </queryRequest>
    </SOAP-ENV:Body>
  </SOAP-ENV:Envelope>
```

In the header, we're basically setting up the path to the HailStorm server, identifying ourselves, and telling HailStorm which service we're interested in and what sort of request we're making. The request itself (three lines contained in the SOAP Body element) is analogous to what we previously put in our XMI file for hspost, and tells HailStorm the details of the request.

Let's see how we put this into code using the Microsoft SOAP SDK:

```
Serializer.startEnvelope "SOAP-ENV", _
                    "http://schemas.xmlsoap.org/soap/encoding/", "UTF-8"
  Serializer.startHeader
    Serializer.startElement "path", strSoapRPNamespace, , "srp"
      Serializer.startElement "action", strSoapRPNamespace, , "srp"
        Serializer.writeString strSoapAction
      Serializer.endElement
      Serializer.startElement "rev", strSoapRPNamespace, , "srp"
        Serializer.startElement "via", strSoapRPNamespace, , "srp"
        Serializer.endElement
      Serializer.endElement
      Serializer.startElement "to", strSoapRPNamespace, , "srp"
        Serializer.writeString strLocation
      Serializer.endElement
      Serializer.startElement "id", strSoapRPNamespace, , "srp"
        Serializer.writeString strMessageID
      Serializer.endElement
    Serializer.endElement
    Serializer.startElement "licenses", strSecNamespace, , "ss"
      Serializer.startElement "identity", strHSCoreNamespace, , "h"
        Serializer.startElement "kerberos", strHSCoreNamespace, , "h"
          Serializer.writeString strUserID
        Serializer.endElement
      Serializer.endElement
    Serializer.endElement
    Serializer.startElement "request", strHSCoreNamespace, , "h"
```

```
            Serializer.SoapAttribute "service", , "myProfile"
            Serializer.SoapAttribute "document", , "content"
            Serializer.SoapAttribute "method", , "query"
            Serializer.SoapAttribute "genResponse", , "always"
            Serializer.startElement "key", strHSCoreNamespace, , "h"
                Serializer.SoapAttribute "instance", , "0"
                Serializer.SoapAttribute "cluster", , "0"
                Serializer.SoapAttribute "puid", , strUserID
            Serializer.endElement
        Serializer.endElement
    Serializer.endHeader
    Serializer.startBody
        Serializer.startElement "queryRequest"
            Serializer.SoapAttribute "xmlns:m", , strServiceNamespace
            Serializer.startElement "xpQuery"
                Serializer.SoapAttribute "select", , "/m:myProfile"
            Serializer.endElement
        Serializer.endElement
    Serializer.endBody
Serializer.endEnvelope
```

Which is frankly, some of the most boring code ever seen in print. Roll on the API, we say. Anyway, we're ready to send it off to HailStorm. Here's how we do that:

```
Connector.EndMessage
```

That's all. Now let's take a look at the response.

Analyzing the Response

We need a SOAP reader now:

```
Set Reader = Server.CreateObject("MSSOAP.SoapReader")
Reader.Load Connector.OutputStream
```

We've now got a whole load of XML sitting in our SOAP reader. If everything's OK let's fish out the entries we need. We can make more use of XPath here to get to the elements that we need, bearing in mind what we saw of the responses we got from the hpost queries. (See? There *was* a reason for showing you that.) We can obtain the XML node corresponding to the SOAP packet's body element like this:

```
Set Body = Reader.Body
```

Now we need to configure the underlying document object model that our SOAP packet is stored in to recognize the namespaces we'll need to use in our XPaths:

```
Set Dom = Reader.DOM
Dom.setProperty "SelectionLanguage", "XPath"
Dom.setProperty "SelectionNamespaces", _
                "xmlns:hs='" & strHSCoreNamespace & "' " & _
                "xmlns:m='" & strServiceNamespace & "'"
```

Now we're ready to pull out the XML nodes corresponding to the elements we're interested in:

```
Set Title = Body.SelectSingleNode _
            "hs:queryResponse/hs:xpQueryResponse/m:myProfile/m:name/m:title"
Set FirstName = Body.SelectSingleNode _
            "hs:queryResponse/hs:xpQueryResponse/m:myProfile/m:name/m:givenName"
Set LastName = Body.SelectSingleNode _
            "hs:queryResponse/hs:xpQueryResponse/m:myProfile/m:name/m:surName"

Set Street = Body.SelectSingleNode _
            "hs:queryResponse/hs:xpQueryResponse/m:myProfile/m:address" & _
            "/m:officialAddressLine"
Set City = Body.SelectSingleNode _
            "hs:queryResponse/hs:xpQueryResponse/m:myProfile/m:address" & _
            "/m:primaryCity"
```

Say Hello

We've got everything we need from HailStorm now, so we can launch into our HTML. The code for this page is structured as three forms: one for confirming our personal details, one for selecting the lot to bid for, and the last for entering the bid. We don't show the first one unless we've got a sensible response from HailStorm. Here's the code controlling that first form. Notice the way it uses the data we've just got from HailStorm.

```
%>

<html>
<body>
<form action="ChangeProfile.asp" method="post" name="details">

<%If Not Reader.Fault Is Nothing Then
   Response.Write "FAULT: " & Reader.faultstring.Text
ElseIf Title Is Nothing Or FirstName Is Nothing Or LastName Is Nothing Then
   Response.Write "Failed to get name"
ElseIf Street Is Nothing Or City Is Nothing Then
   Response.Write "Failed to get address"
Else
%>
<p>
<%= "Hello, " & Title.text & " " & FirstName.text & " " & LastName.text & _
            " of " & Street.text & ", " & City.text %>
</p>
<%End If%>
<input id=submit1 name=submit1 type=submit value="Change Personal Details">
</form>
```

Accessing the Database

The next form makes extensive use of ADO to extract the data from the database. This isn't an ADO book, so we won't be going into this in any great detail. However, it is obviously important to understand what's going on in order to complete the case study, so we'll comment on it briefly as we go through. The code starts by declaring a whole load of variables for later use:

```
<form action="AuctionDemo.asp" method="post" name="select">
<%
Dim strSelectedLot
Dim strNewBid
Dim dblNewBid
Dim SQLConnection
Dim Recordset
Dim Record

Dim strLot
Dim strSelected
Dim strDetails
Dim dBid
Dim nBidUserID
Dim EndDate
```

This form is re-entrant, with a typical transaction taking three passes:

❑ Pass 1 – user hasn't seen anything yet

❑ Pass 2 – user has selected a lot to bid for

❑ Pass 3 – user has made a bid

We establish which pass by examining the data from the Form collection in the Request object. This is similar to the code that we started the initial script with. If it's the second pass, we need to extract the description of the selected lot:

```
strSelectedLot = Request.Form ("lot")

If strSelectedLot = "" Then
  strSelectedLot = Session("selectedLot")
Else
  Session("selectedLot") = strSelectedLot
  Session("bid") = ""
End If
```

If it's the third pass, we need to extract the user's bid:

```
strNewBid = Request.Form ("bid")
```

Now we open up the database:

```
Set SQLConnection = Server.CreateObject ("ADODB.Connection")
SQLConnection.Open
"Provider=sqloledb;Server=dipsy;Database=auction;UID=sa;PWD=sa;"

Set Recordset = Server.CreateObject ("ADODB.Recordset")
Recordset.Open "lots", SQLConnection, 1, 2, 2
```

Note that you should replace the name of the database server with the one that you're using. It's probably the same as the name of your web server, although there's no reason why it needs to be. Also, you should replace the user ID (UID) and password (PWD) with a user ID and password that are valid for your SQL Server installation.

If it's the third pass, we read through all the available lots and update the selected row with the new bid:

```
If strNewBid <> "" Then
  While Not Recordset.EOF
    strLot = Trim (Recordset.Fields.Item ("description"))

    If strLot = strSelectedLot Then
      Recordset.Fields.Item ("bid").Value = CCur (strNewBid)
      Recordset.Fields.Item ("puid").Value = CInt (strUserID)
      Recordset.Update
      Recordset.MoveLast
    Else
      Recordset.MoveNext
    End If
  Wend

  Recordset.MoveFirst
End If
%>
```

Now we create a selection box on the page, and populate it by reading through the database and extracting the description of each lot. If we encounter the currently selected lot, we also extract the details of the current bid (if any) and the closing date of the auction.

```
<select size=10 id=select1 name=lot>
<%

While Not Recordset.EOF
  strLot = Trim (Recordset.Fields.Item ("description"))

  If strLot = strSelectedLot Then
    strSelected = " SELECTED"
    dBid = Recordset.Fields.Item ("bid")
    nBidUserID = Recordset.Fields.Item ("puid")
    EndDate = Recordset.Fields.Item ("enddate")

    If dBid = 0.0 Then
      strDetails = "No bids yet"
    ElseIf CStr(nBidUserID) = strUserID Then
      strDetails = "Best bid is yours, at $" & dBid
    Else
      strDetails = "Best bid is $" & dBid
    End If

    strDetails = strDetails & ", auction ends on " & EndDate
  Else
    strSelected = ""
  End If
%>
```

```
<option <%=strSelected%>><%=strLot%></option>
<%
  Recordset.MoveNext
Wend
%>
</select></P>
<input id=submit2 name=submit2 type=submit value="Show Details of Selected Item">
</form>
```

Entering a New Bid

We only encounter the last form in the case where we have selected a lot to bid for – in other words after the first pass through. This is a very simple form, showing the details of the selected lot, and letting the user input a new bid:

```
<% If strSelectedLot <> "" Then%>
<form action="AuctionDemo.asp" method="post" name="bid">
<%=strDetails%></P>
<table>
  <tr>
    <td>Make your bid:</td>
    <td><input id=text1 name=bid></td>
    <td><input id=submit3 name=submit3 type=submit value="Bid">
  </tr>
</form>
<%End If%>
</body>
```

And that's the end of AuctionDemo.asp.

All we need to do now is create a directory called \EA_Hailstorm\Ch6 under our IIS root directory, move our two files there, and we are ready for action.

Running the Auction Demo (1)

Let's try out what we've got so far and see if it works, shall we? First of all, we need to enter our PUID and server on the entry page:

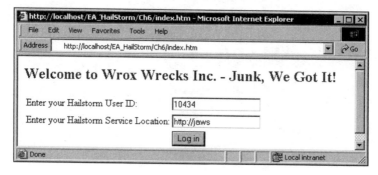

We click on Log in, and this is what we see:

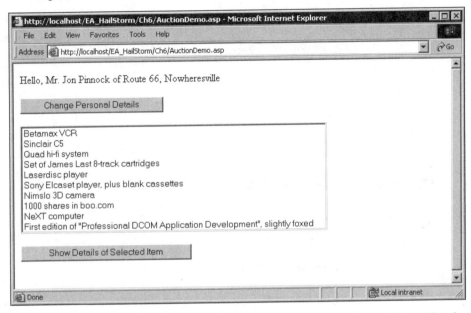

A tasty selection, or what? Well, between you and me, I've always wanted one of those Nimslo cameras, so that's what I'm going for, hit the Show Details... button and then make a bid:

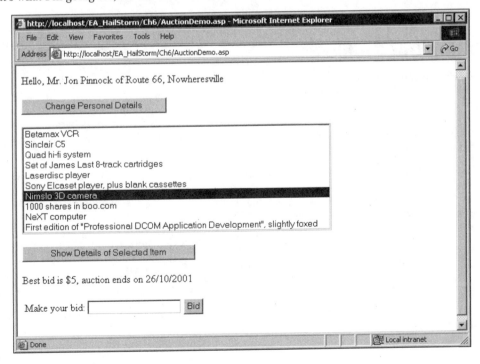

Somebody's obviously beaten us to it, so let's place a bid, and this is what we see:

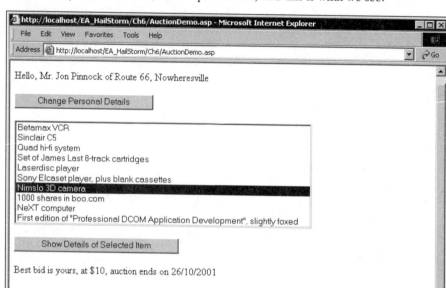

So let's hope that no-one else gets too excited about that one, shall we?

Updating Our Profile

Let's pause to consider what HailStorm's done for us so far. It's retrieved our profile for us, so we haven't had to go through all that tedious process of registering with Wrox Wrecks, like we have to with everyone else we deal with. And we've seen a nice personalized introduction to the site come up, so we have a warm feeling that someone at Wrox knows us and loves us. When we get around to actually paying for all this, the site can also go and fetch our credit card details from `myWallet` for us to confirm before proceeding (we leave this as an exercise for the reader).

But what happens when we move? As things presently stand, we'll have to go to every site we use for e-commerce and change our details. But we don't really want to do that – why can't we do it in just one place? Well, with HailStorm we can do just that. Let's take a look at the third part of our auction site, `ChangeProfile.asp`.

This ASP page is re-entrant like the main auction one. However, there are only two passes:

❑ Pass 1 – Profile data is retrieved and displayed to user. User amends.

❑ Pass 2 – Profile is updated, and success or failure is reported to user.

Much of this code is similar to that in the main page, so we'll skip over the similarities and concentrate on the differences.

Initialization

As before, we start by setting up a whole slew of variables:

```
<%@ Language=VBScript %>
<%

Option Explicit

Dim strUserID
Dim strLocation

Dim strTitle
Dim strFirstName
Dim strLastName
Dim strStreet
Dim strCity

Dim strMessageID

Dim strSoapAction
Dim strSoapRPNamespace
Dim strHSCoreNamespace
Dim strSecNamespace
Dim strServiceNamespace

Dim strMethod

Dim Connector
Dim Serializer
Dim Reader
Dim Body
Dim Dom

Dim Title
Dim FirstName
Dim LastName
Dim Street
Dim City
```

The only new ones are those strings to hold the user input data (`strTitle` and so on) and the string to hold the type of method that we're going to be invoking on HailStorm.

In the next section, we attempt to retrieve the input from the `Form` collection, and determine which pass through this form we're in:

```
strUserID = Session("userID")
strLocation = Session("location")

strTitle = Request.Form ("title")
strFirstName = Request.Form ("firstName")
strLastName = Request.Form ("lastName")
strStreet = Request.Form ("street")
strCity = Request.Form ("city")
```

```
If strTitle = "" Then
  strMethod = "query"
Else
  strMethod = "update"
End If
```

Note that we're intending to use the bulk `update` method on HailStorm, and not the individual `replace` method. We'll see why shortly.

Next, we set up our message GUID and namespace strings as before:

```
strMessageID = "C30D56F0-A91F-11d5-8467-0040957713FA"

strSoapAction        = "http://schemas.microsoft.com/hs/2001/10/core#request"
strSoapRPNamespace   = "http://schemas.xmlsoap.org/rp"
strHSCoreNamespace     = "http://schemas.microsoft.com/hs/2001/10/core"
strServiceNamespace  = "http://schemas.microsoft.com/hs/2001/10/myProfile"
strSecNamespace      = "http://schemas.xmlsoap.org/soap/security/2000-12/"
```

The SOAP Request

The SOAP request to HailStorm is set up in precisely the same manner as before, and most of the header is identical as well. There's one change, which you are invited to discover:

```
Set Connector = Server.CreateObject("MSSOAP.HttpConnector")
Connector.Property("EndPointURL") = strLocation & "/myProfile"
Connector.Property("SoapAction") = strSoapAction
Connector.BeginMessage()

Set Serializer = Server.CreateObject("MSSOAP.SoapSerializer")
Serializer.Init Connector.InputStream

Serializer.startEnvelope "s", "http://schemas.xmlsoap.org/soap/encoding/", "UTF-8"
  Serializer.startHeader
    Serializer.startElement "path", strSoapRPNamespace, , "srp"
      Serializer.startElement "action", strSoapRPNamespace, , "srp"
        Serializer.writeString strSoapAction
      Serializer.endElement
      Serializer.startElement "rev", strSoapRPNamespace, , "srp"
        Serializer.startElement "via", strSoapRPNamespace, , "srp"
        Serializer.endElement
      Serializer.endElement
      Serializer.startElement "to", strSoapRPNamespace, , "srp"
        Serializer.writeString strLocation
      Serializer.endElement
      Serializer.startElement "id", strSoapRPNamespace, , "srp"
        Serializer.writeString strMessageID
      Serializer.endElement
    Serializer.endElement
    Serializer.startElement "licenses", strSecNamespace, , "ss"
      Serializer.startElement "identity", strHSCoreNamespace, , "h"
        Serializer.startElement "kerberos", strHSCoreNamespace, , "h"
```

```
            Serializer.writeString strUserID
        Serializer.endElement
      Serializer.endElement
    Serializer.endElement
    Serializer.startElement "request", strHSCoreNamespace, , "h"
      Serializer.SoapAttribute "service", ,"myProfile"
      Serializer.SoapAttribute "document", ,"content"
      Serializer.SoapAttribute "method", ,strMethod
      Serializer.SoapAttribute "genResponse", ,"always"
      Serializer.startElement "key", strHSCoreNamespace, , "h"
        Serializer.SoapAttribute "instance", ,"0"
        Serializer.SoapAttribute "cluster", ,"0"
        Serializer.SoapAttribute "puid", ,strUserID
      Serializer.endElement
    Serializer.endElement
  Serializer.endHeader
  Serializer.startBody
```

Did you spot the difference? It's that line where we set up the `method` attribute on the `request` element. We pass in the value of the string `strMethod`, rather than hard-code it to `query` as we did before.

The action taken in the case of a query is exactly as it was before:

```
If strMethod = "query" Then
    Serializer.startElement "queryRequest"
      Serializer.SoapAttribute "xmlns:m", , strServiceNamespace
      Serializer.startElement "xpQuery"
        Serializer.SoapAttribute "select", , "/m:myProfile"
      Serializer.endElement
    Serializer.endElement
  Else
```

The Update Request

However, if it's an update, we're into previously uncharted waters. First of all, let's consider what form our SOAP body is going to take for an individual replacement. This is what we'd need to send if we were just replacing the fields in `name`:

```
<s:Body>
  <replaceRequest select="./m:name">
    <m:name>
      <m:title xml:lang="en">Mr.</m:title>
      <m:givenName xml:lang="en">Jon</m:givenName>
      <m:surName xml:lang="en">Pinnock</m:surName>
    </m:name>
  </replaceRequest>
</s:Body>
```

The point is that the `replace` command replaces *everything* below the specified node. We select the XPath of the node that we're going to, and then we specify a complete replacement for its content. The colorization rules therefore mean that we can only replace at a fairly granular level. You can't, for example, just replace the title, because `/myProfile/myName/title` isn't directly addressable.

The converse of this is that if we want to replace both name and address, we can't just issue a replace request on /myProfile, because we'd need to replace the entire profile. (OK, in our example, the name and address do constitute the entire profile, but that won't be the case in real life!) So what do we do? Well, we could simply issue two replace commands, one after the other, but that would be missing an opportunity. Instead, we're going to use the update command to combine two methods in one.

Here's what the SOAP body looks like for an update:

```xml
<s:Body>
  <updateRequest xmlns:m="http://schemas.microsoft.com/hs/2001/10/myProfile">
    <updateBlock select="/m:myProfile">
      <replaceRequest select="./m:name">
        <m:name>
          <m:title xml:lang="en">Mr.</m:title>
          <m:givenName xml:lang="en">Jon</m:givenName>
          <m:surName xml:lang="en">Pinnock</m:surName>
        </m:name>
      </replaceRequest>
      <replaceRequest select="./m:address">
        <m:address>
          <m:officialAddressLine xml:lang="en">Route 66</m:officialAddressLine>
          <m:primaryCity xml:lang="en">Nowheresville</m:primaryCity>
        </m:address>
      </replaceRequest>
    </updateBlock>
  </updateRequest>
</s:Body>
```

Note the three XPaths. The first one identifies the absolute path for the whole update block, whereas the others identify the relative paths for the name and address nodes respectively. You can combine as many replacements, insertions, and deletions as you like in an update block.

So let's code it up. Here's what we end up with:

```
Serializer.startElement "updateRequest"
  Serializer.SoapAttribute "xmlns:m", , strServiceNamespace
  Serializer.startElement "updateBlock"
    Serializer.SoapAttribute "select", , "/m:myProfile"
    Serializer.startElement "replaceRequest"
      Serializer.SoapAttribute "select", , "./m:name"
        Serializer.startElement "m:name"
          Serializer.startElement "m:title"
            Serializer.SoapAttribute "xml:lang", , "en"
            Serializer.writeString strTitle
          Serializer.endElement
          Serializer.startElement "m:givenName"
            Serializer.SoapAttribute "xml:lang", , "en"
            Serializer.writeString strFirstName
          Serializer.endElement
          Serializer.startElement "m:surName"
            Serializer.SoapAttribute "xml:lang", , "en"
            Serializer.writeString strLastName
          Serializer.endElement
        Serializer.endElement
```

```
            Serializer.endElement
            Serializer.startElement "replaceRequest"
              Serializer.SoapAttribute "select", , "./m:address"
                Serializer.startElement "m:address"
                  Serializer.startElement "m:officialAddressLine"
                  Serializer.SoapAttribute "xml:lang", , "en"
                  Serializer.writeString strStreet
                Serializer.endElement
                Serializer.startElement "m:primaryCity"
                  Serializer.SoapAttribute "xml:lang", , "en"
                  Serializer.writeString strCity
                Serializer.endElement
              Serializer.endElement
            Serializer.endElement
        Serializer.endElement
      Serializer.endElement
    End If
```

About as exciting as the query request, but never mind. Let's complete the SOAP work – remember, we only need to extract the data if we're doing a query:

```
Serializer.endBody
Serializer.endEnvelope

Connector.EndMessage

Set Reader = Server.CreateObject("MSSOAP.SoapReader")
Reader.Load Connector.OutputStream

If strMethod = "query" Then

  Set Body = Reader.Body

  Set Dom = Reader.DOM
  Dom.setProperty "SelectionLanguage", "XPath"
  Dom.setProperty "SelectionNamespaces", _
                  "xmlns:hs='" & strHSCoreNamespace & "' " & _
                  "xmlns:m='" & strServiceNamespace & "'"

  Set Title = Body.SelectSingleNode _
        "hs:queryResponse/hs:xpQueryResponse/m:myProfile/m:name/m:title"
  Set FirstName = Body.SelectSingleNode _
        "hs:queryResponse/hs:xpQueryResponse/m:myProfile/m:name/m:givenName"
  Set LastName = Body.SelectSingleNode _
        "hs:queryResponse/hs:xpQueryResponse/m:myProfile/m:name/m:surName"

  Set Street = Body.SelectSingleNode _
        "hs:queryResponse/hs:xpQueryResponse/m:myProfile/" & _
        "m:address/m:officialAddressLine"
  Set City = Body.SelectSingleNode _
        "hs:queryResponse/hs:xpQueryResponse/m:myProfile/m:address/m:primaryCity"
End If

%>
```

Displaying the Profile Data

If we're in the first pass (that is, if the method is "query"), we need to display the data to the user, and let them update it. This is all pretty regular ASP, so we won't make much comment:

```
<html>
<body>

<% If strMethod = "query" Then

If Not Reader.Fault Is Nothing Then
  Response.Write "FAULT: " & Reader.faultstring.Text
ElseIf Title Is Nothing Or FirstName Is Nothing Or LastName Is Nothing Then
  Response.Write "Failed to get name"
ElseIf Street Is Nothing Or City Is Nothing Then
  Response.Write "Failed to get address"
Else%>

<form action="ChangeProfile.asp" method="post" name="profile">
<p>
<table>
  <tr>
    <td>Title:</td>
    <td><input id="text1" name="title" value="<%=Title.text%>"></td>
  </tr>
  <tr>
    <td>First name:</td>
    <td><input id="text1" name="firstName" value="<%=FirstName.text%>"></td>
  </tr>
  <tr>
    <td>Last name:</td>
    <td><input id="text1" name="lastName" value="<%=LastName.text%>"></td>
  </tr>
  <tr>
    <td> </td>
  </tr>
  <tr>
    <td>Street:</td>
    <td><input id="text1" name="street" value="<%=Street.text%>"></td>
  </tr>
  <tr>
    <td>City:</td>
    <td><input id="text1" name="city" value="<%=City.text%>"></td>
  </tr>
  <tr>
    <td> </td>
  </tr>
  <tr>
    <td></td>
    <td><input id="submit1" name="submit1" type="submit" value="Change
profile"></td>
  </tr>
</table></P>
</form>
```

```
<%End If%>
```

If we're in the second pass, we need to establish that the update was successful, before returning the user to the auction:

```
<%Else

If Not Reader.Fault Is Nothing Then
   Response.Write "FAULT: " & Reader.faultstring.Text
Else%>

<form action="AuctionDemo.asp" method="post" name="changed">
<input id=submit2 name=submit2 type=submit value="Return to Auction">

<%End If%>
<%End If%>
</body>
</html>
```

Let's try it all out.

Running the Auction Demo (2)

Let's imagine that we've just logged in as before. Here's what we see:

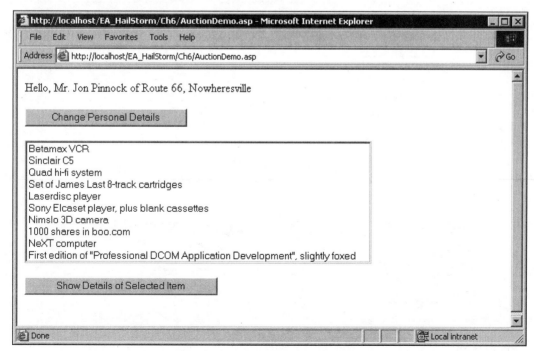

Before we go into the auction, we're going to update our profile, so let's click on the Change Personal Details button. This is what we see:

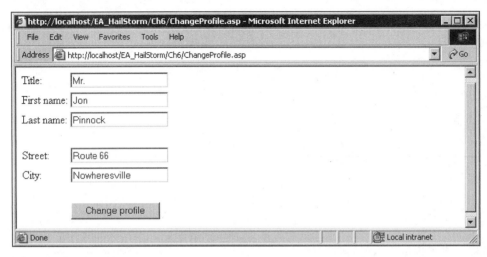

So let's make some changes:

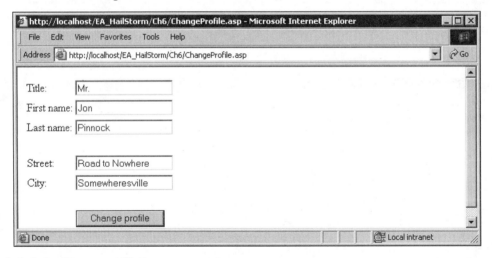

And click the Change profile button:

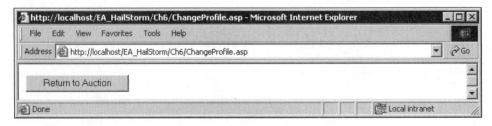

And this is what we see when we return to the auction:

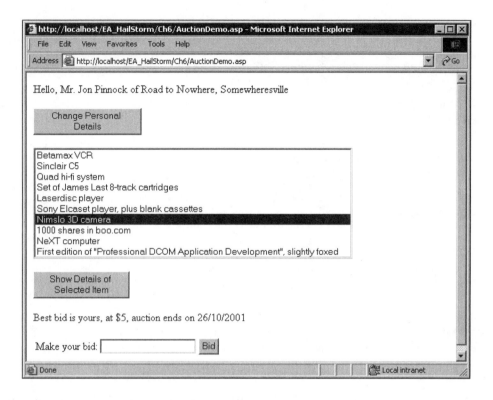

Tell Me When Something's Happened

The reason why the Internet has scaled so impressively is that HTTP is a completely sessionless protocol. Cookies and ASP session objects like the ones we've used in this case study notwithstanding, pretty much every time you request a page, it's like you were just visiting for the first time. Surfing around the net is like having a number of disjointed conversations with people where you're only allowed to ask one question and get one answer each time.

When you stop to think about it, it is extraordinary that anyone has actually managed to make any form of e-commerce work in this kind of environment at all, let alone produce anything as successful as Amazon, or indeed eBay. However, there are some things that just can't be done within the present paradigm. Anyone who has worked with real-time financial data, for instance, will know that the kind of thing you often want to do is set up a watch on a series of financial instruments and get a stream of updates. You can do it using some kind of plug-in, whether Java or some other technology, but you're stuck in one site. You can also do it, of course, by downloading some specialized program to do the watching for you. But that only works if your PC isn't locked down by your management. What you'd *really* like to do is surf around, picking this rate here, that rate there, and so on, maintaining a watch the whole time.

There are more prosaic applications of this type of technology. For instance, wouldn't it be nice to be able to set up a series of watches on news headlines, sports results, and so on? What if that auction site you just placed a bid on would tell you when someone the other side of the world has just doubled your bid for that Nimslo 3D camera? In the latter case, it's not just the users who are keen to get their hands on the technology – real-time notifications mean serious additional business!

Why isn't this happening already, then? To work out why, you have to go back to why the Internet suddenly took off in the 90's when it had already been around for a couple of decades. The answer is the arrival of that simple universal protocol, HTML, which standardized everything and made it possible for everyone to talk to each other. Notifications are still waiting for that standardization moment, but it's possible that HailStorm might provide it.

myAlerts

The initial release of HailStorm only provided four services: myServices, myProfile, myContacts, and myWallet. The really interesting one is still to come: myAlerts. myAlerts is based on an earlier Microsoft technology called Microsoft Alerts.

The idea behind Alerts is that the user can subscribe to one or more alerts offered by a site (such as "Tell me when my bid gets trumped"), in such a way as they receive some sort of notification when the alert event occurs. This can use one of the following mechanisms:

❑ Microsoft Messenger

❑ Mobile device (via MSN mobile)

❑ E-mail

Microsoft Messenger is a client that sits on the user's PC and pops up a window whenever the event occurs. The alert contains a message and, optionally, a URL which can – of course – take the user straight to the site where they can take action about the alert. So within seconds of being notified about that $12 bid, you can have already placed your $13 counter-bid. (See why the dot com's are so interested in this?)

So what's myAlerts going to look like, then? The fact that it's part of HailStorm suggests that the alerts will be centralized on a HailStorm server. This would give the user more control over how he or she elected to receive them. For example, they could receive alerts as and when they happened ("push"), or when they chose to go to their server and fetch them ("pull"). Presumably, given the standardized nature of HailStorm, they could develop a completely different client to receive HailStorm alerts.

On the server side, there is apparently also more control available over where the alerts are directed – they may even be sent elsewhere than myAlerts.

Time to raise a note of caution. How are we to stop spamming then? On the face of it, notifications are a spammer's charter. All you need to do is zap a whole load of notifications into your target's HailStorm account and who needs e-mail? However, there is considerable control left to the user over how he or she goes about subscribing to notifications. It seems that a standard HailStorm colorized schema will be provided, such that subscriptions are made to a given xdb:blue node. The alert will only be sent if something happens below the level of that node.

At the time of writing, a lot of this is sheer speculation. However, one thing is for sure: alerts are a major step forward for web services. Keep an eye on them.

Summary

In this case study, we looked at how HailStorm myProfile could be used to personalize the user's experience of a web site, in the context of a simple electronic auction site. We looked at how to insert and query data using `hspost`, and how to query and replace items using the HailStorm SOAP protocol. Finally, we looked at how notifications are set to revolutionize the way some sites will work in the future.

early adopter

Creating a HailStorm-Compatible Web Service

In this chapter, we'll look at the aspects of creating a HailStorm-compatible web service with emphasis on the procedural steps and coding. What we're aiming to do is provide a simple web service that will send an e-mail, on behalf of a HailStorm user, to all of the people in their myContacts address book. We'll then develop a web site that makes use of this web service. We call this application **MailStorm**.

So, we're building effectively a four-tier application:

- ❑ **Back-end storage**: HailStorm in a Box, standing in for HailStorm itself
- ❑ **MailStorm server**: ASP.NET web services, which we will develop here
- ❑ **MailStorm interface**: ASP.NET web page, which we will develop here
- ❑ **Client**: Any web browser

Obviously, exposing the MailStorm server as a web service means that it is possible to develop other interfaces, perhaps ones that don't rely on a web browser.

As with any multi-tier application, you can deploy the logical tiers on separate machines, or group them however you see fit. For example, you may want to deploy the ASP.NET tiers onto the same machine, and it may even make sense for this to be the same server that HailStorm in a Box is hosted on. Bear in mind, though, that the most realistic scenario for this application is to imagine HailStorm is hosted remotely, that the ASP.NET applications are running in a hosted environment, and that the client could be anywhere.

Provisioning HailStorm Server

The process of provisioning the HailStorm services is fully described in Chapter 2. For this example it's necessary to provision the myContacts service for any user accounts you plan to use.

```
D:/Hailstorm/Bin>hsprov.exe -s myContacts -o username -l http://server_name
```

In the above command example username is the NT Domain username of the person you are provisioning the service for.

Architecture of the MailStorm Application

The vision of Web Services based on open Web standards such as HTTP and XML addresses the challenges of application integration: taking different applications running on different operating systems built with different object models using different programming languages, and turning them into easy-to-use Web applications. A Web Service is simply a URL-addressable resource that programmatically returns information to clients who want to use it. The clients need not know how a service is implemented.

We're going to develop the following elements of the MailStorm application:

❑   The interface, consisting of an ASP.NET page viewable in any browser.

❑   The MailStorm Web Service, which will provide functionality to add entries to myContacts, query myContacts for a list of e-mail addresses, and to send an e-mail to that list.

Building the Web Service using Visual Studio .NET

The MailStorm application will revolve around a web service that will handle all the interactions with the HailStorm myContacts service and perform the functions of populating the HailStorm with new contacts, displaying the contacts, and sending e-mail to all e-mail addresses in that HailStorm store.

The steps for creating the web service and the clients using VS.NET are simple. We need to start a new Visual C# project called MailStorm, in the default location (http://localhost/MailStorm). This will create a new ASP.NET Web service project and add a new virtual directory called MailStorm to our default web server. This virtual directory acts as the root directory for our web service. All the remaining files are placed within this directory. This directory should automatically be flagged as an IIS application directory.

VS.NET provides us by default with a web service with the inspiring name of Service1. We want our service to be called MailStormService, however, so we need to get rid of the default service, and create a new one. First, bring up VS.Net's solution explorer, and delete the Service1.asmx entry in that window (you can bring up a context menu that includes a Delete option by right-clicking on it). Now we can create a new Web Service by choosing Add New Item... from the File menu. Among the options you are presented should be an ASP.NET web service. Enter the name MailStormService for the new web service, and click OK.

At this point, VS.NET has created a great number of files to support this project in the MailStorm IIS directory. The deployment of these files in the IIS directory is shown below:

```
\inetpub
    \wwwroot
        \MailStorm
```

```
AssemblyInfo.cs
MailStormService.asmx
MailStormService.asmx.cs
MailStormService.asmx.resx
licenses.licx
MailStorm.csproj
MailStorm.vsdisco
MailStorm.csproj.webinfo
Global.asax
Global.asax.cs
Global.asax.resx
Web.config
\Bin
      MailStorm.dll
      MailStorm.pdb
      Assemblies utilized by your web service
      that are not in the Microsoft .NET Framework.
```

We need to add the MS SOAP toolkit 2.0 DLL to our project. We do this by right-clicking on the 'References' entry in the solution browser, and choosing **Add Reference....** Choose **Microsoft Soap Type Library** from the **COM** tab of the dialog box, and if you are asked whether VS.NET should generate any files, say yes. Two new entries should appear in the references list: MSSOAPLib, and MSXML2.

The Web Service Files

We are interested only in two files, MailStormService.asmx and MailStormService.asmx.cs. The MailStormService.asmx file will contain only one single line of code:

Service1.asmx

```
<%@ WebService Language="c#" Codebehind="MailStormService.asmx.cs"
Class="MailStorm.MailStormService" %>
```

This file, when requested by a web-browser or web-service client, contains only a <% WebService %> tag, which defines the page characteristics, and tells ASP.NET how to respond. The Language attribute to this tag specifies that we will use C# as programming language throughout the program. The next two attributes are necessary, as the actual C# code driving the service has been set up by VS.NET in a separate file (called a **code-behind** file), MailStormService.asmx.cs. This file contains the definition of class MailStormService that is used as the base class for the web service. The code of MailStormService.asmx.cs file can be viewed by right-clicking on the file name in the Solution Explorer of VS.NET and selecting **View Code.**

Let's take a look at the code generated for the MailStormService.asmx.cs file. The first few lines of the code are a default set of references to standard .NET namespaces (libraries of .NET classes). This is followed by the namespace declaration of our web service, which is MailStorm in this case. These namespaces provide a way to group the web methods and other business logic together. This avoids name clashes between methods in different web services, residing on the same server. Next we see the definition of MailStormService, the base class used for the web service. This class inherits from the System.Web.Services.WebService class.

There is some automatically generated code here that is used to support VS.NET's drag-and-drop component system, which we can ignore – our code doesn't use such components.

The complete code for the Service1.asmx.cs file is shown overleaf:

Service1.asmx.cs

```
using System;
using System.Collections;
using System.ComponentModel;
using System.Data;
using System.Diagnostics;
using System.Web;
using System.Web.Services;

namespace MailStorm
{
    [WebService(Namespace="http://ea.wrox.com/hailstorm/mailstorm/",
Description="This Web Service provides email service to HailStorm myContacts.")]
    public class MailStormService : System.Web.Services.WebService
    {
```

The first task is to create a set of string variables to store a lot of standard strings (namespaces and so on) that we'll be using throughout the class.

```
        private string strSoapEncoding =
                            "http://schemas.xmlsoap.org/soap/encoding/";
        private string strMessageEncoding = "UTF-8";
        private string strSoapAction =
                    "http://schemas.microsoft.com/hs/2001/10/core#request";
        private string strSoapRPNamespace = "http://schemas.xmlsoap.org/rp";
        private string strHSNamespace =
                            "http://schemas.microsoft.com/hs/2001/10/core" ;
        private string strSecNamespace =
                        "http://schemas.xmlsoap.org/soap/security/2000-12/";
        private string strMyContactsNamespace =
                        "http://schemas.microsoft.com/hs/2001/10/myContacts";
        private string strMyProfileNamespace =
                        "http://schemas.microsoft.com/hs/2001/10/myProfile";
        private string strService = "myContacts";
```

We'll be requiring an SMTP server to transmit the e-mail we generate. Substitute the name of a local SMTP server here:

```
        private string strSmtpServer = "mail";
```

The next section is all generated for us by VS.NET. We can actually remove the VS.NET code and our service will function perfectly, but to keep VS.NET happy, we can leave it in.

```
        public MailStormService()
        {
        }

        VS.NET generated code goes here
```

Next there's an important method, that we'll use from within the web service methods to build up a standard SOAP header. We're using the COM interop bridge to access the MS SOAP SDK 2.0 DLL from within our .NET application, since although .NET supports SOAP, it does so only using high-level APIs that won't generate the sort of SOAP packets we need to access HailStorm. The SOAP SDK gives us low-level control over the namespaces and elements involved in the SOAP packet. The code used to generate this header, then, is very similar to the VBScript that used the same COM objects in the previous chapter:

```
public void BoilerplateSoapHeader(MSSOAPLib.SoapSerializer Serializer,
                              string nUserId, string strTo,
                              string strId, string strMethod)
{
    Serializer.startHeader(strSoapEncoding);
    Serializer.startHeaderElement("path", strSoapRPNamespace,1,"",
                                  "", "x");
    Serializer.startHeaderElement ("action", strSoapRPNamespace,
                                  1, "","", "x");
    Serializer.writeString(strSoapAction);
    Serializer.endHeaderElement();
    Serializer.startHeaderElement("rev", strSoapRPNamespace,
                                  1,"","","x");
    Serializer.startHeaderElement ("via", strSoapRPNamespace,
                                  1, "","", "x");
    Serializer.endElement();
    Serializer.endElement();
    Serializer.startHeaderElement ("to", strSoapRPNamespace,1,
                                  "","","x");
    Serializer.writeString(strTo);
    Serializer.endElement();
    Serializer.startHeaderElement ("id", strSoapRPNamespace, 1,
                                  "","","x");
    Serializer.writeString(strId);
    Serializer.endElement();
    Serializer.endElement();
    Serializer.startHeaderElement ("licenses", strSecNamespace,
                                  1, "","", "ss");
    Serializer.startHeaderElement ("identity", strHSNamespace, 1,
                                  "","", "h");

    Serializer.startHeaderElement ("kerberos", strHSNamespace,1,
                                  "","", "h");

    Serializer.writeString(nUserId);
    Serializer.endElement();
    Serializer.endElement();
    Serializer.endElement();
    Serializer.startHeaderElement ("request", strHSNamespace,1, "",
                                  "", "h");

    Serializer.SoapAttribute ("service","",  strService,"");
    Serializer.SoapAttribute ("document", "","content","");

    Serializer.SoapAttribute ("method","", strMethod,"");
    Serializer.SoapAttribute ("genResponse", "","always","");
```

```
        Serializer.startHeaderElement("key", strHSNamespace,1, "","", "h");
        Serializer.SoapAttribute ("instance","", "0","");
        Serializer.SoapAttribute ("cluster", "","0","");
        Serializer.SoapAttribute ("puid","", nUserId,"");
        Serializer.endHeaderElement();
        Serializer.endHeaderElement();
        Serializer.endHeader();
    }
```

Now we come to the first of our WebMethods. Web methods are public methods that are exposed by the web service. In .NET, making a method into a web method is as simple as including the WebMethod declaration before it. Other private methods that are not declared as web methods cannot be accessed by the clients. This provides us security from unauthorised people accessing sensitive data in the HailStorm service by calling any of our internal methods.

This web method simply retrieves all of the data from a user's myContacts store, and extracts all the e-mail addresses from it, returning them as a semicolon-separated list.

```
    [WebMethod(Description="This method retrieves the list of contacts from
myContacts using HailStorm ")]
        public string RetrieveMyContacts(string nUserId, string strServiceLocation)
        {
        string emailadresslist="";
        strServiceLocation="http://" + strServiceLocation;
        string strEndPointURL   = strServiceLocation + "/" + strService;
        string strTo            = strServiceLocation;
        string strId            = "0c69dfd1-6694-11d5-a2bc-00b0d0e9071d";
```

Having configured a few basic variables to begin with, we're now ready to begin building a SOAP request to HailStorm to retrieve the myContacts details. Again, this is very familiar if you've looked at any of the code in the previous case study.

```
        MSSOAPLib.HttpConnector Connector ;
        Connector=new MSSOAPLib.HttpConnector();
        Connector.set_Property("EndPointURL",strEndPointURL);
        Connector.Connect();
        Connector.set_Property("SoapAction",strSoapAction);
        Connector.BeginMessage();
        MSSOAPLib.SoapSerializer Serializer ;
        Serializer=new MSSOAPLib.SoapSerializer();
        Serializer.Init(Connector.InputStream);
        Serializer.startEnvelope("s", strSoapEncoding, strMessageEncoding);
```

Now we can call our SOAP header generating method:

```
        BoilerplateSoapHeader(Serializer, nUserId, strTo, strId, "query");
```

And finally we can get started on building the body of the SOAP request, which will contain a trivial XPath query to select the whole of the myContacts content document.

```
        Serializer.startBody("") ;

        Serializer.startElement("queryRequest", strHSNamespace,"","h");
```

```
Serializer.startElement ("xpQuery", strHSNamespace,"","h");

Serializer.SoapAttribute("select", "","/m:myContacts","");
Serializer.SoapAttribute("xmlns:m", "",strMyContactsNamespace,"");

Serializer.endElement();
Serializer.endElement();
Serializer.endBody();
```

Finally, we can finish off the SOAP packet. Calling `EndMessage()` causes the SOAP packet to be sent.

```
Serializer.endEnvelope();
Connector.EndMessage();
```

Now it's time to read the response. We need to perform a bit of an ugly hack to translate the COM MSXML object that is returned by the SOAP toolkit into a .NET native DOM object. Then we need to configure a `NamespaceManager` to understand the myProfile namespace we need to use to retrieve `email` elements, and select all the `email` elements in the document with a single XPath expression.

```
MSSOAPLib.SoapReader Reader;
Reader=new MSSOAPLib.SoapReader();
Reader.Load(Connector.OutputStream,"");
string u = Reader.Body.xml.ToString();
System.Xml.XmlDocument doc;
doc= new System.Xml.XmlDocument();
doc.LoadXml(u);
System.Xml.XmlElement root = doc.DocumentElement;
System.Xml.XmlNameTable nt = new System.Xml.NameTable();
System.Xml.XmlNamespaceManager nsmgr =
                new System.Xml.XmlNamespaceManager(nt);
nsmgr.AddNamespace("mc", strMyContactsNamespace);
nsmgr.AddNamespace("mp", strMyProfileNamespace);
System.Xml.XmlNodeList elemList =
                root.SelectNodes("//mp:email", nsmgr);
```

Now that we have all of the `email` nodes in an `XmlNodeList`, we can iterate through them all with an `IEnumerator`, adding the addresses to a string:

```
System.Collections.IEnumerator ienum = elemList.GetEnumerator();
while (ienum.MoveNext())
{
    System.Xml.XmlNode address = (System.Xml.XmlNode) ienum.Current;
    emailadresslist = emailadresslist + address.InnerText + ";";
}
```

Finally, we can send back the completed list of e-mail addresses.

```
    return emailadresslist;
}
```

The next method is the meat of the service: it generates an e-mail, and sends it to the list returned by the previous method.

```
    [WebMethod(Description="This method is used to send mail to the contacts
retrieved by the RetrieveMyContacts() Web Method")]
        public string SendMailToMyContacts(string nUserId,
                                           string strServiceLocation,
                                           string messageFrom,
                                           string messageSubject,
                                           string messageBody)
    {
```

First, we use the previous method to obtain a list of contact e-mail addresses:

```
        string emailaddresslist = RetrieveMyContacts(nUserId,
                                                     strServiceLocation);
```

Now we use the .NET mail API to build an e-mail message and send it:

```
        System.Web.Mail.MailMessage msg = new System.Web.Mail.MailMessage();
        msg.To = emailaddresslist;
        msg.From = messageFrom;
        msg.Subject = messageSubject;
        msg.Body = messageBody;

        System.Web.Mail.SmtpMail.SmtpServer = strSmtpServer;

        System.Web.Mail.SmtpMail.Send(msg);

        return "Mail to "+ emailaddresslist + " sent successfully";
    }
```

The last method is used to add contacts to your myContacts data store.

```
        [WebMethod(Description="This method is used to populate myContacts using
HailStorm")]
        public bool addContact(string nUserId, string strServiceLocation,
                               string strFirstname,
                               string strLastname,
                               string strEmail)
    {
        strServiceLocation = "http://" + strServiceLocation;

        string strEndPointURL   = strServiceLocation + "/" + strService;
        string strTo            = strServiceLocation;
        string strId            = "0c69dfd1-6694-11d5-a2bc-00b0d0e9071d";
```

We initialize the SOAP connection to HailStorm as before, except that this time we're performing an insert operation, not a query:

```
        MSSOAPLib.HttpConnector Connector;
        Connector=new MSSOAPLib.HttpConnector();
        Connector.set_Property("EndPointURL",strEndPointURL);
        Connector.Connect();
        Connector.set_Property("SoapAction",strSoapAction);
```

```
        Connector.BeginMessage();

        MSSOAPLib.SoapSerializer Serializer;
        Serializer=new MSSOAPLib.SoapSerializer();
        Serializer.Init(Connector.InputStream);
        Serializer.startEnvelope("s", strSoapEncoding, strMessageEncoding);
        BoilerplateSoapHeader(Serializer, nUserId, strTo, strId, "insert");
```

Having created the header, we build a message body containing a new contact element:

```
        Serializer.startBody("");
        Serializer.startElement("insertRequest", strHSNamespace,"","h");
        Serializer.SoapAttribute("select","","/mc:myContacts","");
        Serializer.SoapAttribute("xmlns:mc","",strMyContactsNamespace,"");
        Serializer.startElement("contact",strMyContactsNamespace,"","mc");
        Serializer.startElement ("name",strMyContactsNamespace,"","mc");
        Serializer.startElement("givenName",strMyProfileNamespace,"","mp");
        Serializer.SoapAttribute("xml:lang","","en","");
        Serializer.writeString(strFirstname);
        Serializer.endElement();
        Serializer.startElement("surName",strMyProfileNamespace,"","mp");
        Serializer.SoapAttribute("xml:lang","","en","");
        Serializer.writeString(strLastname);
        Serializer.endElement();
        Serializer.endElement();
        Serializer.startElement("emailAddress",strMyContactsNamespace,
                                "","mc");
        Serializer.startElement("email",strMyProfileNamespace,"","mp");
        Serializer.writeString(strEmail);
        Serializer.endElement();
        Serializer.endElement();
        Serializer.endElement();
        Serializer.endElement();

        Serializer.endBody();
```

As before, completing the message causes the SOAP packet to be sent.

```
        Serializer.endEnvelope();
        Connector.EndMessage();
```

We now use the SOAP reader to detect whether the insertion succeeded, and return a Boolean value indicating success or failure:

```
        MSSOAPLib.SoapReader Reader ;
        Reader = new MSSOAPLib.SoapReader();
        Reader.Load(Connector.OutputStream,"");
        return Reader.Fault == null;
    }
  }
}
```

That's it for our web services. Now we need to compile the generated C# class, which will create a Dynamic Link Library (DLL) under the bin directory to link to our client projects. Remember, we need not even register the DLL. Just compile the source code and store the DLL in the bin directory. This is sufficient to get access to the DLL by the Web server. The local bin directory and the .NET Framework will pick it up at run time.

We can test out our web service quite easily using a web browser. Pointing a browser at the URL of the machine hosting our web service, followed by /MailStorm/MailStormService.asmx, will bring up the following page:

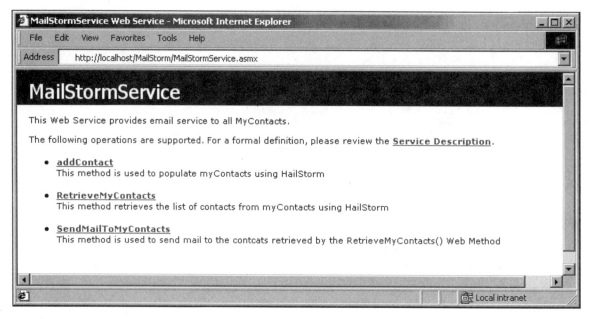

From this screen, we can examine each of the web methods, and test them out.

A Client for MailStorm

We've seen how to create the MailStorm Web Service, which interacts with the HailStorm myContacts service and performs all the HailStorm-specific functions such as populating addresses, displaying addresses, and sending mails. However, we don't want to invoke the web service directly and do all the operations from the web service page on the server. In order to consume web services we need to create proxies and clients so we can access the web methods in the web service. In this example, we'll use a single ASP.NET client to perform all the operations on the web service, which in turn will interact with the HailStorm myContacts service.

Here's what our client will look like:

The top two fields are for entering your HailStorm ID, and the address of your HailStorm server. Having provided this information, you have three options: you can add a new contact, by filling in the fields on the top right; you can list your existing contacts; and you can send an e-mail to your contacts, using the mail form on the left.

This is a complex form, and using most web programming languages it would take a lot of programming effort. We're going to use ASP.NET, however, and the programming logic for this form will consist of about four lines of code.

As for MailStorm, we need to create a new project in VS.NET – this time, an ASP.NET web form project. Call it `MailStormClient`.

As before, Visual Studio has created a default page for us with the unhelpful name of `WebForm1.aspx` – delete it using the solution explorer, and add a new Web Form item called `MailStormForm`.

The MailStorm web form also consists of two separate files: the `aspx` file, and a code-behind file called `MailStormForm.aspx.cs`. This time, however, the `aspx` file will contain more than one line – as well as a reference to the code-behind file, it will contain the HTML that makes up the web page. VS.NET provides three views of an ASP.NET page:

❑ The **code** view – this is the contents of the code-behind file

❑ The **HTML** view – this is the contents of the `aspx` file

❑ The **design** view – this is a visual view of the form as it will look

In the HTML view, we need to set up a table to contain all of the controls we need. Here's the code, slightly muddied by VS.NET's insistence on polluting your HTML with its own work:

```
<%@ Page language="c#" Codebehind="MailStormForm.aspx.cs" AutoEventWireup="false"
Inherits="Mailstorm_Client.MailStormForm" %>
<!DOCTYPE HTML PUBLIC "-//W3C//DTD HTML 4.0 Transitional//EN" >
<HTML>
  <HEAD>
    <meta content="Microsoft Visual Studio 7.0" name="GENERATOR">
    <meta content="C#" name="CODE_LANGUAGE">
    <meta content="JavaScript (ECMAScript)" name="vs_defaultClientScript">
    <meta content="http://schemas.microsoft.com/intellisense/ie3-2nav3-0"
name="vs_targetSchema">
  </HEAD>
  <body MS_POSITIONING="GridLayout" bgColor="buttonface">
    <FORM id="Form1" method="post" runat="server">
      <TABLE height="394" cellSpacing="0" cellPadding="0" width="444" border="0"
ms_2d_layout="TRUE">
        <TR vAlign="top">
          <TD width="1" height="15">
          </TD>
          <TD width="443">
          </TD>
        </TR>
        <TR vAlign="top">
          <TD height="38">
          </TD>
          <TD>
            <TABLE cellSpacing="0" cellPadding="0" width="500" border="0"
height="38">
              <TR vAlign="top">
                <TD>
                  HailStorm ID
                </TD>
                <TD>
                  <asp:TextBox id="txtId" runat="server"
Width="88px"></asp:TextBox>
                </TD>
                <TD>
                  HailStorm Server URL
                </TD>
                <TD>
                  <asp:TextBox id="txtServer" runat="server"
Width="160px"></asp:TextBox>
                </TD>
              </TR>
            </TABLE>
          </TD>
```

```
        </TR>
        <TR vAlign="top">
          <TD height="341">
          </TD>
          <TD>
            <TABLE cellSpacing="0" cellPadding="5" width="500" border="0"
height="340">
              <TR vAlign="top">
                <TD colspan="2">
                  E-Mail Your HailStorm myContacts:
                </TD>
                <TD>
                  First Name:
                </TD>
                <TD>
                  <asp:TextBox id="txtFirstName" runat="server" Width="164px"
Height="24px"></asp:TextBox>
                </TD>
              </TR>
              <TR vAlign="top">
                <TD>
                  From:
                </TD>
                <TD>
                  <asp:TextBox id="txtFrom" runat="server" Height="26px"
Width="164px"></asp:TextBox>
                </TD>
                <TD>
                  Last Name:
                </TD>
                <TD>
                  <asp:TextBox id="txtLastName" runat="server" Width="164px"
Height="24px"></asp:TextBox>
                </TD>
              </TR>
              <TR vAlign="top">
                <TD>
                  Subject:
                </TD>
                <TD>
                  <asp:TextBox id="txtSubject" runat="server" Height="26px"
Width="164px"></asp:TextBox>
                </TD>
                <TD>
                  E-Mail Address:
                </TD>
                <TD>
                  <asp:TextBox id="txtEMail" runat="server" Width="164px"
Height="26px"></asp:TextBox>
                </TD>
              </TR>
              <TR vAlign="top">
                <TD colspan="2">
                  Body:
```

```
                    </TD>
                    <TD>
                        <asp:Button id="btnAdd" runat="server" Width="112px"
Height="24px" Text="Add Contact"></asp:Button>
                    </TD>
                    <TD>
                        <asp:Button id="btnList" runat="server" Width="112px"
Height="24px" Text="List Contacts"></asp:Button>
                    </TD>
                </TR>
                <TR vAlign="top">
                    <TD colspan="2" rowSpan="2">
                        <asp:TextBox id="txtBody" runat="server" Height="208px"
Width="315px" TextMode="MultiLine"></asp:TextBox>
                    </TD>
                    <TD colSpan="2">
                      Status:
                    </TD>
                </TR>
                <TR vAlign="top">
                    <TD colspan="2">
                        <asp:TextBox id="txtStatus" runat="server" Height="162px"
Width="310px" ReadOnly="True" TextMode="MultiLine"></asp:TextBox>
                    </TD>
                </TR>
                <TR vAlign="top">
                    <TD colSpan="4">
                        <asp:Button id="btnSend" runat="server" Height="24px"
Width="88px" Text="Send Mail"></asp:Button>
                    </TD>
                </TR>
            </TABLE>
        </TD>
    </TR>
</TABLE>
    </FORM>
  </body>
</HTML>
```

You can tweak the layout of the page in the design view if you wish.

This will automatically generate some code in the code-behind file, to support the components we've used. But you'll need to tell VS.NET to add handler methods for each of the three buttons. This is done by going to the design view, and double-clicking each button in turn. As you do so, event-handling code is created and inserted into the code-behind file, and a blank method created into which you can insert code that will run whenever that button is clicked.

The code-behind file is quite simple, and the amendments we need to make to it are fairly trivial.

First, we need to import the MailStorm web service. This is done by right-clicking on the References item in the solution explorer, and selecting **Add Web Reference...**. Enter http://localhost/MailStorm/MailStormService.asmx into the address bar, and the service index page we saw before will be brought up. Click the **Add Reference** button at the bottom of the dialog, and the service will be incorporated into the project.

Here's the code that belongs in the code-behind file, with the sections we need to add or amend highlighted:

```
using System;
using System.Collections;
using System.ComponentModel;
using System.Data;
using System.Drawing;
using System.Web;
using System.Web.SessionState;
using System.Web.UI;
using System.Web.UI.WebControls;
using System.Web.UI.HtmlControls;

namespace Mailstorm_Client
{

  public class MailStormForm : System.Web.UI.Page
  {
    protected System.Web.UI.WebControls.TextBox txtSubject;
    protected System.Web.UI.WebControls.TextBox txtBody;
    protected System.Web.UI.WebControls.TextBox txtStatus;
    protected System.Web.UI.WebControls.TextBox txtFrom;
    protected System.Web.UI.WebControls.TextBox txtId;
    protected System.Web.UI.WebControls.Button btnList;
    protected System.Web.UI.WebControls.Button btnAdd;
    protected System.Web.UI.WebControls.TextBox txtFirstName;
    protected System.Web.UI.WebControls.TextBox txtLastName;
    protected System.Web.UI.WebControls.TextBox txtEMail;

    protected System.Web.UI.WebControls.Button btnSend;
    protected System.Web.UI.WebControls.TextBox txtServer;
```

The first code we need to add is a variable to hold a reference to the MailStorm web service.

```
    private MailStormService mailstorm;
```

The next method is generated automatically by VS.NET.

```
    public MailStormForm()
    {
      Page.Init += new System.EventHandler(Page_Init);
    }
```

In the `Page_Load` event handler, we populate our `mailstorm` variable with a reference:

```
    private void Page_Load(object sender, System.EventArgs e)
    {
      mailstorm = new MailStormService();
    }
```

The next two sections are entirely VS.NET generated, and deal with tying up the event handler methods to page events.

```
private void Page_Init(object sender, EventArgs e)
{
  //
  // CODEGEN: This call is required by the ASP.NET Web Form Designer.
  //
  InitializeComponent();
}

#region Web Form Designer generated code
/// <summary>
/// Required method for Designer support - do not modify
/// the contents of this method with the code editor.
/// </summary>
private void InitializeComponent()
{
  this.btnAdd.Click += new System.EventHandler(this.btnAdd_Click);
  this.btnList.Click += new System.EventHandler(this.btnList_Click);
  this.btnSend.Click += new System.EventHandler(this.btnSend_Click);
  this.Load += new System.EventHandler(this.Page_Load);

}
#endregion
```

Finally, the three method frameworks generated by our double-clicks earlier must be populated with programming logic. First, the **Send** button:

```
private void btnSend_Click(object sender, System.EventArgs e)
{
  txtStatus.Text = mailstorm.SendMailToMyContacts(
         txtId.Text, txtServer.Text, txtFrom.Text,
         txtSubject.Text, txtBody.Text);
}
```

This simply gathers information from the various textboxes on the web form, and passes them to a call to the MailStorm service.

Notice that the call to the MailStorm web service looks just like a call to a local component. In fact, we're calling a method on a specially generated proxy object, that wraps our call up in SOAP, and sends it to the service.

Next, the **List Contacts** button:

```
private void btnList_Click(object sender, System.EventArgs e)
{
  txtStatus.Text = mailstorm.RetrieveMyContacts(txtId.Text,
                          txtServer.Text);
}
```

And finally, the **Add Contact** button:

```
private void btnAdd_Click(object sender, System.EventArgs e)
{
  bool success = mailstorm.addContact(txtId.Text, txtServer.Text,
```

```
                              txtFirstName.Text, txtLastName.Text,
                              txtEMail.Text);
       if (success)
       {
          txtStatus.Text = "Successfully added contact " + firstName + " " +
lastName;
       }
       else
       {
          txtStatus.Text = "Error adding contact";
       }
    }
  }
}
```

And that's it. Again, we need to compile the page, then we can bring it up in our web browser.

Conclusions

Hopefully this multi-tiered example of using HailStorm has shown how it is possible to build services that access and use HailStorm on behalf of users. In this case, we created a web service providing the useful function of sending an e-mail to all of your contacts in one go. In addition, we've seen how easy it is to use web services from within .NET applications *once the interfaces to those applications are published in an appropriate form.* At the moment, HailStorm isn't published in a way that VS.NET can use, but this is certainly the plan longer term. When that is the case, programming HailStorm clients will be made considerably simpler.

early adopter

Useful Online Resources

Wrox Sites

- ❏ **Wrox Home** – http://www.wrox.com
- ❏ **Wrox EA HailStorm page** –
  http://www.wrox.com/Books/Book_Details.asp?isbn=186100608X
- ❏ **P2P Discussion Lists**– http://p2p.wrox.com/

Microsoft Sites

- ❏ **Microsoft HailStorm White Paper** – http://www.microsoft.com/net/netmyservices.asp
- ❏ **Microsoft HailStorm News** – http://www.microsoft.com/PressPass/events/hailstorm/
- ❏ **HailStorm SDK Download Site** – http://www.microsoft.com/net/downloads.asp
- ❏ **Microsoft Kerberos Page** –
  http://www.microsoft.com/windows2000/techinfo/howitworks/security/kerbint.asp
- ❏ **Microsoft Kerberos Implementation** –
  http://www.microsoft.com/windows2000/techinfo/howitworks/security/kerberos.asp
- ❏ **Passport Developer Information** – http://www.passport.com/devinfo/
- ❏ **SQL Server 2000 Evaluation Edition** –
  http://www.microsoft.com/sql/evaluation/trial/2000/default.asp

- ❑ **Windows 2000 Advanced Server Evaluation Edition** – http://www.microsoft.com/windows2000/edk/default.asp
- ❑ **Windows Script Host** – http://www.microsoft.com/msdownload/vbscript/scripting.asp
- ❑ **Microsoft SOAP Toolkit** – http://msdn.microsoft.com/soap

Standards

- ❑ **SOAP** – http://www.w3.org/TR/SOAP/
- ❑ **SOAP Routing Protocol** – http://www.gotdotnet.com/team/xml_wsspecs/soap-rp/default.htm
- ❑ **SOAP Security Extensions** – http://www.w3c.org/TR/SOAP-dsig/
- ❑ **Using SOAP with MIME** – http://www.w3c.org/TR/SOAP-attachments
- ❑ **DIME** – http://www.gotdotnet.com/team/xml_wsspecs/dime/default.htm
- ❑ **Kerberos** – http://web.mit.edu/kerberos/www/
- ❑ **XPath standard** – http//www.w3c.org/TR/xpath
- ❑ **XPath online tutorial** – http://www.zvon.org/xxl/XPathTutorial/General/ examples.html
- ❑ **SOAP API directory** – http://www.soapware.org/directory/4/ implementations

HailStorm-Related Sites

- ❑ **Ready-to-Run Software** (It is porting the Passport SDK to non-MS platforms) – http://www.rtr.com

General Web Services Sites

- ❑ **Web Services Zone at DeveloperWorks** – http://www-106.ibm.com/developerworks/webservices/
- ❑ **SOAP Web Services Resource Center** – http://www.soap-wrc.com/webservices/default.asp
- ❑ **Web Services Architect** – http://www.webservicesarchitect.com/
- ❑ **Microsoft's Web Services Page** – http://www.microsoft.com/webservices
- ❑ **Sun's Open Net Environment Homepage** – http://www.sun.com/sunone/

HailStorm Mailing Lists and Newsgroups

- ❑ **P2P HailStorm list** – http://p2p.wrox.com/list.asp?list=hailstorm
- ❑ **Microsoft's Web Services Newsgroup** – news://msnews.microsoft.com/microsoft.public.msdn.webservices
- ❑ **Microsoft's SOAP XML Newsgroup** – news://msnews.microsoft.com/microsoft.public.xml.soap
- ❑ **Advocacy Group for an Open HailStorm** – http://groups.yahoo.com/group/webwide

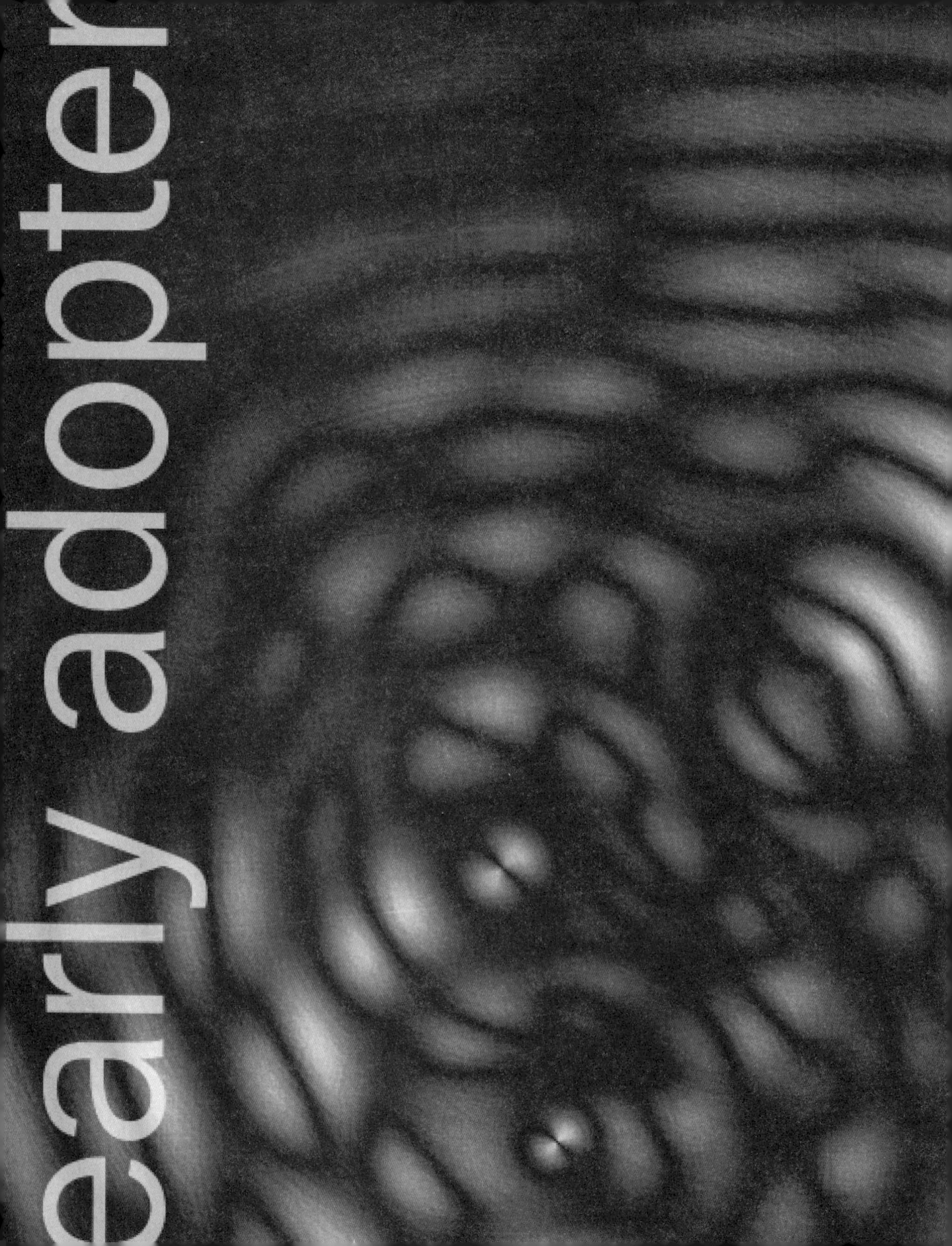
early adopter

B

Stop Press

This appendix details any late-breaking changes to the forthcoming release of HailStorm in a Box that could not be incorporated into the main body of his book before shipping to the printers.

Services to be Available at PDC (October 2001)

The current list of services touted to be available at PDC is:

- ❑ myAlerts
- ❑ myApplicationSettings
- ❑ myCalendar
- ❑ myCategories
- ❑ myContacts
- ❑ myDevices
- ❑ myFavoriteWebSites
- ❑ myLists
- ❑ myLocations
- ❑ myPresence
- ❑ myProfile
- ❑ myServices
- ❑ myWallet

Note that they too have had a name change, with the 'my' prefix being replaced by '.NET'. So myAlerts is now called .NET Alerts, myCalendar is now .NET Calendar, and so on.

The HailStorm Runtime Library

It would see that the HailStorm Runtime Library and its C API might ship with the first version of HailStorm in a Box for October 22 2001. However, it remains unclear as to whether or not it will be documented.

WSDL Support

The October release of HailStorm in a Box may have WSDL support to use web service references in Visual Studio.NET.

p2p.wrox.com
The programmer's resource centre

A unique free service from Wrox Press
with the aim of helping programmers to help each other

Wrox Press aims to provide timely and practical information to today's programmer. P2P is a list server offering a host of targeted mailing lists where you can share knowledge with your fellow programmers and find solutions to your problems. Whatever the level of your programming knowledge, and whatever technology you use, P2P can provide you with the information you need.

ASP Support for beginners and professionals, including a resource page with hundreds of links, and a popular ASP+ mailing list.

DATABASES For database programmers, offering support on SQL Server, mySQL, and Oracle.

MOBILE Software development for the mobile market is growing rapidly. We provide lists for the several current standards, including WAP, WindowsCE, and Symbian.

JAVA A complete set of Java lists, covering beginners, professionals,and server-side programmers (including JSP, servlets and EJBs)

.NET Microsoft's new OS platform, covering topics such as ASP+, C#, and general .Net discussion.

VISUAL BASIC Covers all aspects of VB programming, from programming Office macros to creating components for the .Net platform.

WEB DESIGN As web page requirements become more complex, programmer sare taking a more important role in creating web sites. For these programmers, we offer lists covering technologies such as Flash, Coldfusion, and JavaScript.

XML Covering all aspects of XML, including XSLT and schemas.

OPEN SOURCE Many Open Source topics covered including PHP, Apache, Perl, Linux, Python and more.

FOREIGN LANGUAGE Several lists dedicated to Spanish and German speaking programmers, categories include .Net, Java, XML, PHP and XML.

How To Subscribe

Simply visit the P2P site, at **http://p2p.wrox.com/**

Select the 'FAQ' option on the side menu bar for more information about the subscription process and our service.

wrox

Programmer to Programmer™

Wrox writes books for you. Any suggestions, or ideas about how you want information given in your ideal book will be studied by our team. Your comments are always valued at Wrox.

Free phone in USA 800-USE-WROX
Fax (312) 893 8001

UK Tel.: (0121) 687 4100   Fax: (0121) 687 4101

Early Adopter Hailstorm – Registration Card

Name _____

Address _____

_____

_____

City _____ State/Region _____

Country _____ Postcode/Zip _____

E-Mail _____

Occupation _____

How did you hear about this book?

☐ Book review (name) _____

☐ Advertisement (name) _____

☐ Recommendation _____

☐ Catalog _____

☐ Other _____

Where did you buy this book?

☐ Bookstore (name) _____ City _____

☐ Computer store (name) _____

☐ Mail order _____

☐ Other _____

What influenced you in the purchase of this book?

☐ Cover Design ☐ Contents ☐ Other (please specify):

_____

How did you rate the overall content of this book?

☐ Excellent ☐ Good ☐ Average ☐ Poor

What did you find most useful about this book? _____

_____

What did you find least useful about this book? _____

_____

Please add any additional comments. _____

_____

What other subjects will you buy a computer book on soon?

_____

What is the best computer book you have used this year?

_____

Note: This information will only be used to keep you updated about new Wrox Press titles and will not be used for any other purpose or passed to any other third party.

wrox

Programmer to Programmer™

Note: If you post the bounce back card below in the UK, please send it to:

Wrox Press Limited, Arden House, 1102 Warwick Road,
Acocks Green, Birmingham B27 6HB. UK.

Computer Book Publishers